GEORGE WASHINGTON'S HAIR

GEORGE WASHINGTON'S
HAIR

How Early Americans Remembered the Founders

KEITH BEUTLER

UNIVERSITY OF VIRGINIA PRESS
Charlottesville and London

University of Virginia Press
Printed in the United States of America on acid-free paper

First published 2021

9 8 7 6 5 4 3 2 1

Library of Congress Cataloging-in-Publication Data
Names: Beutler, Keith, author.
Title: George Washington's hair : how early Americans remembered the
    founders / Keith Beutler.
Description: Charlottesville : University of Virginia Press, 2021. | Includes
    bibliographical references and index.
Identifiers: LCCN 2021015814 (print) | LCCN 2021015815 (ebook) |
    ISBN 9780813946504 (hardcover) | ISBN 9780813946511 (ebook)
Subjects: LCSH: Collective memory—United States—History—19th century. |
    Founding Fathers of the United States—Biography. | United States—
    History—1783-1865—Historiography. | United States—History—1783-
    1865—Antiquities. | United States—Biography—History and criticism. |
    United States—History—Societies, etc.
Classification: LCC E300 .B48 2021 (print) | LCC E300 (ebook) |
    DDC 973.3092/2—dc23
LC record available at https://lccn.loc.gov/2021015814
LC ebook record available at https://lccn.loc.gov/2021015815

Cover art: From U.S. $1 banknote. (National Numismatic Collection at the
Smithsonian Institution / CC-BY-SA-4.0)

For Melissa Goin Beutler

CONTENTS

PREFACE

At Philadelphia's Independence National Historical Park, combing through documents held by the National Park Service, I related to a member of its staff the question that had lured me to the archives. Did early Americans have beliefs about the nature of memory itself that, by giving shape to their efforts to remember their nation's birth, affected foundational patriotic American memory and identity? Afraid of boring my attentive auditor, I quickly described evidence I was finding that in the young United States, between 1790 and 1840, "memory" was defined in increasingly popular physical terms. Physicalist understandings of memory demanded concrete placeholders to preserve the nation's founding memories. Many artifacts that early Americans collected as such—including locks of George Washington's hair—are with us still. Yet, we no longer understand them as our forebearers did.

At my mention of surviving fragments of George Washington's mane, the archivist's eyes brightened. If the Founders' follicles were what I sought, there was, she volunteered, a little known—and, by present-day lights, bizarre—collection of Washington's and other early Americans' tresses at Philadelphia's Academy of Natural Sciences. Intrigued, I proceeded across town as fast as public transport would allow to the Academy's library at the intersection of 19th Street and the Benjamin Franklin Parkway. Within minutes, a curator, visibly pleased that someone wanted to see the then-obscure collection, showed me the extant "hair pile" and "Presidential Hair Book" of Academy alumnus Peter Arrell Browne. In the mid nineteenth century, Browne used his wealth and connections as a prominent attorney to gather hirsute specimens. He hoped to develop scientific calculi by which to read people's moral character from the physical attributes of their hair. Dying in 1860, the jurisprudent left his hairy trove to the Academy. Now, leafing through his presidential hair book, one page at a time, one lock at a time, one chief executive at a time, I encountered actual surviving filaments clipped from the heads of U.S. presidents from

George Washington through James Buchanan. The surreality of that whole experience made my own hair stand on end.

What I could not know then was that I was more or less surrounded by George Washington's hair. Scores of institutions hold locks from his mane. Especially along the northeastern portion of the Interstate 95 corridor, one is never very far from that Founder's fragments. To drive the ten-hour stretch from Richmond, Virginia, to Portland, Maine, is to pass within fifty miles of a lock of his hair nearly four dozen times—an average of about once every fourteen minutes. Like breadcrumbs leading us back to the scenes of the Revolution, the debris field, as I have since mapped it, stretches from the East Coast across the Midwest, verges into baldness in sparsely populated areas in the West, then reappears on the West Coast. George Washington's Hair is a guidebook into key features of early American patriotic memory culture that spawned this remarkable, now little-remembered bodily diffusion. The new United States' culture of commemoration was not merely passionate. It was also intellectually sophisticated. To recover it historically is to comprehend anew the origins and leading elements of early American nationhood and identity.

A complete list of all who aided in the research, writing, and publication of George Washington's Hair would fill a too-large portion of this book. Several exemplary figures, however, deserve special thanks. First is David Konig. David's kindness, patience, erudition, and friendship have given me strength for years, and he has read my work repeatedly, always supportively, with remarkable enthusiasm and a sharp editorial eye. I also want to thank the editors at University of Virginia Press, especially Richard Holway who acquired this project and Nadine Zimmerli who inherited it at an advanced stage. They both made this book far better than it would otherwise have been, and were personally and professionally supportive from start to finish.

Early in my research, Iver Bernstein took me under his wing, offering crucial advice. Conevery Bolton Valencius believed in this project from its inception and saw it whole. In her inimitable way, she shared unstintingly from her vast fund of knowledge, and offered lavish encouragement. Garland Allen, Peter Kastor, and James Wertsch all gave excellent advice. Matt and Elizabeth Timmons lent to us their

Chicago-area home for a month, allowing me access to the Newberry Library's archives. Rebecca Klussman, Dee Andrews, Thomas S. Kidd, Matthew Easter, Lindsey Hill, Mary Ellen Fuquay, Jon Han, Matt Heckel, Charles Ackerson, Michael Cobb, Christina Mathena Carlson, Lowell Walters, Trent Dougherty, Charles E. "Scully" Stykes, and Brett Woods all helpfully read, and commented upon, large portions of the manuscript. The press's anonymous readers too deserve thanks for offering critical guidance.

I am indebted to, and thankful for, numerous academic organizations that generously awarded fellowships to support my research: the Virginia Historical Society, the Gilder Lehrman Institute of American History, the New-York Historical Society, the Massachusetts Historical Society, the Pennsylvania Historical Society, the Library Company of Philadelphia, the American Philosophical Society, the International Center for Jefferson Studies at Monticello, the Fred W. Smith National Library for the Study of George Washington at Mount Vernon, the College of Physicians of Philadelphia, the David Library of the American Revolution, Washington University, and Missouri Baptist University. Staff at each of these remarkable institutions patiently guided me into relevant sources, and I am grateful for their help and friendship. Special thanks is owed to the staff at the Monroe C. Gutman Library at Harvard University who gave me permission to roam freely for weeks amid the stacks of their priceless Historical Textbooks Collection.

Colleagues in academia too numerous to list, including discussants at professional conferences, research fellows with whom I was in residence at some of the archives mentioned above, and students and coworkers at Washington University and at Missouri Baptist University helped mightily, offering kind encouragement and spot-on suggestions. My mentor from my undergraduate days, the late Homer H. Blass, remains an inspiration, along with Mark Steinhoff, Terry Lindley, and Bruce Wheeler. David Poor sent hilarious faux letters of rebuke to my office, now and again, just to remind me that I needed to finish this book. Special thanks is owed to Missouri Baptist University presidents Alton Lacey and Keith Ross; to provosts Arlen Dykstra and Andy Chambers; and to my division's chair, Janet Puls; to colleagues David Hechler, Justin Watkins, Matt Heckel, and Jim Kellogg who filled in for me in my absence; and Missouri Baptist University's trustees, all of whom made it possible for me to take much-needed research and writing sabbaticals.

I am inexpressibly thankful for my family's unfailing love and encouragement. My parents, my late father, Tony, and my mother, Bernadette (who bought me more books as I was growing up than she probably should have); my siblings, Barbara Beutler Baker and Julie Beutler Dahl, and their families; my in-laws, Larry and Edie Goin; as well as numerous aunts, uncles, nieces, nephews, cousins, and other family members, have all provided boundless love and support. Above all, I am thankful for my wife, Melissa Goin Beutler; and for our wonderful children, Grant and Kylie, both of whom grew up hearing, albeit in good humor, an inordinate amount about George Washington's hair, for which I apologize. We are blessed too with canine companions—Sheena, Max, and Mindy—who provide solid protection services and much love. Melissa does the most to fill our home with joy. It is a privilege to dedicate to her, along with all of my love, *George Washington's Hair.*

GEORGE WASHINGTON'S HAIR

INTRODUCTION

In January of 1800, as America mourned George Washington's recent death, twenty-year-old Elizabeth Wadsworth wrote from Portland, Maine, to her father, U.S. congressman and former Revolutionary War officer Peleg Wadsworth, then serving in Philadelphia. "Papa[,] I will tell you what I want more than anything I think of at present." It was something that even her well-connected father, she knew, would probably find "impractable" to obtain: a lock of General Washington's hair. "Papa," asked Elizabeth, "had he hair?"[1]

George Washington had indeed had tresses. "Eliza" was only one of many Americans now jockeying for surviving strands. The competition notwithstanding, Peleg Wadsworth wrote back in triumph. "You expressed a strong desire for" a "relic of General Washington," a "Lock of His Hair." Holding "the laudable wishes of my children sacred," the congressman had requested a strand from George Washington's former secretary, Tobias Lear. In "the inclosed" Eliza could see her father's success. "I will not detain You longer, but leave you to unfold the Secret."[2]

As the congressman's family eagerly opened his letter, Eliza hoped against hope that it would fulfill her "first wish." She was not disappointed. Papa's missive included "a separate packet" for Eliza. She broached the parcel "with veneration and awe," tremulously removing its "Sacred" contents. "How shall I duly honor the relic?" she wondered upon seeing the hair. "I feel as if it" is "too great for me to possess. I want to give thousands who have never had the happiness of seeing General Washington" the "satisfaction of viewing this lock."[3]

A Problem with Histories of Memory

It would be a long time (not until 1899) before thousands would see Eliza's prized relic.[4] However, her assumption that masses of Americans would appreciate viewing it was reasonable. Americans notoriously venerated "The Father of His Country." Yet, their clamor for George Washington relics revealed more than primitive patriotic nostalgia. Between 1790 and 1840, Americans thought a lot about how memory works. They acted accordingly. New theories of memory, especially then-emerging scientific theories about the physics of memory itself, informed their earnest efforts to preserve and instill memories of their nation's natal happenings, its Revolution and Founding. We cannot understand historically their performances of patriotic memory, including Eliza Wadsworth's request to her father for a lock of George Washington's hair, without noticing that Americans' changing beliefs and assumptions about the workings of "memory" per se were, in that same era, inspiring popular "scientific" arguments for using relics, such as locks of hair, as concrete memory aids.

Applications of new ideas about memory to patriotic remembrance in the young nation proved to be anything but politically neutral. Some Americans were better positioned than others to deploy the memory-evoking relics that au courant memory theory increasingly recommended. The cachet of politically provocative performances of nationalistic "memory" by diverse groups, including war veterans, African Americans, women, museum-keepers, historians, evangelicals, and others, was thus affected by changing popular assumptions about the nature of memory itself. Significantly, by 1840, it was sometimes the least privileged persons whose efforts to identify themselves as worthy objects of patriotic memory most benefited. To that extent, new understandings of memory itself helped, however accidentally, to democratize American memory.

Historians have noticed the gradual democratization of patriotic memory in the new nation. However, they have generally treated it too casually as an effect of overall democratization in Jeffersonian and Jacksonian America such that "a more democratic vision of the past started to make sense."[5] This book, by contrast, reveals that a physicalist evolution in how Americans understood memory, by influencing who could credibly remember the Revolution, did more than reflect the democratization of American culture. Rather, popular redefinition of the faculty of memory itself causally contributed to the young nation's democratization.[6]

Classical Roots

Had you traveled widely in the early American republic, you might have noticed that many American place names had obvious commemorative significance. Some locales' appellations, such as "Washington" or "Franklin," indicated pride in the nation's own past. Others, such as "Utica" or "Troy," hinted at American indebtedness to Classical culture.[7] The juxtaposition of storied American and Classical names on the young nation's landscape is a useful clue about how Americans thought about memory. As they labored to preserve and pass on memories of their own nation's beginnings, their view of memory itself was informed by received thinking about the Greeks and Romans.

Much early American theorizing about memory drew upon a Classical tale known to Americans primarily by way of Cicero.[8] The latter reported that the ancient Greek poet Simonides of Ceos had "invented the science of mnemonics" inadvertently. While at a large banquet, Simonides was called out to receive a message. In his absence, the roof of the hall wherein the dinner was being held fell in, crushing the occupants. Later, friends of the dead who "wanted to bury them" were "unable to know" one body from another, for all "had been completely crushed." Yet, Simonides "was enabled by his recollection of the place in which each of them had been reclining at the table to identify" each corpse "for separate interment." From his feat of memory, Simonides inferred "that the best aid to clearness of memory consists in orderly arrangement," and that "persons desiring to train this faculty must select localities and form mental images of the facts that they wish to remember and store those images in the localities, with the result that the arrangement of the localities will preserve the order of the facts, and the images of the facts will designate the facts themselves."[9]

Simonides assumed that the images and loci prescribed by his system could efficaciously exist as abstractions in the mind. Some subsequent commentators argued otherwise. As the American theorist of memory William Burnham saw in 1888, and as the more recent scholarship of Frances Yates and of Dowe Draaisma has confirmed, well into the modern period thinking about memory in the West, while continuing to be influenced by "local memory" theory à la Simonides, oscillated between less physicalist and more physicalist renditions. Less physicalist Neoplatonist understandings conceived of memory as essentially of the "soul," belonging "not to the sensory" domain, "but to the intellectual part of the mind," and assumed with Simonides that effective places of memory, or loci, could exist as abstractions. Competing moderately physicalist, neo-Aristotelian views of memory—the sort that inspired the physically real "memory palaces" of the Renaissance—treated memory as essentially a sensate, bodily activity of material brains, and, adapting Simonides' system, relied more upon the concreteness of real-world loci and relics as effective memory props.[10]

The Physicalist Memory Revolution in Early America

As the first chapter of *George Washington's Hair* reveals, in the period between 1790 and 1840 transatlantic thinking about memory, still in the local memory tradition, was tacking in a sharply physicalist direction.[11] Influenced by such ideas as physiognomy, brain localization, and their popular combination as phrenology, Americans increasingly embraced reductive materialist views of memory, ways of conceiving of memory as self-consciously physicalist. Americans concerned with preserving and passing on memories of the nation's birth were thus inspired to privilege the memory-inducing power of physical loci or props of memory, including the "living relics" of the Revolutionary War, its surviving military veterans.

By 1840, however, Revolutionary War veterans did not represent a cross-section of their former military units. Purely actuarial realities, the demography of death, entailed that in a typical American community those still alive were former privates. There had, of course, been far more rank-and-file troops than officers in the Patriot armies. In addition, officers had tended to be older than enlisted men. Thus, as the Revolutionary War veterans in a given locale passed away, it was generally the officers who departed first. So, in the 1830s, as American memory culture, veering in a physicalist and physiognomic direction, began to privilege "living relics" of the Revolution as foci of patriotic remembrance, previously undistinguished Revolutionary War privates

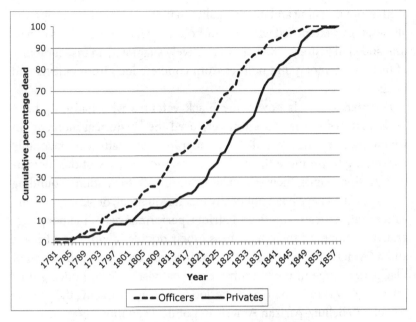

Demography of death of veterans of the American Revolution, 1781–1860.
The sample cohorts for this analysis were 120 randomly selected veteran officers of the Revolution and 120 randomly selected veteran privates of the Revolution for whom definite years of birth and death are listed in Daughters of the American Revolution, *DAR Patriot Index: Centennial Edition*, 3 vols. (Washington, DC: National Society of the Daughters of the American Revolution, 1990). I wish to thank Scott Hendrickson, of the Political Science Department of Washington University in St. Louis, for assistance in graphing my results.

suddenly found themselves venerated as the last living leaves on the Revolutionary tree.[12]

Transforming effects that the evolving popular memory of the U.S. Founding was having, or might have, upon the body politic alarmed some. Chapter 2 explores how between 1790 and 1840 elite conservatives founded historical societies to shape and correct popular American memory with learned history based on written archival primary sources. Their new historical societies were themselves deeply influenced by the popular turn toward physicalist local memory theory. The Massachusetts Historical Society, the New-York Historical Society, and the Virginia Historical Society were incorporated as perpetual legal entities meant to outlast the bodily loss of the nation's Founders.

With more meaning and intentionality than the current historiography allows, they juxtaposed within their holdings texts and artifacts of natural and civil history. Thus, they effectively suggested an inseparability of history, memory, and politics from concrete loci, from objects and landscapes.

Chapter 3 reveals how some Black veterans who had only been lowly privates in the war effectively used the "historical moment" in which memory theory and the demography of death were favorably converging to promote themselves as embodied relics of the Revolution. At first glance, their self-identification with the nation's Founding may appear to have been politically inconsequential, or simply conservative. Yet, African American Patriots' performances of memory suggestively conveyed their "two-ness," their double identity as Africans and as Americans, and such veterans inspired the rising generation of Blacks to engage in more controversial activism. Thus, noticing how "memory" was redefined in the period is crucial for tracing the genealogy of antebellum African American political agitation.

Blacks were not the only Americans whose ability to affiliate themselves with the nation's Founding was transformed by the physicalist turn in theories and practices of memory and the demography of death in the Revolutionary generation. As Chapter 4 explains, Christian evangelicals too rode the wave of changing demography and memory conventions, as, for their own reasons, they joined the cultural contest to draw upon America's birth stories. During the Revolution, evangelicals, especially Methodists, had been religious outsiders widely suspected of Toryism. However, after the Revolution and Founding, between 1790 and 1840, in what has been termed an "evangelical surge," America's middling and lower classes especially embraced evangelical Christian theology. At the same time, rank-and-file veterans from those same classes, now disproportionately evangelical, were becoming emblems of the Revolution. Not too surprisingly, then, it became easier and more popular than ever before to "remember" the American Revolution and Founding, however ahistorically, as essentially works of, by, and for evangelicals. Thus, with changing theories and practices of memory pious patriotic myth took hold.

Changing memory theory and memory of the Revolution would not have had the powerful, intertwined influences that they did upon American culture in the half century from 1790 through 1840 were it not for the fact that members of the rising generation of Americans were being schooled to concern themselves with how human memory works and with concomitant implications for practices of patriotic memory. Chapter 5 explores how textbooks taught young learners new, adamantly physicalist memory theory, and, by both precept and implication, commended reliance upon relics and monuments to support nationalistic American memory. It also explains how American textbook writers deployed physicalist pedagogies of memory to "scientifically" buttress traditional arguments for privileging women as teachers, and, by implication, for women learning, and holding forth upon, the nation's guiding memories. In that way, changing memory theory in the new nation had an important, if indirect, influence in contestation over the proper role of women in American society.

In 1800, as Eliza Wadsworth opened the gift of George Washington's hair conveyed to her by her congressman father, gaining entrée to such "sacred" patriotic relics befit her elite station and she likely could not have imagined anyone of lower rank receiving a similar relic. Yet by the 1820s, the unfolding demography of death and the growing popularity of materialist understandings of memory were incidentally, but effectively, having a democratizing affect upon patriotic memory culture in America.

Shifting demographics meant that, after 1820, in almost every American community, the last surviving veterans of the Revolution would be common rank-and-file enlisted men, most of whom were from middling to lower classes. As au courant physicalist understandings of memory demanded physical props, these surviving veterans of the Revolutionary War were suddenly celebrated as living relics of the Revolution. In honoring those mostly lower-class men as patriotic icons, the whole nation, at least implicitly, acknowledged that patriotism was not the preserve of only well-heeled economic, cultural, and political elites such as the Wadsworth family. Rather, popular physicalist memory theory, in prioritizing sensory perception of physical objects such as relics, construed memory, including performances of patriotic memory, in egalitarian, democratic terms, accessible to every sensate person, without reference to gender, race, or class.

In fact, diverse groups of Americans—proto-feminists, Blacks, Christian evangelicals, and others—took to gathering up for themselves in the 1820s and 1830s—quite without help from any congressman fathers—patriotic relics of the United States' natal happenings, including, in a number of celebrated cases, extant hanks of human hair, purportedly preserved from the pate of the *Pater Patriae*, the Father of His Country, George Washington. Consistent with, and often informed by, then-popular mnemonic physicalism, they pointed to their possessing sacred patriotic relics to insist on possessing as well cultural authority in the early Republic.

Thus, may this book be summarized analytically. Yet, as a work of history, it is intended not only to make persuasive arguments, but also to tell compelling stories. Readers will meet such characters as a museum owner interested in preserving the Founders' bodies, an African American storyteller brandishing a lock of Washington's hair, an evangelical preacher burned in effigy for voicing his impolitic understanding of the Founders' religious beliefs, and a schoolmistress who politicized memory theory to privilege women as conveyors of patriotic memory. Let the stories begin. It is mid-1789. One of Philadelphia's most revered residents is gravely ill . . .

PART I

CONSERVATIVE ROOTS OF AMERICAN MEMORY FROM THE 1790s

1

THE TAXIDERMIST

In July of 1789, Benjamin Franklin—bedridden in his Philadelphia home—was physically failing. On the 17th, the American Philosophical Society, pained at the impending loss of its founder, "*Resolved*, that a portrait of Dr. Franklin, the president of the society[,] shall as speedily as is convenient be executed in the best manner—to be perpetually kept in one of their apartments: and that [the Society] . . . shall apply to Mr. Peale to prepare and execute the same."[1] News of their request reached Charles Willson Peale—a Philadelphia museum owner, portraitist, and taxidermist with a penchant for natural history—as he was washing "birds and beasts" in arsenic, preparing the dead specimens for inclusion in his museum's displays.[2] Eager to accommodate the Philosophical Society, of which he was proudly a member, Peale was soon at Benjamin Franklin's bedside. Too ill for a formal sitting, Franklin asked the artist to model the new portrait after a likeness that Peale had rendered years before. Should he regain strength, the expiring sage promised, the newer painting could be finished from life.[3] As it was, Benjamin Franklin endured only one fifteen-minute session. Peale largely recopied his 1785 rendition of the old man's famous visage, and the Philosophical Society passed on acquiring it—preferring another one of Peale's earlier portraits of their founder.[4]

Several months later, on 17 April 1790, Benjamin Franklin was in the throes of death. The doctor's relative Samuel Vaughan, who four years earlier had sponsored Charles Peale's admission to the Philosophical Society, felt overwhelmed.[5] Vaughan tried to control himself, tried to suppress his "grief" at what he was witnessing at the old man's bedside.

Yet, having "never before been so much affected," he suffered "histerick fits," and had to withdraw. Later, he wrote to his wife conveying a "melancholly tale": though at first Franklin "squeezed my hand, his eyes remarkably bright and piercing," his body was giving out. The doctor "brought up much phlegm, taken from his mouth in handkerchiefs," his "hand convulsed," and there was a distinct "rat[t]ling in his throat." Soon, Dr. Benjamin Franklin, "Our Dear Friend the Philanthrophist, Philosopher, Patriot, and Politician" was "no more."[6]

Philadelphians lamented en masse. Vaughan witnessed a procession to Franklin's burial that was "half a mile in Length, the streets on each side lined with people five or six deep, the whole way. The doors and windows all crouded, numbers upon the . . . tops of houses & even chimnies."[7] As Charles Willson Peale later wrote, it seemed that "the whole City . . . collected at" Franklin's "interment."[8] In the evening, one of Charles's sons—Rembrandt Peale—kept vigil on a wall overlooking the burial ground at Christ Church where Franklin's body—one of the most physically recognizable in the world—had just been entombed.[9] Grief-stricken, Vaughan sought an extant relic from that body—a bit of the deceased scientist's "venerable hair." He hoped that one day those remains would be part of a larger personal collection of locks that would include hair from two other "Worthies" of the American Revolution: George Washington and Patriot financier Robert Morris.[10]

For his part, Charles Willson Peale—perhaps recalling his own frustrating efforts to artistically capture a dying Franklin's features—went on to insist that more of the good doctor could and should have been preserved than tresses or an image on painted canvass. In 1792, Peale published a broadside boasting of his museum's displays of animal specimens preserved by taxidermy and arranged beneath "portraits of many of the persons . . . highly distinguished . . . in the late glorious [American] revolution." Contrasting the efficacy of painting to taxidermy as means of memorialization, Peale allowed that though it was by means of "Good and faithful paintings" that "the likeness of man is . . . with the greatest precision handed down to posterity," there were also "other means," such as "use of powerful anticeptiks," to materially "preserve, and hand down to succeeding generations, the reliks of such great men," and to protect "their bodies from . . . being the food of worms." Admittedly, taxidermical preservation of the United States'

Founders might, from a purely aesthetic standpoint, not achieve "that high perfection of form, which the well-executed painting in portrait and sculpture can produce," yet all "who reverence the memory of such luminaries" would prefer to preserve and display the "*actual remains*" of the Framers. "Sorry I am," Peale lamented, "that I did not propose the means of such preservation to that distinguished patriot . . . Dr. Franklin, whose liberality of soul" would have encouraged him to "suffer the remains of his body to be now in our view."[11]

Peale meant what he wrote; his words were not hyperbole. The museum founder was indeed evincing enthusiasm for preserving the bodies of the Founders, like so many arsenic-soaked "birds and beasts."[12] Anyone who would name one son Titian, and others Rembrandt, Linnaeus, and Franklin, was presumably serious in advocating such a commingling of art, zoology, and patriotic commemoration, as his scheme for embalming and displaying Franklin and other Founders in his museum would have involved.[13] Though Peale did not specify the protocol he had in mind, stuffing "Dr. Franklin," or any of the Founders, would necessarily have been invasive. He might have to do, as he had done with numerous animals, the following: take "off the skin from the carcase [sic] except from the head and feet, from which all the flesh that could be taken with a knife or hooks" is "removed"; then, "with a . . . blunted hook," pull out more "flesh"; cut "away . . . interior parts of the skul [sic]," remove "the brains, Eyes, and tongue"; insert "into the body, where the bowels had been taken out, a piece of cork"; rub special antiseptic powders "into the skin"; and push them "into all" of the body's evacuated "cavities."[14]

Physiognomy

Admittedly, Peale's first efforts to juxtapose natural history specimens with painted likenesses of leading American Revolutionary leaders in his museum had been, at least in part, an effort to boost attendance at his gallery after the artist's brother in-law, Colonel Nathaniel Ramsay, observed that paintings were one thing, exotic natural artifacts quite another. Few could be expected to make great efforts to see the former. Many would willingly travel twenty miles to behold the latter.[15] Yet, whatever his initial motivations in collecting them, Charles Willson Peale's private correspondence makes clear that he soon developed a quasi-religious reverence for the facility of natural history specimens in his museum to exult "the soul to" God, and inspire "congenial goodness, and that love of order so indispensable to public and private prosperity."[16]

While the organization of Peale's "world in miniature," as the Philadelphian styled it, was that of a great chain of being, with the American Founders at the top spatially, and, by implication, ideally, the epistemology of Peale's "school," as the latter was also wont to call his museum, was suffused with the physiognomic theories of Swiss clergyman Johan Caspar Lavater (1741–1800).[17] Lavater defined physiognomy as "the science

Charles Willson Peale, *The Artist in His Museum*, 1822. (Pennsylvania Academy of Fine Arts, Philadelphia)

or knowledge of the correspondence between the external and visible man, the visible superficies, and the invisible contents." "Each part of an organized body," he insisted, "is an image of the whole." Metaphorically, "The human body is a plant, each part of which has the character of the stem." Any part of a person's body could be interpreted physiognomically to reveal the "internal motives" of its possessor "which would otherwise be first revealed in the world to come." Though he was a clergyman, Lavater argued that "physiognomy is more indispensable than the liturgy. It is . . . alike profitable for doctrine, exhortation, comfort, correction, [and] examination." High priests in the emerging physiognomic faith were portraitists, such as Peale. Lavater wrote that "Portrait painting, is the most natural, manly, useful, noble, and . . . difficult of arts." Because the face is where a human soul's "emanations" appear most legibly, as "Sacred to" the portrait painter "should be the living countenance as the text of holy scripture to the translator."[18]

Lavater further held that "national character" was reflected in "national physiognomy." Displaying his penchant for reasoning from parts to wholes, he argued that individual "countenances discover more the characteristic of a whole nation, than a whole nation does that which is national in individuals."[19] Embracing Lavater's epistemology, Peale believed that representations of individual Founders in his museum would facilitate "a sort of" physiognomic "converse with distinguished [American] Characters" that would encourage museum-goers to cultivate their own latent potentialities as republican citizens. Thus, he kept admission prices to his exhibits low, wishing to make such transforming encounters affordable to visitors from every walk of life.[20] Echoing Lavater's passion for portraitists, Peale enthused that the portrait painter "who can produce a perfect illusion of sight," so that the "spectator . . . believes the real person is there" deserved "to be caressed by the greatest of mortal beings."[21] A further debt was owed to the able artist for being a skillful practitioner of memory—for drawing upon a "good memory" of physical features of painted subjects to portray their bodies, thereby physiognomically unveiling and archiving their characters for "ages to come."[22]

Like Lavater, Peale held that heads were uniquely revelatory. In portraiture, Peale's first rule was that "the general proportions of the features and other parts of the head should be exact, . . . even in a head size canvis [sic] the air of the head is all important."[23] Comporting with

Lavater's teaching that each part of a body transparently expresses a force of character that animates the whole body, Peale thought that at the first sketching of a person's face, "it must be determined what will be the [facial] expression, and in this must every feature accord; a unity of the whole." If "there is a smile in the mouth, the eyes, the nose, the cheeks, and even the forehead must have its share."[24] Thus rendered accurately, "the features of the man" will "represent" that subject's "mind," for the "temper of man . . . moulds the features; the constant exercise of any one passion[,] the governing muscles being in constant action[,] fixes the growing form."[25]

In 1802, influenced by Lavater's assertion that tracings of the shadow of a person's profile were "the . . . truest representation that can be given of man," Peale began to employ a device called a "physiognotrace," by which visitors to his museum could have their profiles made.[26] In effect, Peale was giving his guests opportunities to scrutinize physiognomically their own characters against the standard of nature's great chain of being, effectively represented by his museum as an American body politic with the Founders at its pinnacle. Following recommendations by Lavater, Peale had visitors' silhouettes cut out on doubled-over paper.[27] This allowed the museum owner to archive a copy of each likeness. By December of 1808, he was boasting to Thomas Jefferson: "I have upwards of 8,000 profiles on sheets of paper[,] which furnishes a very rational amusement."[28] As Charles Willson Peale physically sorted these records according to what he believed they revealed physiognomically, he was effectively annexing museum visitors to his natural history exhibits—literally putting them in place taxonomically. Ideally, he explained in an 1816 letter to Philadelphia's Select and Common Councils, visitors would judge themselves. By contemplating concrete natural history "objects" in Peale's museum, they would come to scientifically "know themselves, and their dependence on others." In short, Peale meant to use his museum to persuade visitors of a relatively traditional and hierarchical view of the body politic over and against the sort of emerging democratic egalitarianism espoused by his friend Thomas Jefferson.[29]

Mnemonic Physicalism

Peale believed that the fact that objects in his museum were materially well organized made them more memorable than they would have been otherwise. In 1805, he explained that "a museum fit for a regular system of the Study of Nature" must "contain in good preservation some specimens of every department, arranged in some methodical mode, not huddled together without order with respect to their several Natures. . . . otherwise the more numerous a collection is, the more it will distract the Minds of its Visitors: if it gives [a] little information, that little will soon be obliterated because [of] not [being] stored in its proper place."[30] Popular memory theory agreed. An essayist in an education journal explained: "we" should not clutter the "storehouse" of memory with "all of the broken and useless furniture that we can find room for."[31] A Methodist magazine reprised a seventeenth-century Puritan minister's assertion that "when notions are heaped incoherently in the memory without order . . . , they confound and overthrow the memory."[32] The *Massachusetts Magazine* evoked "apartments . . . in which memory stores its merchandize" in an orderly fashion, and the *New York Magazine* praised Simonides, the ancient Greek father of Classical memory theory, for realizing "how necessary order is in memory."[33] Following Simonides, teachers of memory in the West had long instructed students to imagine rooms, or loci, in their minds in which they were to mentally organize objects representing particular ideas. In the case of Peale's natural history museum, the locality was an actual physical place, filled with real physical objects—reflecting the fact that concrete, material objects were coming to be regarded as essential props to memory.

Indeed, memory itself was being understood in increasingly physicalist terms. Physicians, for example, were associating memory with specific anatomic loci. Thus, an article in the 1815 *New-England Journal of Medicine and Surgery* explained that "Unusual pressure of the skull upon . . . both anterior lobe of the brain" was associated with "loss of memory," and an 1808 issue of the *Medical Repository* had reported on a physician in Paris who conceived of the remembering brain as extending outward through the body's nerves, and insisted that strong memories were simply those that resulted from highly effective transmissions of physical sensations to the brain.[34] Later, as education

journals burgeoned in the 1830s, they too stressed the utility of physical memory props. An 1837 essayist in the *American Annals of Education*, writing on memory and pedagogy, went so far as to unashamedly
acknowledge: "Of late [in my own teaching] I have sometimes sub-
stituted Natural History for Civil History, because the former can
best be illustrated by sensible objects."[35] For Peale that dilemma was
a false one. He emphatically integrated natural and civil history in his
museum, proudly teaching both with striking material props, ranging
from zoological specimens to intriguingly, perhaps locks of George
Washington's hair.[36]

By the time of Charles Willson Peale's death in 1827, his son Rembrandt had also demonstrated enthusiasm for conveying the memory of
the Founders in ways consistent with a physicalist assay of memory
and memorialization. The younger Peale, who proudly shared a birthday with the general, immodestly assigned to himself the "mighty" task
"of resuscitating the form of [George] Washington," by then deceased
for nearly a quarter century.[37] The result was Rembrandt Peale's well-
known 1823 painting, *Patriae Pater*: a composite of earlier portraits of
Washington that had been painted from life by Rembrandt himself,
the elder Peale, and Gilbert Stuart; as well as a bust of Washington by the
Frenchman Houdon, based, in turn, upon a life mask taken at Mount
Vernon in 1785 directly from George Washington's face. Rembrandt
Peale believed that each of those prior productions had some true
insights, but that each, his own work included, was also significantly
flawed. Houdon's life mask, for example, while indicating "the exact
proportions & . . . forms of the solid parts," of the general's face, was
doubtless "defective in the expression of the soft parts."[38] Rembrandt
argued that, by comparison, *Patriae Pater*—as a synthesis of the most
accurate aspects of each of these earlier works—was the most authentic portrayal of Washington's features ever rendered. It deserved to be
regarded as the "Standard Likeness" of George Washington and might
reliably be used to scientifically deduce the first president's moral and
mental characteristics from his physical features.[39] To his father's belief
in physiognomy as a science by which character could be read from
bodies, Rembrandt Peale syncretistically added enthusiasm for newly
popular theories of phrenology.[40]

Phrenologists traced the genesis of their discipline to the work of
Viennese cranial anatomist Franz Joseph Gall. Since the time of Galen

in the second century, western physicians had imagined that the brain's most significant functional parts were its ventricles, and that the surrounding gray matter forming the cerebral cortex was merely protecting the ventricles from injury. In the 1790s, Gall departed from this received tradition and argued that the essential functions of the brain took place not in its ventricles, but at its surface, in the cerebral cortex. Gall further claimed that specific mental functions were localized in different regions of the cortex as distinct organs. He asserted that the development of each psychological function was proportional to the size of its corresponding organ in the cerebral cortex, reasoning that protuberances in skulls were caused by such variations in organ size. By inference, analysis of the topography of a person's skull would reliably reveal details of its possessor's mental composition.[41]

In March of 1805, Gall and his pupil Johann Gaspar Spurzheim began an ambitious lecture tour that lasted three years and took them throughout much of Europe as evangelists for Gall's anatomical theories, collectively termed "craniology." In 1813, however, the two had a falling out: Gall held to the Christian doctrine of original sin—an inherent, inherited human capacity for evil—and he physically reified that doctrine, labeling one region of the human brain, for example, "murder." By contrast, Spurzheim contended that all human faculties were intrinsically good, and, if used for evil, were simply misused. What is more, while Gall conceived of "craniology" as a purely scientific discovery and eschewed speculating about its social implications and uses, Spurzheim sought to apply insights from "craniology" to social, political, and religious questions.[42] Spurzheim's adaptation of Gall's view—dubbed "phrenology," from the Greek words for mind and discourse—was particularly appealing in the early republic, where Calvinist religious beliefs in essential human depravity were increasingly giving way to more optimistic conceptions of human nature. As the American population grew and moved around, the promise of phrenology to make even strangers' individual's characters readily, and objectively, legible proved to be irresistible.[43] Particularly quick to embrace this new "science" was bustling Philadelphia, where the first phrenological society in the United States was founded in 1822.[44]

Phrenology and Physicalism

Parrying criticism that phrenology, by focusing on physical brains rather than upon abstract minds, smacked of atheistic materialism, phrenologists claimed to be mind-body dualists and emphasized their supposed discovery of a material organ in the human brain designed for use in adoring God.[45] Yet, there was no denying that their epistemologies assumed the priority of physical objects in the order of knowing. Thus, in 1840, J. L. Pierce, a Philadelphia physician, invoked what was fast becoming a commonplace: given the findings of phrenology, educators should promote learning in pupils not through enforced rote memorization, but by presenting instructive physical objects to "their external senses."[46] Although prior popular memory theory in the early United States had stressed the "association of [abstract] ideas" in the mind, an 1822 review in the *Philadelphia Journal of the Medical and Physical Sciences* publicized the countervailing opinion of a leading phrenologist that association of ideas was epiphenomenal; associated ideas were merely products of a prior "association of faculties," reducible, in turn, to physical interactions among corresponding organs in a rememberer's brain.[47]

Classical and Renaissance memory theory had prescribed efforts to buttress memory by mentally associating or pairing abstract ideas with imagined loci in the mind.[48] Phrenologists similarly described memories as concretely resident in various specific anatomic loci of the brain. Memory, according to most phrenologists, was not confined to one organ within the brain. Rather, it was distributed among the numerous localized organs of the brain, with each individual brain organ containing memories related to its own unique function.[49] Consider the example of a "PHRENOLOGICAL ANALYSIS, Showing the Development of Brain, Power of Mind, Temperament, and Prominent Features of Character" performed on Charles Willson Peale's grandson of the same name in New York on 2 November 1836.[50] It featured a list of thirty-five "Phrenological Organs" in the brain, with the relative protuberance of each of these organs in Peale rated numerically on a scale one to twenty-one. Each organ was assigned a corresponding number designating that organ's location in the human head, as illustrated in graphics near the top of the page in the extant original. Peale was given a high rating for organ twenty-seven, "Locality." As a lecture by the Rev. J. M. Graves, printed in 1838, explained, "One possessing this organ very large will notice and easily recollect incidents that transpire from the local impressions made by different objects connected with them—will readily recollect the position or location of things when traveling, that will enable him to find his way back without inquiry—will remember where and in what position he leaves things . . . &c."[51] As made clear above, utilizing a human capacity for "local memory," for memory of objects in relation to specific loci, had been a key strategy in western memory theory since the time of Simonides, and that Classical understanding of loci was well known in the United States of the 1830s. As phrenologist Amos Dean declared in 1835, "We are all familiarised to the phrase, 'local memory', and can no doubt bring to mind or recollect strong instances of the possession of it."[52] By the 1830s, phrenology had reified the concept of loci, arguing for a physical localization of faculties within the human brain, corresponding physical localization of memories within the brain, and—as Dean noted—phrenologists even posited the existence of a physical organ in the brain dedicated solely to comprehending "locality" per se, including phrenological locality.[53] A more thorough physicalist recasting of the received "local memory" tradition is hard to imagine.

The influence of the new physicalist epistemology on efforts to remember the U.S. Founders was manifest in the well-known Scottish phrenologist George Combe's published account of his 1838–40 visit to the United States. Consistent with physicalist phrenological imperatives, Combe gave particular attention to material objects he had seen on his trip that were associated with the Founders—such as a chair of Benjamin Franklin's, and another in which Jefferson had sat to draft the Declaration of Independence.[54] Drawing upon likenesses of deceased Founders' skulls, Combe argued that phrenology could demonstrate their greatness scientifically.[55]

Phrenologists courting an American audience often gave flattering posthumous interpretations of U.S. Founders' crania. The example of Combe suggests that doing so could be an effective way to gain a hearing for phrenology in the United States. One source upon which Combe relied to analyze Washington phrenologically was the art of Rembrandt Peale. The phrenologist recorded in his diary on 18 January 1839 that he "visited the studio of Mr. Rembrandt Peale," who was "the son of the earliest portrait-painter that America can boast of." Like his father, the younger Peale was "personally acquainted with General Washington, and painted a large . . . portrait" of him. Combe noted further that he had heard—from Rembrandt Peale, no doubt—that "the likeness has been pronounced to be faithful." "Washington's head as here delineated is obviously large," observed Combe, especially the "anterior lobe of the brain," which "is large in all directions." The "organ of Benevolence is seen to rise; but there the moral organs disappear under hair."[56]

Whether Rembrandt Peale noticed Combe's frustration with the fullness of George Washington's hair, it is doubtful that the latter would have apologized for the prominence of that feature in his painting. Nearly two decades later, Peale bragged that he had a privileged knowledge of Washington's tresses. He recalled that when he first painted Washington from life: "By sitting . . . early in the morning, I had his hair before it was curled and powdered by the barber, after which hour," Peale peevishly added, "Mr. Stuart's portrait was painted."[57] Conventional phrenology, as such, did not allow for physiognomic analysis of hair. However, Rembrandt Peale—while embracing phrenology—also accepted Lavater's physiognomic theories, as endorsed by his father. Lavater had taught that: "As is the hair[,] so are the muscles, as muscles, so the nerves, as the nerves, so the bones; as some or all of these[,] so the powers of the mind to act, suffer, receive and give"; thus, from "the hair . . . we may make deductions . . . concerning the nature of the mind"—a truth of which even "the least accurate observer may convince himself . . . by daily experience." Indeed, "From the hair alone we may know the man."[58] Lecturing on phrenology the same year that Combe visited his studio, Rembrandt Peale asserted that, in his eagerness to part the "tresses" of a person to uncover their skull for analysis, the orthodox phrenologist might inadvertently be brushing past revealing physical features.[59]

Delaplaine's *Repository*

In 1818, Rembrandt Peale's brother received a request from Philadelphia publisher and art gallery proprietor Joseph Delaplaine "to have the honor of placing the portrait of your very worthy & most respected father in my National Gallery of portraits of distinguished Americans. It is a mark of distinction to which I think he is . . . entitled."[60] It makes sense that Delaplaine wanted to enshrine the elder Peale. Like Peale and his progeny, Joseph Delaplaine was on a passionate, patriotic quest to record the Founders' physical features with such taxonomic precision that their—presumably exalted—characters would forever be verifiable by physiognomic analyses.

In 1816, Delaplaine began publishing the most ambitiously conceived illustrated biographies that had ever been printed in the United States. *Delaplaine's Repository of the Lives and Portraits of Distinguished American Characters* argued that Classical Greco-Roman biographies— "monuments of genius" on their own terms—suffered from "an eminent defect which detracted . . . from their interest and value. They contained no likeness of the great men whose lives they so ably recorded. To a delineation of the mind they did not subjoin portraiture of the body."[61]

It was critical, argued Delaplaine, that this deficiency in American memorialization be remedied. It was "well known" that "efforts have been made by the writers of Europe to degrade the character of the natives of America. The people of the west, although the immediate descendants of European ancestors, have been declared to be inferior, both in body and intellect, to those who are now in the eastern hemisphere."[62] From the time of the great eighteenth-century naturalist Georges-Louis Buffon, French philosophes and other Old World intelligentsia had argued that something debilitating about the climate of the New World ensured that animals and human inhabitants in the western hemisphere would be physically inferior to their counterparts in Europe.[63] Thomas Jefferson had protested that Buffon's assay of the Americas had "more eloquence than sound reasoning"; mammoth bones in the western hemisphere, among other evidences, proved the vitality of the region.[64] Jefferson delightedly told of a party in France at which the abbé Raynal "had got on his favorite theory of the degeneracy of animals, and even of man, in America," leading Benjamin Franklin to propose that French and American guests all rise "to see on which side nature has degenerated." The Americans present, "Carmichael, Harmer, Humphreys, and others," were "of the finest stature and form." Those "on the other side were remarkably diminutive, and the abbé himself, was a mere shrimp."[65] Now, Delaplaine maintained that published engravings of the United States' Founders could furnish similar "evidence that cannot be resisted, that, by a removal to the new world, man has sustained no deterioration[,] either in body or in mind." "Perhaps," he conjectured, "even the reverse will appear most probable."[66]

The Philadelphian characterized his published "series of portraits" as "perfect resemblances of the leading worthies of our country," showcasing the "advanced state of science and of the arts" in the United States while enabling "its sons to rescue from oblivion every lineament of its benefactors, and along with their deeds, to consecrate their features to endless commemoration."[67] One "science" by which engravings in the *Repository* might be analyzed was physiognomy. Delaplaine believed that a "skillful physiognomist" might deduce "a generalized outline" of the "prevailing disposition" of an individual from a portrait in the *Repository,* but he doubted that physiognomical analysis alone could reveal more than "an obscure intimation of the predominant passions" of a subject's heart. To understand the innermost person, "something more is requisite: the moral being must be described as well as the physical—and the personal portrait be accompanied with a characteristic biographical sketch of the man intended to be commemorated." Thus, in the *Repository* it was by "combined operations of the type and the graver that a correct image of the whole man" was "exhibited to view."[68]

The introduction to the *Repository* concentrated on defending scientifically legible portraiture of national worthies as rooted in an ancient impulse; "old coins, medals, busts, and medallions, containing likenesses of the personages of antiquity" were pointed to as evidence of the "universality" of a desire to remember the faces of the dead.[69] Describing time-honored "natural principles" favoring memorialization of bodily features, Delaplaine shaped an apologia that simultaneously spoke to conditions, anxieties, and axioms of nationalistic memory culture particularly relevant in the early American republic.[70] First, he contrasted "mis-shapen" memorial efforts that, according to Delaplaine, must historically have been produced by societies of "unlettered savages" to the refined *Repository*—in which every portrait was "in a shape so respectable as to ensure permanent care."[71] Thus, the American publisher portrayed his commemorative efforts as artistically creditable at a time when many Americans feared that their own memorializing suffered by comparison to European exertions.[72] As Delaplaine acknowledged directly in an 1818 prospectus for the gallery, his work was meant to help America to "pass by" Old World "dotards in refinement," and to "become their tutor in the true art" of expressing national feeling.[73]

Secondly, Delaplaine stressed that—as attractive, tangible keepsakes—copies of his *Repository* would perpetuate the memory of leading American benefactors "for centuries beyond . . . their physical existence"—a significant claim at a time when Americans were anticipating the imminent physical loss of the founding generation as an entire cohort.[74] Thirdly, Delaplaine suggested that a portrait in his *Repository* "at a single glance, presents to the untutored mind, that of which the scholar can obtain but an obscure view by . . . reading and reflection."[75] Thus, the publisher deployed a leading argument for physical memorialization: that physical objects—as one essayist wrote in 1820—conveyed "impressive lessons" to "every class."[76]

Lastly, Delaplaine stressed that a memorial on the order of the *Repository* "brings the most distant objects close to our eyes, and enables us, when removed to distant parts of the earth, to keep company with those whom we venerate."[77] Thus the publication could be viewed as an antidote to a developing problem: deleterious effects on collective memory that might result from the nation's ongoing physical expansion beyond geographic loci where the Revolution had been fought. As Americans surged westward following the Louisiana Purchase, it was conceivable that settlers would become unmindful of natal American events that had occurred in locales now far to the east.

In the early 1820s, a group of sojourners in New Hampshire implicitly acknowledged and addressed that problem by assigning surnames of early U.S. presidents to peaks in the White Mountains.[78] During Lafayette's 1824–25 memory tour of the United States, the former compatriot of Washington was hailed most deliriously as an embodied relic of the Revolution in frontier regions, and a decade later was still revered as "a sort of God among the [settlers in the] woods of the Ohio and the West."[79] In 1831, a citizen from "the humble walks of life," Vermonter Thomas Southgate, wrote to Maryland's Charles Carroll of Carrollton to report a personal effort to shore up Revolutionary recollection on the frontier: "knowing you to be the last worthy surviving signer of the declaration of Independence[,] I named a son after you[,] wanting to have one of the name in Vermont."[80] Two years later, Boston's Robert C. Winthrop—speaking of generational transition in the new nation—welcomed Kentucky's Henry Clay with a play on words that effectively highlighted a popular patriotic memory strategy on the frontier—giving new settlements names evocative of the Revolution: "Lexington in Kentucky and Lexington in Massachusetts—the *Clay* of both contains blood devoted to the cause of American Independence."[81] The next year, an essayist in the *North American Review* hoped that "as [their] wagons rattle" westward, descendants of those who fought the British at Concord will still "cherish . . . the example of the past."[82] At the same time, in Kentucky, Presbyterian minister John D. Shane evidenced determination that his own westward travel would not alienate him from collective memorialization of the Revolution. Reverend Shane began a scrapbook that would eventually contain hundreds of clipped news accounts and other articles focusing conspicuously upon the importance of recalling Revolutionary battles and of honoring Revolutionary veterans. Later, he undertook a series of interviews of western pioneers, underscoring the same themes. A clipping in his scrapbook stressed that: "When removed to regions far distant from the place of our birth, from the home of our youth, and from those loved in life who no more cheer us in hours of trial, we may in the turmoil of business forget the past, but there are objects, which . . . rouse recollections . . . and force us . . . to retrace scenes long forgotten."[83] *Delaplaine's Repository* had the potential to be just such a portable, memory-provoking physical object.[84]

Yet, critics contested its reliability. Baltimore's *Portico* commended Delaplaine for attempting to preserve "in remembrance the features of the deceased," but charged that many of the *Repository*'s engravings, far from representing the Founders' features with scientific precision, rose "little above the level of mediocrity." In the image of Fisher Ames, for example, "the hand resembles nothing human." Ames's left eye appeared to be "nearly an eighth of an inch higher than the right one, giving to the face the ludicrous appearance of smiling on the one side, and frowning on the other." The frontispiece featured "busts of Washington, Franklin, Jefferson, and somebody else, who, from the resemblance, might be taken as the twin brother of Jefferson." Washington's face "can only be known to be his, from its occupying the most conspicuous station," for it "resembles that of a baboon, much more nearly than it does the human countenance."[85] By contrast, Philadelphia's

Analectic Magazine, and Naval Chronicle held that "most of the engravings" in the *Repository* were "highly creditable."[86]

While differing on the physiognomic veracity of the *Repository*, both periodicals took issue with the physical arrangement of Delaplaine's first volume. They protested that its biography and accompanying portrait of Washington should have come before treatments of lesser notables. In any case, some organizing schema should have been adopted. "We are," declared the *Analectic Magazine,* "altogether at a loss to account for the arrangement" of the book. "We had" no idea "that a *repository* was like a receptacle of superannuated furniture, where all the articles are carelessly thrown together, without any regard to chronological priority, or to the claims of superior excellence."[87] At first blush, such criticism of the *Repository* as disorderly might seem unjustified. Yet, readers at the time could understand it as the predicate of a reasonable argument against the *Repository*'s efficacy for evoking memory. Like Charles Willson Peale, discussants of memory theory in the New Republic pictured memory and physical order as coeval.

Both *The Portico* and the *Analectic Magazine,* while arguing that Washington had been disrespected in the *Repository* by not being given first place physically among his contemporaries, contended that the written description of the general's physiognomy in Delaplaine's book was hagiographic. The narrative had asserted that the general's "appearance was strongly indicative of his character," exhibiting "the most striking representation of greatness and majesty, that we have ever seen attached to the person of a mortal." Though the "lineaments of his face" were "never to be forgotten by those who had once seen them," they "were almost lost to the beholder while examining them, in the impress of his spirit and the expression of his intellect." Indeed, no artisan had ever succeeded in capturing Washington's physical greatness: "The pencil and the chisel have vied . . . in a laudable attempt to perpetuate his likeness," but "Washington has never been correctly delineated."[88] In the opinion of the *Analectic Magazine* such claims in the *Repository* were merely "hyperbolical eulogium" of the sort that even the "ancients, with all their superstitious apotheoses" would have blushed to proffer.[89]

Late in 1816, a booklet defending *Delaplaine's Repository* from the *Analectic Magazine*'s "unfounded attack" went to press in Philadelphia. Ostensibly written by one of the authors whom Delaplaine retained to compose character sketches for the *Repository*, the pamphlet reasserted that Washington had never been accurately portrayed: "His bust by Houdon wants animation: that by Ciracci [*sic*] has too much sternness." Even "Our countryman Stuart, the ablest portrait painter . . . the world has ever produced," has "fallen short" in his "attempt to give a likeness of Washington," as "I could easily" show "were his painting before me."[90] The tract also parried criticism of the physical placement of the Washington profile in the *Repository*. Revealing that a determination had been made to begin the volume with a portrait and biographical sketch of Columbus as the discoverer of the Americas, it noted: "in many . . . kinds of arrangement, the two places highest in honour are the first and the last." Since "the portrait [of Washington] could not appear in the first, it was determined that it should occupy the second place of honour—the end of the volume."[91] Delaplaine's defender continued by arguing from a conflation of Washington the historical person and the artistic physical representation of the general in the *Repository* that "The portrait of Washington is the representative of himself. *Like* himself, therefore, all places are indifferent to it. Whatever situation it may occupy," whether it be "first or last," it "consecrates and honours by the impress [of Washington's physiognomy] which it bears."[92]

A "Panzographia"

Three years later, Joseph Delaplaine sought to found a gallery in which to display the portraits collected for publication in his *Repository*, and future productions that would similarly capture the Founders' "features on the canvass" before those "aborigines of American greatness" became one with the "physical amalgama" of the soil. Delaplaine envisioned his gallery—his "Panzographia"—as nothing less than a "school of morality" in which "day after day" both sexes of the rising generation would "delight to sojourn amidst the forms of the fathers of their country, and [would] depart from the exhibition with newer and stronger aspirations." Perhaps recalling that his published *Repository* had been criticized for not exemplifying the imperative of orderliness, Delaplaine was at pains to emphasize that his Panzographia would be a "well arranged" locus of nationalistic memory, combining physical order and bodily representations of the Founders to inspire the

right mental associations. He pledged that the arrangement of the portraits would reflect "a careful discrimination of character. Statesmen
will occupy one department; military genius another; naval heroes, a
third . . . &c." Thus, "the eye of the spectator will not be confounded
by an injudicious association of pictures." Moreover: "Each division
will also be surmounted by an emblematical device, which . . . will . . .
serve as a pilot to the curiosity of the observer."[93] In effect, Delaplaine
envisioned the space as a memory palace materially reifying an objective, hierarchical—or, at least, well-differentiated—body politic, and
doing it arightly by using icons, "emblematical" devices as accessible,
sensate guides to the entire organizational schema for which he was
evangelizing.

An anonymous observer—perhaps Delaplaine himself—dubbed
the arrangement a success. A letter from "An American" published in the
city's *Literary and Musical Magazine* in April of 1819 reported that, on
a recent visit to Philadelphia, the correspondent undertook "to view
the various exhibitions which it offers to the eye of the stranger," and
declared: ". . . I should feel that I was guilty of an omission of my duty
as an admirer of the Fine Arts, did I not make some public acknowl-
edgement of the satisfaction I received from a view of Mr. Delaplaine's
National Gallery of American Portraits." Indeed, "placed in the center
of" an awe-inspiring "assemblage of the worthies of my country, my
feelings were irresistibly subdued, and my soul elevated far beyond
its ordinary level" as "I gave way to the workings of my imagination,
and considered myself actually encircled by that great band of warriors, statesmen, and divines, &c. who have laid the foundations of our
glory." Thus transported, the observer concluded "that every American ought to bring his children to this collection, as the finest school of
patriotism, which this or any other country can produce."[94]

Notwithstanding that accolade for evoking nationalistic memory
"irresistibly"—seemingly deus ex machina—the Panzographia, along
with the *Repository*, was a commercial failure. Though Delaplaine invested thousands of dollars of his personal fortune into the projects,
they remained unprofitable.[95] The reasons were likely several. First,
as has already been noted, Delaplaine cast doubt upon the efficacy of
the *Repository* as a memory prop by not physically arranging its parts
according to a readily comprehended schema. Secondly, Delaplaine's
epistemic claims for the memorializing art that he promoted were

uninspiring for being unelaborated. By contrast, Rembrandt Peale would miss no opportunity to hold forth on the physiognomic accuracies of his renditions of George Washington.[96] Thirdly, Delaplaine's work was poorly adapted to the market revolution in the early republic, and to the growing middle class to which the new economy catered.[97] The prospectus for the Panzographia had an off-putting elitist tone, and, at eight or nine dollars per volume, collecting the entire projected series of the *Repository* was too expensive for most consumers to countenance.[98] The Peales, too, were elitists, but Charles Willson Peale purposefully kept admission fees at his gallery low, offering personal profiles from the "physiognotrace" at a nominal fee, and Rembrandt Peale sold cheap engravings of his rendering of Washington—advertised with Henry Clay's dictum that "every house in the United States, should have the likeness of Washington in it."[99] In the end, however, Delaplaine's and the Peales' memorializing institutions were both swept away by market forces. Competition from Peale's museum undercut the Panzographia. In time, Rubens Peale purchased Delaplaine's collection.[100] Eventually, Phineas T. Barnum bought much of the Peales' assortment.[101] In the 1830s, Barnum's cynical marketing of elderly African American Joice Heth as the putative former wet nurse of young George Washington demonstrated that popular interest in Revolutionary memory—even if credulous—could be lucrative.[102] For Delaplaine, however, it was a path to poverty. In April of 1824, he wrote to friends asking for help: "You know my National Gallery . . . I lost by it, every dollar of my fortune, $25,000. I am reduced to beggary."[103] By the end of the year, the Philadelphia publisher was dead.

John Fanning Watson, Local Impressions, and Body-Centered Memory

Perhaps no one mourned Joseph Delaplaine's passing more than his close friend—local banker and antiquarian John Fanning Watson. More than a decade later, Watson was still lamenting the loss of one in whom he had found "such affinities of intellectual pursuits and pleasures."[104] One important aspect of their intellectual correspondence had been a shared interest in the effectiveness of physical objects for evoking historical memory. In the 1830s, Watson, remembering that "the late

Mr. Delaplaine" had encouraged the banker "to see some such work . . . effected," published *Annals of Philadelphia,* a popular history notable for its stress on memory-provoking artifacts.[105] Watson was irrepressible in his enthusiasm for what he termed "relics of the olden time."[106] He was extreme, too, in his impulse to repeatedly explain his antiquarian fanaticism within conventions of memory popular in his time, and is, in hindsight, a particularly legible signpost to relationships between theories and practices of memory in the early nineteenth century.

Watson's voluminous public and private writing on history drew frequently upon heavily freighted contemporaneous language of memory theory to highlight and extol physical "remembrancers."[107] On the opening page of the second volume of *Annals of Philadelphia,* Watson explained that "relics are . . . earnestly sought and sedulously preserved," because—and here Watson quoted an unspecified source— "they are full of local impressions and transfer the mind back to 'scenes before.'"[108] Thus, as in many of his writings, he alluded directly to the Classical notion of loci, abstract in Greco-Roman memory theories, but, by Watson's time, physically reified by phrenologists and others.

In his *Annals,* Watson boasted of his vast personal collection of relics—including "sixteen pictures hanging up" in his house in "frames of relic wood, preserved as remembrancers." He listed each "picture," including: a copy of the Declaration of Independence framed with pine wood from the table on which the Declaration was signed; a rendering of the house in which President Washington lived when the federal government was headquartered in Philadelphia, set in "yellow pine, of his door, and corners of mahogany in his levee door"; and a portrayal of the frigate *Alliance,* framed in oak of the *Alliance* with corners made of Cook's ship *Endeavour.*[109]

Not content merely to describe abstractly physical remembrancers to readers, Watson effectively invited them to bask first-hand in the auras of specific memory-evoking relics. He devoted several pages to indices of extra-illustrated manuscript editions of his *Annals* that he had deposited at the Historical Society of Pennsylvania and at the Library Company of Philadelphia, indicating at precisely what pages of which archived manuscripts one might personally see and touch specific pasted-on historical artifacts.[110]

Even today, nearly two centuries later, the system works. Go to the Philadelphia Library Company reading room. Request Watson's manuscript. Turn to page 170, as the print edition of his *Annals* instructs. There—as promised—you will find a swatch of black fabric, with a handwritten note from Watson himself: "The black-silk velvet below, was once in the Coat of Dr. Franklin. It is S[ilk] Velvet with the pile uncut—very thick and heavy."[111] Walk next door to the Pennsylvania Historical Society. Look on page 460 of the volume there. Just as indicated in the *Annals* is a silk badge worn as a commemoration by Commodore James Barron during Lafayette's 1824 visit to Philadelphia.[112]

Though Watson did not make the point explicitly, Lafayette's celebrated memory tour of the United States in 1824–25 was itself emblematic of a turn toward the physical in memorialization of the American Revolution. Historians have noted the proliferation of material mementos—such as Commodore Barron's badge—during the tour, but there was more to the story.[113] In 1791, as a touring George Washington was about to pass through Charlotte Courthouse, Virginia, Richard Venerable had mused in his diary about a "great anxiety in the people to see Gen[eral]. . . . Washington—strange is the impulse which is felt by almost every breast to see the face of a Great good man." The next day, he reported: "All crowding the way where they expect him to pass[,] anxious to see the Savior of their Country and object of their love."[114] Yet, while the crowd might have gathered to gape at the president, they dared not touch him—certainly not to shake his hand. As Watson noted decades later, part of Washington's calculated dignity was that he avoided shaking hands, "even with best friends."[115] Lafayette's tour was characterized by an entirely different—and new—grammar of physical interaction, wherein the body politic might have its celebrities, but only such as every member felt confident and competent to literally handle. Thus, Philadelphian Sarah M. Haines confessed to being "shocked at the unceremonious manner in which he [Lafayette] was treated[;] one of the committee after having read to him a grossly flattering address, then took the General by the arm and said to the audience the General will walk round for the *ladies to look at*." The living link to Washington "passed close by me and many near me without any introduction shook hands with him." Haines had her hands "raised for the purpose but the thought arose whether or not it would not be evincing my regard for him more firmly to spare him that shake than to give it." It was as if "humanity" itself had "decended [sic] in his presence ...; it seemed from what I saw that he must suffer from such violent exercise of arm."[116]

By the 1830s, as Watson was writing his *Annals*, Lafayette and Washington—having both died and been buried—were forever physically out of reach.[117] Or were they? In his *Annals*, Watson enthused: "I have the hair of Washington in a gold locket," and "it consists of two parcels; the principal body was cut off in 1781, by Martin Pierre, his hairdresser, and was given to me in 1830 by his son, John, in Philadelphia," while the "small circle of two long gray hairs, tied together by silk thread, was a part of that preserved by Gen. Mifflin, and was given to me in 1828, by Samuel Chew."[118] On the Fourth of July, 1835, in a diary extant at the Winterthur Museum, Watson reported: "There being a military company going from our home to Trenton, to pass the day in its celebration. I availed myself of the occasion, to offer a trip of recreation and observation to my Son ... by going in the company," and "to make the occasion the more impressive to the Military, I lent them my Hessian tassel taken from the flag captured at the memorable Battle of Trenton," and "a golden locket, containing Washington's hair, & a picture on the reverse of the passage of the Delaware," with the locket being "suspended round the neck of the Captain at the time of dining & drinking their toasts."[119] Watson and the captain were not alone in venerating Washington's hair—nor was a desire to do so necessarily eccentric. In the early American republic, holding on to the hair of remembered loved ones or heroes, a part of memorial culture since time immemorial, was gaining fresh popularity—both as a means of reconnecting with the bodies of the departed, and of posthumously inferring their moral character, à la Lavater, from their hair's physiognomy.[120]

In the 1830s, Watson garnered yet another Washington relic from a location where bodily association with the deceased first president was inescapable—the Mount Vernon estate where Washington's corpse was buried. In December of 1837—as Watson explained in his *Annals*—Washington's body was disinterred there and transferred to an improved "sarcophagus" made "of marble, made and presented by Mr. Struthers of Philadelphia."[121] *The Knickerbocker* later reported Struthers's description of the exhumation:[122]

The coffin containing the remains of Washington was in the extreme back part of the vault . . . the case which was much decayed (and near which was found a silver breast-plate on which was engraved the date of his birth and his death,) was stripped off, and the lead of the lid was discovered to have sunk very considerably from head to foot; . . . this fractured part was turned over on the lower part of the lid, exposing to view a head and breast of large dimensions, which appeared, by the dim light of candles, to have suffered but little from the effects of time. The eye-sockets were large and deep, and the breadth across the temples, together with the forehead, appeared of unusual size. There was no appearance of grave clothes. The chest was broad; the color was dark and had the appearance of dried flesh and skin adhering closely to the bones. We saw no hair. . . .

The absence of tresses on Washington's corpse may have resulted from an earlier action by John Struthers, who—if his descendants' family lore is to be believed—had already taken advantage of the occasion to snatch a lock—still extant today—from the general's decomposing scalp.[123] In any case, Watson's *Annals* breathlessly reported Struthers's account of the cadaver's appearance, including—perhaps as a positive phrenological indicator—the detail that the corpse had a "high brow"—and adding triumphantly: "A piece of his coffin has been given to me by a lady."[124]

Perhaps the unnamed female benefactor was one of the many Americans in the era who, while visiting Mount Vernon as pilgrims, stole away with such relics. Such visits to the general's estate were very common and collectively contributed to the construction of national identity in the early republic.[125] Visitors to memory-evoking loci at Mount Vernon may easily have understood their practices of memory in terms of then-prevalent memory theory. In 1822, one pilgrim, reporting to an uncle about a visit to Mount Vernon, noted: "There [is] something so powerful in the principle of association [given] that our feelings are often powerfully wrought upon by scenes, which would otherwise be uninteresting." What, then, "must be the sensations of him, who stands upon the tomb of that man who has bequeathed to posterity his conquests and fame"?[126] In an era when principles of association and loci were progressively reified, being physically present at Washington's tomb—or being presented either a physical relic from his coffin, or a lock of his hair, both of which Watson acquired—could seem axiomatically ideal for provoking nationalistic memory.

To say the least, the example of Watson, and of others who post-humously collected Washington's hair problematizes Gary Laderman's claim: "The Protestant roots of American culture discouraged any activity resembling the Catholic tradition of venerating the relics of saints in the treatment of Washington's body . . . and the material re-mains" of George Washington "would not be shared with the rest of the nation."[127] In the context of ideas circulating at the time, the simplest explanation for why Watson and other Protestant Americans—their church's longstanding theological concerns about "popish" recourse to relics notwithstanding—unabashedly sought relics of the Founders may be that in increasingly popular physicalist memory theory they had found a purely secular rationale for, and definition of, reliquary.[128]

From Bodies to Monuments

During the summer of 1828, Watson felt evocative powers of asso-ciation and loci wash over him as he visited a place near Philadel-phia synonymous with the bodily sacrifices of Washington and his men in the Revolution: Valley Forge. In his journal, the antiquarian recorded his "deep emotions at all the necessary *association of ideas*" as he passed over ground where Patriot troops had encamped in the winter of 1777–78.[129] Sixteen years before Watson's visit, Philadelphia's *Freemasons Magazine* had called for the construction of a commem-orative monument at Valley Forge, as part of a larger effort to mark with monuments "Mountains[,] valleys[,] plains[,] forests [,] rivers[,] cities[,] and villages[,] which saw our fathers fight for independence" so that they will be recognized for their "nobility," while "those ignoble mountains[,] valleys[,] plains[,] forests [,] rivers[,] cities[,] and vil-lages[,] which have never witnessed the feats of our heroes will remain neglected and unknown."[130] In essence, the anonymous essayist pro-posed that the concept of loci be literally, physically applied, through pointedly selective construction of monuments that would memorably inscribe judgment on the nation's landscape.

One can see affinities to such logic in a treatise by J. R. Murden, published in New York in 1818 as *The Art of Memory, Reduced to a Systematic Arrangement Exemplified under the Two Leading Principles,*

Locality and Association. Murden instructed readers in the traditional Classical method of associating the ideas that one wanted to remember with imagined "sensible objects," which were then mentally placed into imagined loci.[131] A good example of a memory-locating sensible object, he observed, would be a monument.[132] Historians have noted increased interest between the War of 1812 and 1840 in building nationalistic monuments in the United States, and they have ascribed such interest to an upsurge in patriotism following the Battle of New Orleans.[133] That is probably correct—so far as it goes. Yet, additional factors were also evident in Watson's time.

First, such monument building was consistent with Watson's and other Americans' general awareness of Classical "local memory" theory. Thus, an 1831 committee in Fredericksburg, Virginia, seeking to build a monument to "rescue from oblivion" the "hallowed spot" where "lie interred the remains of the Mother of Washington," acknowledged that from "the remotest antiquity" monuments had served to give "a local habitation" to "those glorious deeds which would otherwise have perished from human memory." Given that the locality of Mary Ball Washington's burial "is known," her body should not be relocated to a nearby church, as others had planned. Rather, the "local sanctity" of her remains should be recognized as strictly "inviolable."[134]

A second, emotionally charged factor that, by the 1820s, encouraged efforts to construct monuments, was the progressive physical loss of the nation's natal generation. In 1828, as Watson recounted his visit to Valley Forge, he noted that only a handful of veterans who served there during the Revolution were alive to witness a recent commemoration at the site.[135] Two years earlier, at a commemorative ceremony at Groton Heights in Connecticut, Charles Griswold had also noted the paucity of living veterans. Griswold assured the survivors that they were "becoming more and more the objects of our deep attention." Yet, a cruel fact had to be faced. The roll of veterans was "fast diminishing." Nonetheless, he vowed, even after the body of the last survivor of that conflict had been translated into eternity, memory of the Battle of Groton Heights would live on.[136]

In an era when popular science, including the phrenology fad, was reifying received local memory theory, and reductively treating the human body and its sensate perceptions of physical objects as *necessarily* central in forming memories, the loss of the physical bodies of the founding generation—as Charles Willson Peale, Rembrandt Peale, Joseph Delaplaine, John Fanning Watson, and Charles Griswold all knew—was the loss of so many physical props supporting the memory of the Revolution. How then could Griswold prophesy that the rising generation would not forget the fast-dying war veterans? Revealingly, Griswold's public rationale for his confidence applied language affiliated with up-to-date, scientifically premised, physicalist renditions of Classical local memory theory to the embodied veterans. A monument, Griswold promised, would be built on the exact spot of the fight at Groton Heights and become a new "center of attraction," remaining as "an object of our senses" long after the bodies of the deceased veterans had been buried in the earth.[137]

The idea that the disappearing bodies of veterans needed to be replaced as physical cues to patriotic memory by constructed monuments was evident as well in an 1825 press account of the laying of the cornerstone of the Bunker Hill Monument. Reviewing Daniel Webster's dedicatory oration at Bunker Hill, in which Webster justified the monument on the grounds that "local association" was "fit to affect the mind of man," the United States Literary Gazette, in words strikingly consistent with the bodily preoccupations of memory theory in that era, exulted that "venerated remains" of the fallen at Bunker Hill—officers and privates alike—were disinterred with "religious care" to make room for the monument's foundation of "stones of massive granite" that were "hewn to take the place of the . . . [bodily] relics thus removed."[138] A contemporaneous news article, deploying popular pedagogy, offered a parallel defense of the monument: as an enduring physical structure on the exact "spot where his ancestors fought," it would stand as an "outward testimonial" that taught onlookers that though "their bodies may molder in the dust, the gratitude of their countrymen will not suffer their name to perish from off the earth."[139]

Whatever consolation Americans found in the idea that they could replace dying Revolutionary veterans with monuments as physical memory props, the era from 1820 to 1840 was one of heartfelt emotion as Americans literally grasped not only for Lafayette's hand, but for bodily contact with other aged veterans as well.[140] In his report of the 1828 commemorative ceremony at Valley Forge, Watson noticed that "only *two* officers of the old encampment were then present!"[141] The officers were almost all deceased. By the 1820s, an even higher percentage of the survivors of the Revolution were former enlisted men than that group's original majority share of the whole cohort of veterans. The present writer's own statistical comparison of mortality rates by year of 120 randomly selected rank-and-file Revolutionary veterans, compared to death rates by year of 120 randomly selected officers, finds that by 1840 93 percent of the officers had died, but only 76 percent of enlisted men had died.[142]

Given the turn toward physicalist memory theory and the concomitant currency of relics, there is every reason to infer that increasing celebration of surviving Revolutionary War privates in the 1820s and 1830s as living relics resulted in part from an intersection of the demography of death and a popular physicalist redefinition of memory itself, which, in combination, contributed significantly to the democratization of popular patriotic memory. Yet, well-connected high-society types, such as the Peales, would be neither easily, nor completely, displaced as ombudsmen of America's natal memories. Helping to solidify the hold of their class on America's founding stories would be historical societies begun, for the most part, by their fellow patricians.

2

THE ARCHIVIST

In late August of 1790, Massachusetts clergyman and historian Jeremy Belknap recounted in a letter to Ebenezer Hazard that prominent New York merchant "Mr. Pintard . . . strongly urged the forming of an American Society of Antiquarians. Several other gentlemen have occasionally spoken to me on the same subject. Yesterday, I was in . . . company where it was again mentioned." So, "[t]his morning I have written" a prospectus for such an organization "and communicated it to . . . gentlemen" who have "wished that a beginning could be made." If "it should come to anything[,] you shall hear farther." Belknap closed in words that only seem incongruous at first reading: "I send a few specimens of the Sandwich Island cloth, fish hooks, and cordage made of the fibres of cocoa shell."[1]

Belknap's hoped-for "American Society of Antiquarians" was begun several months later as the Massachusetts Historical Society. It was the first of its kind in the country, the forerunner of the more than ten thousand historical societies in the United States that today still preserve a lion's share of the evidence upon which professional historians depend to write the nation's history.[2] Why, though, might Belknap have sent along "fibres of cocoa shell" in a letter envisioning the nation's first historical association? Was the juxtaposition insignificant, or does it provide a useful clue about the concerns and assumptions of the archivists who began the historical society movement in early America?

At first glance, it may seem that the Massachusetts Historical Society and its institutional progeny were the antithesis of the increasingly object-based nationalistic memory culture that Charles Willson Peale and his co-laborers and successors in Philadelphia exemplified. The historical association that Belknap and several other antiquarians began in 1791, as well as similar organizations founded in the half-century that followed, such as the New-York Historical Society, the Pennsylvania Historical Society, and the Virginia Historical Society, intentionally put a higher premium on manuscripts than on relics. Yet, if those historical societies were thus seeming exceptions to materialistic vectors of memory culture in the new nation, they were only such as would prove the physicalist rule. After all, the first historical associations in the new nation deliberately displayed, along with their carefully gathered written sources for history, material objects quite like the "fish hooks, and cordage made of the fibres of cocoa shell" that Belknap had enclosed in his letter to Hazard. Indeed, their concentration on gathering written sources was in a wider context of profound appreciation for what the Reverend Belknap celebrated as the "artificial and natural [physical] curiosities . . . which may elucidate . . . natural and political history."[3] Those who initiated historical societies in the new nation carefully crafted their organizations as antidotes to the unhappy effects on America's national memory caused by the fast-diminishing physical presence of the founding generation *and* by the progressive physical loss and destruction of natal American artifacts and documents. To Belknap and others who began historical societies, such documents were emphatically material relics.

Belknap's Revolution

By 1790, Jeremy Belknap, at forty-six years old, was himself becoming a relic of the American Revolutionary era that had deeply shaped his outlook on history and historical preservation. Amid the War for Independence, as a Congregationalist preacher, Belknap was one of the "black regiment" of clergy who supported separation from Britain.[4] Events during the war only strengthened his Patriot convictions and anger at the British. He had been appalled in 1775 when redcoats occupying Boston's Old South Church scattered the late Rev. Thomas Prince's extensive collection of Americana. Prince had been Belknap's mentor and dear friend. The dispersal of Prince's storied "New England Library," one of the most extensive collections of historical manuscripts in America, was, to Belknap, unforgivable. Years later, he was still mourning the irretrievable loss "to the friends of science and of America" effected by "British barbarity." "Had we suffered it at the hands of Saracens," rather than Britons, he opined, "the grief had been less poignant!"[5]

There were other destructions of historical documents that haunted him too: the burning of the courthouse in Boston in 1747, and of Harvard's library in 1764; the plundering of the Court of Common Pleas by imperial forces in Boston in 1776; the ransacking by a Boston mob in 1765 of royal governor Thomas Hutchinson's home, which had been brimming with original materials Hutchinson was using to write a history of the Bay Colony. It was with such "instances" of destructions of documents "which . . . occurred within our own memory" in mind that Belknap and seven like-minded members of the Massachusetts gentry met in late January of 1791 to form a historical society. Its purpose would be to gather written primary sources, and to effectively safeguard their material existence by physically "multiplying copies" of the historical documents, methodically reprinting and distributing them in such quantities that neither accidents, nor natural disasters, nor the ravages of war would ever threaten their survival as concrete primary evidence for historians.[6]

For Belknap, and many of the society's other elite founders, reading staid, rational written histories seems to have afforded a respite from the contemporaneous political tumult in that Age of Revolutions.[7] In their younger years, the fathers of the Massachusetts Historical Society had been enthusiastic supporters of the American Revolution. Later, however, they felt threatened by the leveling forces that the Revolution had unleashed. The 1786 rebellion in western Massachusetts led by Daniel Shays, a veteran of the American Revolution, confirmed their darkest fears: Massachusetts and the nation had embraced revolutionary principles to an unfortunate extreme and were careening into disorderly egalitarianism. By unreasonably disrespecting traditional, hierarchical, and social distinctions as natural bases of societal structure, the emerging egalitarian culture, they became convinced, was becoming uncivilized. Thus, George Minot, one of Belknap's co-founders of the Historical Society, depicted the uprising as bitter fruit of a "relaxation of manners" in the Revolution's wake.[8] Belknap believed that Shays's Rebellion was terrible "mischief." He rejoiced when a contingent of the rebels was repulsed by "a few old Continental officers," members of the Revolutionary elite, who had "formed an association"—a sort of body politic, with the right people at its head—in defense of traditional government.[9]

The historical association that Belknap, Minot, and their colleagues founded was similarly meant to serve progovernment purposes. They promoted the Massachusetts Historical Society as an encouragement to nationalism, a contribution to reforming the nation under the aegis of the new federal Constitution, which, they hoped, would remedy systemic political and cultural weaknesses of the sort that had been made all too obvious by the Shaysite uprising.[10] Their Massachusetts Historical Society was to be a platform from which cultured men of leisure, such as themselves, would beneficently reveal to the American public rational truth about the nation's history, simultaneously winning merited respect for the United States among Europe's educated elite. Belknap was determined to see a proliferation of societies on the order of the Massachusetts Historical Society that together would constitute a great federation of American learned societies, a "Republic of Letters" mirroring the nation's new republican political system.[11] The Massachusetts Historical Society, he hoped, would be in the vanguard of these developments, laboring to ensure that, after "25 years of controversy and Revolution" the United States would at last "settle" down and develop in "virtue and good order," building upon its epic past.[12]

Enlightenment

A devotee of Enlightenment ideals, Belknap regarded reason as the right lodestone, whether in historical studies or in theology. In the world as the Reverend Belknap understood it, even the deity generally acted in compliance with predictable principles of Newtonian physics.[13] Thus, the most miraculous milestones in the Christian chronology were, the Reverend Belknap assumed, eminently rational and susceptible to historical proof. When in *The Age of Reason* Thomas Paine rejected the historicity of the resurrection of Christ, Belknap responded in a treatise that maintained that Jesus's resurrection could be verified by precisely the same species of historiographic logic by which it could be shown that the United States' Founders had issued the Declaration of Independence. With reference to both events, texts and syllogisms, not popular memory or tradition, afforded historical certitude, if not certainty.[14] Belknap and the other founders of early American historical societies generally posited that popular memory both could and should be corrected by historians' use of the sort of written sources with which the historical societies were determined to fill their archives.[15] Yet, even as historical associations were thus setting themselves over and apart from popular memory in the new republic as objective, independent arbiters, they were, in fact, deeply influenced by, and implicated in, the general contemporaneous turn toward physicalism and reliquary in American memory culture.

As enlightenment philosophes, Jeremy Belknap and his fellow founders of historical societies commonly thought of the world as a closed physical continuum. Every object was related to every other object by discoverable laws of physics. Historical happenings were presumably explicable in terms of visible, earthly, natural cause-and-effect relationships, even though God was the final cause of reality itself. Reading Cotton Mather's writings on witchcraft, Belknap found laughable the Puritan divine's description of obtrusive spiritual causes for physical effects in the natural world. To Belknap, who with many new England clergymen in the late eighteenth century was becoming increasingly liberal in his theology, witchcraft appeared to be a figment of people's imaginations, a grand deceit.[16] When he wrote history, it was far from providentialist. Rather, Belknap's accounts emphasized humans' choices within, interactions with, and determination by natural material environments. His *History of New-Hampshire* eschewed explanations of happenings as products of divine agency, while delving deeply into the natural features and history of New Hampshire. It featured tables listing the advanced ages to which particular residents of New Hampshire had lived, suggesting that state was a hospitable environment for human habitation, no small implication in a time when leading European naturalists, such as France's Georges-Louis Buffon, were notoriously deprecating the New World environment as fit only to produce biologically inferior men. Such constitutionally inferior men, it was supposed, could only have inferior histories.[17] Belknap and his colleagues in the new historical societies sought to answer from evidence that the New World is as "well stored with all useful materials as the old."[18] Vindicating its physical environment and its natural history, Belknap and his allies would, they well appreciated, effectively be striking a blow for the greatness of the western hemisphere's civil history too—natural and civil history being, in then-prevalent Enlightenment ontologies, intimately related, even of a piece.[19]

Accepting that a land and its people could only be fully understood in relation to each other, Belknap insisted that practicing historians must be practicing geographers, too. They must explore firsthand the physical terrain upon which their historical narratives would unfold. In 1789, after walking the Bunker Hill battlefield site in Charlestown, Massachusetts, he wrote to Ebenezer Hazard: "I have lately been on the ground" upon which the "battle of Charlestown" was fought, and "surveyed it with my own eye, and I think it was a most imprudent affair on both sides. . . . This is a general observation. There are several [more] which occurred from the sight of the ground, which I could not have had without [it]; and I think it essentially necessary to an historian" to "visit the spot where any transaction passed, and minutely examine every circumstance."[20] Thus, consistent with mnemonic physicalism, Belknap, in effect, urged his fellow historians to literally ground historical understandings and memory in the terra firma of historic landscapes explored as memory palaces.

Cabinets of Curiosities

Where Belknap and other historical researchers could not or would not go to survey land in person, specimens from natural environs might still be brought to them. Thus, from its founding onward the Massachusetts Historical Society collected not only manuscripts for the use of its members, but also artifacts of natural history, which were held in its display cabinet.[21] Historical societies founded subsequently did similarly. Much later, some histories wrote off those collections as relatively meaningless, as eccentric examples of an impulse among the learned in that era to practice "*omnium gatherum,*" as sideshows compared to the historical societies' rich textual acquisitions, which historians still mine.[22] Yet, "cabinets of curiosities" in historical societies, and the way that they were juxtaposed with accumulated texts, will repay closer consideration.[23]

It helps to recall the longer history of such collections. Cabinets of curiosities, in anything like the form that Belknap and his associates thought of them, had first become popular in late Renaissance Europe

among the upper classes, especially royalty. Often, a monarch's cabinets included specimens that had been contributed by far-ranging explorers who retrieved them from newly discovered realms. Resulting
collections served psychologically to associate the royal with all things
wondrous, suggesting the wide compass of the monarch's influence
and authority, extending even to a bewildering New World.[24]

In the Enlightenment, such cabinets gained increasing scientific significance. They were elaborately arranged by their keepers to exhibit
the natural "chain of being" in a region while simultaneously showcasing the artificial productions of its human inhabitants. In the eighteenth century, such hierarchical, carefully organized displays could
also be interpreted by elites as reassuringly parallel to a new political
orderliness, in contrast to the civil wars and violent uprisings that had
shaken Europe in the sixteenth and seventeenth centuries. Soon, private collectors in Europe among the rising bourgeoisie were assem-
bling cabinets of their own, implying that they had enough erudition
and sophistication to join the cultural elite.[25]

The founders of the Massachusetts Historical Society, and of similar associations in Enlightenment America, likewise saw their main-
tenance of "cabinets" as markers of their cultural accomplishment. As
European keepers of curiosity cabinets in the eighteenth century appear to have used the order of their natural history cabinets to suggest the value of social order, elite American collectors such as Jeremy
Belknap may well have understood their collections of juxtaposed
American natural and artificial history specimens as reassuring evidence that the Age of Revolution had finally passed in the New World.
Objects from the Revolutionary era they displayed as *relics*, demonstrating visually that the Revolution, and perhaps the leveling spirit
it had brought, was literally objectively past, finished, over, no more.
Hierarchically arranged, natural history specimens could also suggest
that "natural law," which had been commonly invoked to justify the
American Revolution, ultimately favored not social leveling, but a naturally hierarchical body politic. In short, cabinets of curiosities might
have aided elite conservative intellectuals like Belknap to undercut,
preempt, and otherwise delimit arguments from nature for egalitarianism in the wake of the Revolution.[26]

Like their European forerunners in the Age of Exploration, American cabinet keepers on the eastern seaboard of North America were

being presented with bewildering natural history finds picked up by explorers and pioneers who had gone westward. A decade after the founding of the Massachusetts Historical Society, the Lewis and Clark expedition brought back to the East Coast all manner of surprising, awe-inspiring natural and ethnographic artifacts. Atlantic Coast founders of the leading early historical societies could use their curiosity cabinets, as European rulers had in the Age of Exploration, to comprehend—and thus, manage psychologically—the complexities of their society's geographical extension westward into the unknown. At the same time, by evidencing their continent's natural richness *and* evoking historically great Americans, cabinets of juxtaposed civil and natural history relics effectively answered Old World natural historians in the European intelligentsia, such as France's Buffon, who insisted that America was a land of inferior natural resources, and hence of physically degenerate inhabitants of second-rate historical importance.[27]

Looking at specific pre-1840 holdings in the cabinet of the Massachusetts Historical Society, and at the limited extant direct evidence of what its membership thought of the artifacts, helps to confirm that the society's cabinet, like Charles Willson Peale's Philadelphia museum, juxtaposed objects illustrative of American natural and civil history at least partially with a view toward coherently and concretely bolstering America's ranking among leaders in the transatlantic Enlightenment elite. The society's original 1791 constitution, echoing the prospectus for the organization that Belknap had drawn up the summer before, committed the association not only to gathering historical manuscripts, but also to making a "collection of . . . specimens of natural and artificial curiosities. . . . which can improve or promote the historical knowledge of our country, either in a physical or political view."[28] By mid-February of 1795, "several natural curiosities" had "already" been "collected" by the society, and were on display in its Massachusetts "apartment," along with books of history and "Piles of Gazettes" that, at least by comparison, afforded "the eye little entertainment."[29] Artifacts on view presumably included all of the donations "For the Cabinet" that the society had accepted at its most recent quarterly meeting in January: "Specimens of Petrafications found at Brookline, from John Lucas, Esq. An Indian Bow and Arrow, and a Basket of Curious Workmanship, from Mr. John Dolbeare. The horns of a large

Buck and those of a small Buck, from Mr. Timothy Green. Four Young Sharks. The First Ball fired at Lexington on the 19th of April 1775, from Mr. John Soren. An Ellegant Mezzotinto print of Dr. Franklin, handsomely framed and glazed from Thomas K. Jones."[30] Consider how each of those objects could effectively have contributed to make the Massachusetts Historical Society's cabinet a nationalistic museum of American natural and historical greatness evocative of Peale's better-known menagerie. "Petrifications" could show the antiquity of America, implying that no matter how foreshortened the written record of the New World appeared, the western hemisphere actually had a full natural history. American Indian artifacts, especially the "Basket of Curious Workmanship," could remind viewers that American artistry existed even among the continent's aboriginal peoples, presumably even in its prehistory. Thus, Massachusetts Historical Society member William Jenks averred in 1831 that "remains of our Indians . . . found in the cabinet of curiosities which the Society is forming" offer "proofs of industry and skill" in Native American cultures.[31] The "horns of a large Buck" could be viewed as evidence that America had biological specimens no less hardy than their Old World counterparts, a point Thomas Jefferson had made in 1787 by shipping antlers from American deer directly to Buffon.[32] "Four Young Sharks" could have brought to mind the vast transatlantic environs and history that Europeans and Americans shared. "The First Ball fired at Lexington" might commemorate the triumphant fact that in the recent Revolution the American people had bested Europe's leading military power. The "Ellegant Mezzotinto print of Dr. Franklin," the most internationally respected American intellectual, could evoke the greatness of Boston, where Franklin was born and where his parents were buried, and conveniently link the spirit of the Revolution in which Franklin figured largely, and which members of the Historical Society loved to recall as a completed event, to printing, Franklin's vocation and the Massachusetts Historical Society's strategy of choice for preserving and disseminating historical knowledge. In 1836, the society accepted "a case containing matrices for types formerly the property of Mr. Franklin," with the request that the donation be "carefully preserved," and a suggestion "that any articles once the property of so distinguished a son of Boston (especially if connected with the art of printing) must be" regarded as particularly valuable.[33]

Numerous other patriotic artifacts also made their way into the society's cabinet in the early nineteenth century, including a "pen with which several signatures" were written upon the Declaration of Independence, a suit of "clothes worn by the immortal Franklin in the YEAR he signed the Treaty with France," and a "pair of epaulets, which were in habitual use by General Washington at the successful siege of Yorktown, in Virginia, and which were worn by him on the day when he resigned his commission as Commander-in-Chief to Congress at the Close of the Revolutionary War."[34] With such relics illustrative of American history set alongside American natural history specimens, in keeping with the society's 1791 formal regulation that "American coins and curiosities" must "be kept by themselves in the best part of the cabinet," the Massachusetts Historical Society created a collection illustrating the nation's past that, as one of its supporters, Thomas Hall, explained triumphantly in 1802, was quite like Charles Willson Peale's nationalistic museum in Philadelphia.[35]

Hall hoped that there would, however, be at least one crucial difference. Peale's museum, he complained, as "private property," could "be sold by" Charles Willson Peale "tomorrow, if he pleases, to the Emperor of Russia or to the Great Mogul," and "thereby frustrate all the endeavors of the liberal benefactor." Hall wished that the Massachusetts Historical Society, by contrast, would be built upon a less "narrow, precarious basis."[36] He need not have worried. In the first place, the Massachusetts Historical Society was a true association, not the personal fief of Belknap or anyone else in the way that the Peale museum was for Charles Willson Peale and his family. It is hard to imagine Belknap, his disproportionate influence on the historical society notwithstanding, presenting himself as its personification in anything like the way that Peale effectively identified himself with his museum's collection in his 1822 self-portrait, *The Artist in His Museum*. Belknap was too insistent that associations of individuals, not solo efforts, were needed among collectors for "securing what they have got together after they have quit the stage," for there was strength in numbers: "Solomon was not mistaken when he said. 'Two are better than one.'"[37] Belknap was hardly alone in recognizing benefits in association. In the half century following the Revolution, Americans became increasingly enamored with what Alexis de Tocqueville termed "the science of association." By the 1830s, that famously observant French visitor could report, "Americans of all ages, all conditions, and all dispositions constantly form associations."[38]

Formalizing the Massachusetts Historical Society's status as a historical association, the Massachusetts state legislature, in 1794, acknowledged that "the collection and preservation of materials for a political and natural history of the United States is a desirable object," and that "the institution of a Society for those purposes will be of public utility," and so granted the "Society by the name of the Massachusetts Historical Society" the right to exist "forever" as a "Society and body politic and corporate."[39] As artificial bodies of potentially endless duration in the law, corporations, in principle at least, could prevent losses of collective memory and material holdings as successive human generations hastened to the grave.[40] Thus, during the era of the early republic, incorporation became an increasingly popular strategy of choice among Americans who were seeking to effectively transmit favored values, activities, or undertakings further forward into the republic's history than the founding generation could hope to. The 1820s and 1830s especially would witness, though not without controversy, a general loosening of barriers to incorporation in the new nation, and a proliferation of incorporated historical associations, which, like the Massachusetts Historical Society, worked to preserve "the memories" of the "fathers" of the new nation as "the curtain of age will soon be drawn over their lives."[41]

Publishing Local Memory

Time and again, Belknap and others in the new association vowed that it would preserve written historical sources by publishing them. To John Adams, Belknap insisted in 1791: "The only sure way of preserving . . . things is by printing them."[42] A circular letter written by Belknap, and disseminated by the society in November of 1791, noted that the Massachusetts Historical Society's members "have . . . given their encouragement to . . . publication . . . in which will be given the result of their inquiries into the natural, [and] political . . . history of the country."[43] The use of the singular term "the result" is significant. It reflected Enlightenment confidence in the unity of knowledge, as did the content of the historical society's earliest printed offerings, which, though topically wide-ranging, still had overarching themes. In particular, comporting with contemporaneous vectors in memory culture, the society's first half century of publications stressed remembrance of past events as physically sited in ways that evoked local memory techniques of recollection.

Thus, in an 1813 address before the society, published in its 1814 *Collections*, member John Davis pointed out that while their organization had displayed "as valid memorials" in its "museum" the "utensils, . . . arms, and . . . trophies" of great Massachusetts men, "We have but few sepulchral monuments of our ancestors." Yet, he declaimed, the landscape itself can stand in support of their memory: "when familiar with their history, and fortunately it is most minute, this metropolis, its hills, harbour, and islands . . . and every neighboring village will bring their revered images to view." Inviting his audience to perceive the evocative powers of the local memoryscape firsthand, he declared: "On the spot where we are now assembled, we may behold Johnson at a little distance, [and] Cotton at the governour's garden."[44] Similarly, an 1815 publication by the society, a "Historical Sketch of Charlestown, Mass.," featured comparisons between locations of buildings prominent during the 1775 battle of Bunker Hill and those of the structures on the site in 1815.[45] A decade later, the Bunker Hill Monument would begin rising on the old battlefield, a brainchild, as the society proudly noted in its 1835 minutes, of William Tudor Jr., one of its members and the son and namesake of the man in whose house the society's inaugural meeting had been held in January of 1791.[46] At the monument's dedication on 17 June 1825, it would be lauded by society member Daniel Webster as important because "local association" is "fit to affect the mind of man," and the head of the Massachusetts Historical Society would represent the society in the day's celebratory parade.[47]

Exemplifying the Physicalist Turn

The Massachusetts Historical Society in its first half-century was thus very much in, and sometimes an influential part of, American memory culture as the latter was moving toward physicalism. Even Jeremy Belknap, a lettered rationalist disposed to prize the written word over "the senses," once urged the national Congress to construct "an apartment for the trophies taken from the enemy at various times in the late war," the "sight of which serves to fan the flame of liberty and independence."[48] The society that Belknap founded claimed in its 1792 "Introductory. . . . Address to the Public" that the "art of printing affords a mode of [historical] preservation more effectual than" monuments, such as those of "Corinthian, brass, or Egyptian marble."[49] Yet, vectors toward physicalism that affected American memory culture in the decades that followed not only pushed the society and its members toward suggesting and supporting the Bunker Hill Monument. Inevitably, these tendencies also influenced how the epistemic authority of the medium for preserving knowledge of the past that the society preferred—written history—would be judged.

Illustrating that epistemologies that affect memorialization, such as the physiognomic emphases of the phrenologist and the exegetical bent of the documentary historian, were never hermetically separated, is an 1834 letter by H. A. Griswold. Griswold reported to George Bancroft, a leading member of the society, an earnest patron of its manuscript and print archives, and, as one of the most popular and respected historians in the nation, virtually the personification of urbane, literate historiography: "Dr. [Charles] Caldwell [of Kentucky] gives [your historical writings] a very high character, even before he has seen [them]"; "because the author is *phrenologically* pre-disposed for a historian; he is sure [that a work of history by you] *must* be all that a historical work should be."[50] In other words, it was Bancroft's skull shape, not the latter's self-conscious devotion to German-style *criticism*, or *Kritik*, of written historical sources, that, for Caldwell, vindicated Bancroft's written histories.[51]

Clearly Jeremy Belknap, the Massachusetts Historical Society, and its patrons were affected by the bodily turn in late eighteenth-century and early nineteenth-century American memory culture, as memory and memories came to be understood and judged in increasingly physical terms informed by claims about human biology. From its inception, well before inherited popular local memory theory was actually reified by the likes of phrenologists, the Massachusetts Historical Society, with its emphasis upon understanding history in relation to localities and its cabinet brimming with juxtaposed artifacts of American civil and natural history, was anticipating, much as Charles Willson Peale's Philadelphia museum was in the same "historical moment," the physicalist direction in which practices among patriotic American rememberers would continue trending in the ensuing decades. What, though, of other historical societies that followed? Did their practices of memory develop similarly? A look at the early histories of three more of the most important early American historical societies, the New-York Historical Society, the Historical Society of Pennsylvania, and the Virginia Historical Society, may make the answer evident.

The New-York Historical Society

John Pintard, well before he spearheaded the 1804 founding of the New-York Historical Society, had begun drawing attention to artifacts as sources of nationalistic instruction. As an officer in New York's republican Tammany Society in 1790, Pintard founded its American Museum that featured relics illustrative of the new nation and its natural environment, a collection that would in time be taken over by showman P. T. Barnum. In 1808, giving similar attention to reliquary, Pintard's Tammany Society superintended what it touted as a long-overdue interment of American soldiers who had died on British prison ships during the Revolution.[52] At a personal level, Pintard experienced the power of bodily relics in 1821 while witnessing the repatriation of the body of executed British Revolutionary War soldier Major Andre "to receive the honour due to the memory of a brave and valiant soldier," and in 1830 as he was moving corpses of his deceased relatives to a new family crypt.[53]

Taken in by relatives after his parents' deaths not long after his birth in 1759, Pintard had learned that "dreadful secret" from the lips of his dying aunt: he was not being raised by his biological parents. By 1780, however, as he still excitedly remembered six decades later, while rearranging relics in the family vault, his grief was substantially assuaged when he discovered something precious: remnants of his birth mother's "long black hair, which I brought home and gave to my wife—[and] it remains [a memento of her] to this day."[54]

The ideological and interpersonal links and overlaps between Jeremy Belknap, the father of the nation's first historical society, and John Pintard, the father of its second, and between the respective historical organizations that they began, were many. Like Belknap's, Pintard's patriotism was forged in the crucible of the Revolution. When the entry of British troops into New York prompted a call-up of the New Jersey militia, Pintard, then a student at Princeton, tried to join the ranks. Ordered not to do so by "Professor Houston," who taught mathematics at the college, Pintard fell out. However, the next day he reconsidered and marched off to the Patriot camp where he soon faced his instructor, now Captain Houston. The "instant he saw me," Pintard remembered, Houston growled, "I thought that I ordered you to remain at home and mind your studies!" Feeling "like a Cock in his own dunghill, I recovered my arms, and replied, 'Sir! Could I see my native city attacked and not turn out in its defence?'" When his enlistment expired, Pintard returned to Princeton fully expecting to be expelled. Instead, he received his degree, and a warm handshake from Professor Houston as congratulation for his academic achievement and an acknowledgment of his wisdom in having made patriotism a priority. "I never look back at this period of my eventful life," Pintard later recounted wistfully, "but with much pleasure," and so it was with the New-York Historical Society, which, like its founder, honored and emphasized the memory of the Revolution.[55]

Pintard was among those who first prevailed upon Belknap to begin the Massachusetts Historical Society. Like Belknap, Pintard fretted over the physical fragility of aging historical documents and argued that printing multiple copies of them was the surest way to preserve them as primary sources. Like Belknap, Pintard accepted that while artifacts could be illuminating and inspiring, tangible written sources were most essential for conveying authoritative historical memories across time. A maxim that Pintard copied into his commonplace book made the point pithily: "Trust not everything to memory; half a word taken on the spot, is worth a cartload of recollection."[56]

Significantly, Pintard's New-York Historical Society offered "for the inspection of the curious, and for the reference of the man of research" opportunities to consider its manuscript and print holdings alongside of, and presumably as if in conversation with, material artifacts representing American civil and natural history.[57] A striking example of the society's civil-history mementos was "a piece of the original Coffin of General Montgomery," a much-mourned American casualty during the U.S. invasion of Quebec in the Revolution, which, at a meeting of the society on 11 August 1819, was "laid on the Table . . . placed in a vase with a glass covering for its Security" along with a certificate that attested to its authenticity, and noted that, presumably at the time of the corpse's transfer from Canada and its reburial at Saint Paul's Church in New York in 1818, the fragment was procured "by John Trumbull, one of the Vice Presidents of the Historical Society, to be deposited, in their collections."[58] Exemplifying the New-York Historical Society's attention to natural history artifacts was its effort, announced in 1817, to collect mineralogical samples from every state in the Union, and to house them in cabinets, one-per-state, "after the manner adopted in the national collection at the Ecole des Mines at Paris."[59]

Insisting that the American landscape should be used to preserve national memory was the message of "the first scholarly paper on American place names" ever "read before a learned society," an offering by Egbert Benson, one of the original founders and the first president of the New-York Historical Society.[60] In December of 1816, Benson argued before the society that "Naming counties, towns, villages, streets, forts, and so forth after the heroes and other worthies of our land, by formal public authority" constituted "a sort of legislative monument, which has this to recommend it to republican economy, that it comes cheap."[61] John Pintard could hardly have failed to agree. In the wake of the Revolution Pintard lobbied successfully for New York City to rename streets bearing royalist appellations from the colonial era, "such as King, Queen, Duke, Princess, and Crown," with good republican monikers.[62]

Also encouraging nationalistic pride in American environs was DeWitt Clinton. In 1811, as the New-York Historical Society's vice president, he used language evocative of local memory theory while celebrating "that curiosity we feel in tracing the history of the nations, which have occupied the same territory before us, although not connected with us in any other respect." After all, Clinton exclaimed: "'To abstract the mind from all local emotion,'" as "an eminent moralist" said, "'would be impossible, if it were endeavored, and it would be foolish, if it were possible.'"[63] Two years later to the day, an address to the society on American botanical history by Samuel Mitchill concluded that "American plants. . . . during the verdant period . . . surpass those which grow in other quarters of the globe" in "autumnal hues," providing "a spectacle . . . our artists might portray for the purpose of giving a national style and character to their landscapes," an imperative which would soon become associated with New York's Hudson River School of American painters.[64]

The Historical Society of Pennsylvania

The turn among patriotic American rememberers toward physical relics and physicalist memory theory, which affected the Massachusetts Historical Society and the New-York Historical Society, also influenced the Historical Society of Pennsylvania. This association, essentially an offshoot of the American Philosophical Society, which itself juxtaposed natural and civil history artifacts, was begun in mid-1820s Philadelphia in the wake of an episode in that city's history during which relics, both vintage and newly minted, were conspicuously utilized to celebrate and capture the patriotic moment of Lafayette's 1824 visit to Philadelphia on his famous memory tour.[65] As Hampton L. Carson noted in a 1940 history of the society, during Lafayette's visit to their city Philadelphians excitedly produced and brandished commemorative mementos of every sort, including cotton handkerchiefs depicting Lafayette's reception at Independence Hall, "white kid gloves stamped with portraits of Lafayette, 'Lafayette Snuff-boxes,' 'Lafayette Stocks,' 'Lafayette Cravats,' and 'Lafayette Flasks' for brandy."[66]

One person who treasured such a relic, a "Lafayette Badge," was John Fanning Watson, the Philadelphia antiquarian whose intertwined enthusiasms for local memory theory and patriotic reliquary knew no bounds.[67] Watson was not technically a founder of the Historical Society of Pennsylvania, but, as one of its actual founders remembered in 1826, at the meeting that launched the society two years earlier, it was "well understood that . . . John F. Watson, though personally absent" was "to be considered as present" and "therefore in the category of foundation members" of the Historical Society.[68]

Characteristically, in his contributions to the society's efforts to elucidate "the civil . . . and natural history" of Pennsylvania by collecting manuscripts, "medals, coins, or any other article deriving value from historical or biographical affinities: Indian idols, ornaments, arms, or utensils, &c.," Watson evidenced his pronounced passion for using historical relics as local memory props.[69] An extra-illustrated manuscript of his *Annals of Philadelphia* that he donated to the Historical Society, replete with inserted historical artifacts—including his "Lafayette Badge"—with transcribed historical documents, historical narrative, and references to "local memory," amounted to an annotated cabinet of curiosities, and was itself the very artifact of the juxtaposition of texts and relics in early American historical societies.[70]

Roberts Vaux, a supporter of fellow Philadelphian Joseph Delaplaine's physiognomically oriented efforts to honor the founders of the United States and one of the Pennsylvania Historical Society's eventual founding members, successfully requesting that Watson donate his manuscript to the projected Pennsylvania Historical Society, predicted in an 1824 letter to the latter that the extra-illustrated manuscript of Watson's *Annals* would "form a starting point" for the future society's efforts "& would no doubt insure the foundation of such an association."[71] In his other correspondence with Watson, the two shared their affinity for historical relics, comprehending their value with reference to local memory theory. After Watson wrote excitedly to Vaux of a surviving tree from William Penn's forest in the City of Brotherly Love, Vaux answered: "It gratifies me much to learn, that within the limit of Phil[adelphia] anything still *lives*, which had *life* at the time our adventurous ancestors originally committed themselves to the perils of the wilderness." Vaux continued: "When I next go to the City, I will visit 'the *Last Tree of the Forest*,'" and "it will give me pleasure to make some arrangement for rendering it an object of interest to the present, & for succeeding generations." Drawing Philadelphians' attention to the tree as a relic would, Vaux intimated, address a serious problem in that burgeoning city: "We have nearly lost our *local impressions*, '*strangers feed our flocks, & aliens are our wine dressers*', it is high time something was done to awaken worthy feelings concerning our honorable forefathers & the thing of their day." If he "could enjoy the consolation of having done as much as thy self," Vaux wrote to Watson, "toward bringing *the olden time* in review, I should think I had not lived in vain."[72]

Three weeks later, Vaux reported to Watson, "It has not yet been in my power to see the proprietor of the Elm on Race & . . . 7th St." to work out some way of marking it publicly as a historical object. "But the tree itself I have visited & contemplated it with no ordinary interest & pleasure. Something must be done to perpetuate so valuable a relick of the ancient time."[73] The next year, Vaux acknowledged Watson's "valuable present" to him of a box made of pieces of relic wood "which associate so many interesting recollections . . . and would prove a passport for its possessor to the good will of all the Antiquaries on the Globe." That box, Vaux gushed, "could not be committed to hands which will preserve it with more (I had almost said) *religious care* than my own, for as I grow older, my attachment to the Ancient time, & its memorials, increases & strengthens."[74]

In a report on "Memorials of Country Towns and Places in Pennsylvania" read to fellow members of the Historical Society of Pennsylvania at its 17 February 1830 meeting and published in its *Memoirs*, John Fanning Watson offered a first-person account of the joys of remembering Pennsylvania's history through visiting its historic loci and collecting related souvenirs. He noted that "Penn's furniture remained long at Pennsbury after his death," and "a gentleman of Bucks County told me . . . that for years it was deemed a kind of pious stealth to bear off some of the articles—one of them had the mantle piece, much prized, and another had his plush breeches; his clock and secretary desk are still known." In 1826, Watson explained, he had visited Pennsbury himself, and, like "those who had preceded me, I brought away a relic—a piece of the carved capital of the pilaster once at the front door."[75]

Watson was far from alone in preferring to view history through relics comprehended in terms of received local memory theory, which recently had been recast in particularly biological, physicalist terms. He had enjoyed a close personal relationship with Joseph Delaplaine, whose effort to commemorate in print the physical features of the Founders accompanied with narrative depictions of their lives was, like Watson's extra-illustrated *Annals of Philadelphia* and the first American historical societies, *both* a repository for written history and a sort of cabinet of curiosities. In his 1830 report to the Historical Society of Pennsylvania, while describing relics from Penn's estate at Pennsbury, Watson mentioned another friend, Deborah Logan, who, like Delaplaine, Roberts Vaux, and Watson himself, held enthusiastically to increasingly au courant physicalist presuppositions about relics and memory. On a visit to Pennsbury, Watson reported, Logan saw there William Penn's "quilt of white Holland quilted with green silk in figures."[76] In her diary, Logan, like the contemporaneous historical societies, gave priority to the written word as a prop of memory, but, also like the historical societies, she was fascinated with relics comprehended in light of the local memory tradition. Her diary, as Logan herself understood it, was itself a relic, in which she gave her memories "a local habitation." In that journal, Deborah Logan stressed how full her world was of evocative relics with "local charms" that effectively brought to mind associated memories.[77] Given their shared epistemic assumptions about memory and history, it is perhaps unsurprising that in his *Annals*, Watson dubbed Logan "the female historian of Pennsylvania."[78]

Watson's empathetic connections were not only with nostalgic fellow Pennsylvanians like Deborah Logan and members of the Historical Society of Pennsylvania. In the "Republic of Letters" that Jeremy Belknap presciently envisioned would link America's emerging historical societies across state lines, Watson became a leading citizen. Besides being a prominent member of the Historical Society of Pennsylvania, he was also a corresponding member of the New-York Historical Society and of the Massachusetts Historical Society. He wrote to the latter in 1832, acknowledging his election to its corresponding membership, sending along a "box of relic-wood formed of the last remaining walnut-tree of the primitive forest standing before the Hall of Independence at Philadelphia (*vide* page 350 of my Annals of Philadelphia)," and, in Watson's irrepressible way, he espoused his enthusiasm for "*means* of acquiring knowledge of olden-time events in given localities."[79] As the Massachusetts Historical Society noticed when it eulogized Watson in its 1861 *Proceedings*, he wrote in such terms not only to the Massachusetts Historical Society and to the Pennsylvania Historical Society, but also "to other historical societies of the country."[80] Watson's well-received, enthusiastic interest and involvement in leading early American historical societies, including the Pennsylvania Historical Society, is transparent evidence that it is accurate to view the practices and outlooks of those societies as deeply influenced by the turn toward physicalism in the popular memory theory of the day.

Virginia's Historical Society

Yet, the point should not be over-argued. Memory theory did not exist in a vacuum, simply dictating the formation and practices of the historical societies. A look at the Virginia Historical and Philosophical Society, the last of the four leading state historical societies to be formed in the pre-1840 era, is an instructive reminder that battles over memory, while clearly influenced by changing memory theory, also turned upon more earthy cultural and political developments.

In August of 1796, Virginia jurist St. George Tucker wrote to Jeremy Belknap lauding the accomplishments of the Massachusetts Historical Society while complaining that there was no equivalent society in the "country" of Virginia, with the unfortunate implication that "[t]he archives of this country are almost as little known as its natural history; and the characters of men perish with their corporeal existence." However, he insisted, "this country produced men of genius and of learning, and of virtues sufficient to have obtained them a fair seat in the temple of fame, had it been their fortune to move in any other sphere."[81] Three-and-one-half decades later, on 29 December 1831, St. George Tucker's son, George Tucker, a professor of moral philosophy at the University of Virginia, took the floor at a meeting of leading Virginia gentry assembled in the old hall of the Virginia House of Delegates for the purpose of founding a state historical society. Echoing his father's earlier concern, Tucker noted that no two states "had so much agency in bringing [about] the [American] Revolution as Virginia and Massachusetts." However, unlike Massachusetts, Virginia had no historical society "collecting valuable facts and memorials of its history." The antidote that Tucker proposed, and which the assembled group approved, was the Virginia Historical and Philosophical Society. It would, Tucker vowed, "collect and preserve materials for the civil and physical history of Virginia," with special attention to the Revolution as it had occurred in the Old Dominion. Tucker prophesied that "the time would come when our Revolution" will "be looked at as the most important event in fixing the destinies of the hundreds of millions who would inhabit this Continent, but also in influencing those of all mankind." In short, Virginia would one day have its due honor in the national memory. Its new historical society would help to hasten that day. Simultaneously, the society would draw attention to the natural greatness of Virginia, including "useful minerals" abundant in its mountains.[82] Several months later, the society issued an "Address to the Public" recapping Tucker's themes. The state, it proclaimed, was at last awakening from "lethargy," and, led by the Virginia Historical and Philosophical Society, would contend for that place of honor "among her sister States to which her moral worth . . . and past achievements" fully "entitle her."[83]

If the Tuckers and the new society seemed at once nostalgic and defensive, they almost certainly were. Virginia had been progressively losing political, cultural, and economic influence in the new nation since even before St. George Tucker's 1796 epistolary comments to Belknap enviously praising the Massachusetts Historical Society.[84] A long agricultural decline, as the state's overworked soil lost fecundity, was forcing Virginians to leave their native state and emigrate westward. Their exodus was draining the Old Dominion of assets and population, and hence of representation in the federal government. The gentry especially felt their state's plight. They lamented: "No one can make money or live like a gentleman in Virginia. We have lost all our honor. . . . Things grow worse and worse." Virginia "is a ruined country. It will see no felicity in our time[,] if ever."[85] George Tucker, seven years before helping to found the historical society, warned clearly, if implicitly, of Virginia's decline in *The Valley of the Shenandoah*. In that novel, "Colonel Grayson, a meritorious officer of the 'continental line' in the war of the revolution," gazing upon his family's old Virginia estate is "reminded . . . of the fall of his family from their former opulence and consequence to the most absolute poverty; and the tender . . . melancholy he had formerly experienced, was exchanged for a bitterness of feeling, and soreness of the heart, which had nothing in it consolatory or agreeable."[86] A like theme of nostalgia for Revolutionary Virginia pervaded another novel, *Edgehill*, which had been published in 1828 by James Ewell Heath, who in December of 1831 was, with Tucker, among the society's founders.[87]

In the latter year, Virginia's gentry was shaken by news of the bloody August uprising of Nat Turner and other enslaved people in Southampton County, Virginia. Delayed by illness, Turner intended to begin his insurrection several weeks earlier, on July Fourth, the high, holy day of American patriotic memory, timing that might have been meant as both a rebuke to the United States and an ironic nod at its Revolutionary history.[88] Future founders of the Virginia Historical Society were heavily involved in putting down the rebellion. Governor John Floyd, who in December became the society's first vice president, authorized dispersal of state weapons and militia against Turner; shuddered at reports "of the conduct of the negroes, the most inhuman butcheries the mind can conceive of"; and insisted in his diary that "white people shot them in self defense."[89] John Hampden Pleasants,

James H. Gholson, and William Henry Broadnax, all of whom would soon be among the first members of the society, helped to carry out Virginia's lethal military response. The *Lynchburg Virginian* reported that Broadnax's forces alone killed "upwards of 90 blacks," and, apprehending a leader of the insurrection, unceremoniously "shot him, cut off his head and limbs, and hung them in different sections, to inspire a salutary terror among the slaves."[90]

In 1832, after the rebellion had been suppressed, fiery debate ensued in the Virginia legislature over whether or not to abolish slavery in the state, drawing several legislators who had lately become charter members of the Virginia Historical and Philosophical Society into tense arguments about the applicable lessons and authority of state and national history and memory. Gholson, for example, thus rebutted fellow legislators, including Thomas Jefferson's grandson, Thomas Jefferson Randolph, who argued in support of abolition from memory of the Founders. "Will you believe it," Gholson asked sarcastically, "when I tell you that these great men of the revolution owned slaves. . . . Yes, actually owned slaves, and worked them too?"[91] Gholson was particularly put out that Randolph's plan for gradual emancipation would have begun on the Fourth of July 1840, which, to Gholson's thinking, would have forever sullied the patriotic associations of Independence Day.[92]

Historical society member George W. Summers, by contrast, framed emancipation as a bold stroke "worthy of the land of" Patrick Henry.[93] Broadnax, however, chortled that legislators contending for emancipation on the supposition that it would spare Virginia from future bloody rebellions might as speculatively, and uselessly, labor to prevent some future, fantastical dystopia in which travelers will forlornly search the ruins of Virginia's capitol building for relics of Jean-Antoine Houdon's statue of George Washington, which, in 1832, still had pride of place in the building. After legislative debate ended in a loss for the emancipationists, newly minted Virginia Historical and Philosophical Society member Thomas R. Dew published a triumphant postmortem summary of the controversy, celebrating the preservation of legally sanctioned slavery in the Old Dominion, and rejecting with particular disdain antislavery arguments that compared Nat Turner to "Lafayette" or to other revolutionists whose memory was revered in the dominant White culture.[94]

Perhaps, because it was, for him, too extreme or painfully obscene even to imagine, Dew did not consider the most provocative possible such comparison, one that, in the years that followed, would regularly be made by pro-abolitionist admirers of Turner: that of Nat Turner, as a would-be liberator of slaves, to the most revered freedom fighter in American and Virginian history, George Washington.[95] As the historically minded Dew perhaps knew, a like comparison was said to have been made in the aftermath of an earlier slave rebellion in Virginia, one led by Gabriel Prosser in 1800. At its conclusion, one of Prosser's band of rebels reportedly declared in court: "I have nothing more to offer than what General Washington would have had to offer, had he been taken by the British and put to trial by them."[96]

On 17 February 1832, shortly before Dew published his polemics against Turner and the emancipationists' uses of history and memory, Virginia Governor and Vice President of the Philosophical and Historical Society John Floyd conveyed news to the state legislature of what seemed to Floyd to be a contemplated material crime against the memory of Washington and the dignity of Virginia. "I have heard with painful emotion," he wrote, that, as part of the "preparations now going forward to celebrate the centennial birth-day of our countryman, George Washington," the "Congress of the United States are about to cause the remains of that distinguished citizen to be disinterred," removed "beyond the limits of Virginia," and placed permanently in a crypt within the federal Capitol building in Washington, DC, an expropriation that Floyd hoped that every legislator, as "descendants of those men whose blood was poured out and mingled in the soil of Virginia," would vociferously resist. The House of Delegates swiftly voted unanimously to join Floyd's protest.[97] In Congress, one Virginia representative lamented the effort to deprive his suffering state "of the last consolation of being the depository of" George Washington's bones, and another acknowledged that though, in the past, "Gentlemen had been pleased to call Virginia the fruitful mother of great men," she "has little left her but the pride of by-gone days"; the nation ought to "leave to Virginia her pride, and not to rifle from her arms the dust of her dearest, noblest son." In the end, the threatened plan died, as Washington's heirs roundly rejected the federal government's request to remove his corpse from Mount Vernon, where, as another member of Virginia's congressional delegation opined, "every stalk, every stone" is a relic of "the memory of the man."[98] The Old Dominion would hold on to George Washington's body, but the Virginia Historical and Philosophical Society was beginning its work in an era of extreme self-doubt among the Virginia gentry about their ability to preserve inviolate memories of their storied past.

That historical association, as it set about collecting relics and documents pertaining to Virginia's natural and civil history, was meant to resist Virginia's decline at a time when, as Thomas Gilmer declared before the society in 1837: "Few among us regard themselves as settled, fewer still succeed to places which were occupied by their families." Yet Gilmer hoped that though Virginia's youth now take "no time for forming local attachments," the Virginia Historical and Philosophical Society might have an ameliorative effect.[99] Gilmer's reference to "local attachments" was conventional in its use of the terminology of local memory theory, and, in practice, Virginia's historical society was generally conventional, self-consciously mimicking "similar institutions" as it simultaneously collected both natural and civil history artifacts.[100] Hobbled by extracurricular pressures and burdens, though, it did not flourish as well as its rivals in the Northeast. In 1838, plagued by a lack of funds, the society began nearly a decade of dormancy.[101] By then, its members' fear that Virginia was being pressed to the margins of collective American memory was all the more well founded.

When Belknap wrote to Ebenezer Hazard in 1790, sending along natural history artifacts from the greater western hemisphere, and broaching the idea of a Massachusetts Historical Society, he was betraying an Enlightenment worldview in which spatial, material, and temporal contexts—places, objects, and time—were of a piece, as local memory theory, particularly in its increasingly physicalist forms, effectively implied. Working from similar suppositions the later founders of the Virginia Historical and Philosophical Society saw with alarm that the Massachusetts Historical Society, the New-York Historical Society, and the Pennsylvania Historical Society were laboring with success to ensure that their states, and the North generally, would have archives of documents and artifacts sufficient to ensure their states' prominence in collective American memory. Those historical societies did so in ways that evidenced a theoretical and practical appreciation of the material foundations and props of memory and history. Two centuries later, historical understandings and popular memory alike are still profoundly affected by the magnitude of their success.

From the 1790s, and over the next half century, elite founders of historical societies; proprietors of museums and galleries, such as Peale and Delaplaine; and well-heeled literati, such as banker John Fanning Watson, worked diligently to conserve their privileged place in American memory, seeking to ensure, as Virginia Historical and Philosophical Society Member Thomas W. Gilmer said in an 1833 address: "the past at least is safe."[102] Yet, from the elite's standpoints the past really was not safe all, for by the 1820s and 1830s, people hailing from less privileged social classes or categories—including African Americans, Christian evangelicals, and proto-feminists—were taking strategic advantage of the turn to the physical, to relics and to loci, in memory culture to materially assert, and insert, themselves as central figures in America's patriotic pantheon. Among these able insurgents would be an irrepressible Revolutionary War pensioner in Middletown, Connecticut, with a flair for performing political street theater, always with himself in the unlikely starring role: Hamet Achmet.

PART II

DEMOCRATIZING TOUSLING OF AMERICAN MEMORY FROM THE 1820s

3

THE FREEDMAN

On 11 June 1827, more than one hundred boys who had come to Middletown, Connecticut, from all parts of the United States to study at the American Literary, Scientific, and Military Academy expressed their admiration and sympathy for local Revolutionary War veteran Hamet Achmet by subscribing ten to thirty cents apiece to a fund for his benefit.[1] At first blush, their act may seem surprising. Achmet had only been a drummer in the Revolution. No one remembered him for dramatic battlefield heroics. Admittedly, by the late 1820s, it was possible for nearly any veteran of the War for Independence to draw attention simply by remaining alive. It was also an era in which physical bodies, organic and inorganic, became key integers in American memory culture.[2] Enlisted men were generally the last embodied remnants of the Revolutionary armies, and suddenly seemed destined, as W. H. Prescott wrote to George Bancroft in 1835, to be "carted about" for exhibit at patriotic celebrations as "long as their bones" held together.[3] In such a climate, even a veteran drummer boy might be hailed as a living relic of the nation's founding conflict. Yet, if the demography of death favored honoring Achmet, a factor obvious to residents of Middletown could easily have precluded his popularity with the cadets: Achmet was African American, a member of a racial minority persecuted throughout the nation, including in Connecticut, where few Blacks remained legally enslaved but thousands still faced ubiquitous de jure and de facto discrimination.[4]

A manifestation of racial prejudice in the period was an inclination among White Americans to devalue or forget the Revolutionary War military services of Black Patriots such as Hamet Achmet.[5] In 1830, a long-promised monument to Patriots who had perished in 1781 at Fort Griswold was finally erected in Groton, Connecticut, some thirty-five miles east-southeast of where Achmet was living. Prominent in that memorial was a marble tablet upon which were inscribed names of eighty-four of the fallen. Noticeably "below" the other appellations, "by themselves," in "genuine keeping with the 'Negro Pew' distinction" common in American churches, under the heading "Colored Men," were listed two Black Patriots who had died at Fort Griswold, "Sambo Latham" and "Jordan Freeman."[6] Several days after the shrine's dedication, African American William Anderson, of New London, Connecticut, reflected upon how it memorialized prejudice, noting that the first name of his Black relative *Lambert*, also "called Lambo" Latham was indelibly rendered in its marble as a diminutive, "the *American classic appellation of 'Sambo.'*"[7]

Six years later, in New York, in the fall of 1836, an old African American man was taken into custody by a White watchman for being inexplicably "inhabited in the uniform of a revolutionary soldier." Seemingly unaware of Blacks' military services in the Revolution, the watchman simply assumed that he had chanced upon "an old fool, madman, or mountebank." However, that false "supposition was ultimately dispelled" by the African American himself, who offered "a short but clear account of his career in the revolutionary war," transforming himself from an enigmatic detainee into an object of public memory, soon celebrated in news accounts—however bemusedly—as a bona fide Black "Veteran of the Revolution."[8]

Similarly, Hamet Achmet's notoriety as an African American Revolutionary War veteran was effected by his own agency, his self-representation. Had you visited Middletown, Connecticut, in the 1830s, you might have heard the Revolutionary War pensioner relating that, as a child, he was kidnapped in Africa, sold into bondage across the Atlantic, eventually becoming a slave to none other than George Washington. In Washington's service he was tasked with holding the general's horse, and, as he grew older, with serving as his waiter. He subsequently fled to escape the clutches of Martha Washington—who disliked him—and served as a Patriot drummer in the Continental Army.[9]

A Penchant for Reliquary

In 1893, Emilie Stedman, a granddaughter of one of Middletown's leading citizens, enumerated the physical props with which Achmet corroborated his stories, an assemblage of material evidence proving to Stedman's satisfaction that "Hamet was undoubtedly a servant of Washington."[10] Among the Black man's treasured artifacts were several that he claimed had been personally vouchsafed to him by the Washingtons: "a tiny silver box, shaped like a coffin, inclosed in a wooden case of similar shape," containing "a lock of General Washington's hair," a "rapier, or small dress sword, engraved" with the initials "G.W.," and a "waistcoat of flowered silk, which 'the general' had worn."[11] Stedman was not alone in being impressed by Achmet's reliquary. In 1839, the *Hartford Review* enthused: Achmet "retains a perfect recollection of his massa and missus Washington, and has several remembrancers of them. Among these, is a lock of the General's hair, and his (the General's) service sword."[12]

While Hamet Achmet's use of artifacts to link himself to the nation's beginnings thus became an aspect of his popular notoriety in the 1830s, his recourse to Founding-era relics as evidence of his own history had begun earlier out of practical legal necessity. Achmet's Revolutionary War pension application included an 1818 deposition disclosing "that the declarant has the Drum which he used & the cap which he wore" during his service. His pension file also held a copy of an 1820 letter from Judge Pierpont Edwards—colonial-era preacher Jonathan Edwards's youngest son—to Secretary of War John C. Calhoun. Edwards's memo reiterated that Achmet "now has his *leather cap* and his *drum* with the distinctive marks of the United States painted on them."[13] Annexed to Achmet's application was a schedule of property mentioning "1 Drum which he had in the army," and disclosing that the Black man possessed "1 old Sword," the latter being, perhaps, an oblique reference to the blade of George Washington's that Achmet would eventually claim had been presented to him.[14]

The claim to have known Washington was likely to interest Achmet's Middletown audience. With the rest of the nation, that community had mourned Washington's December 1799 death. Two months after his passing, on 22 February 1800, at a solemn ceremony honoring Washington's birthday, a poem read to Middletown's assembled citizens highlighted lingering grief over the loss of their commander-in-chief among Revolutionary War veterans like Achmet: "Why droops yon veteran soldier's hoary head," his "honest pride, his wonted ardour fled?"[15] In 1826, just over two and a half decades later, the cadets at the American Literary, Scientific, and Military Academy, too young to have served under Washington with Achmet's generation, or even to remember the national shock as reports spread of Washington's death, were, nonetheless, effectively initiated into the cult of lamentation over Washington's decease. That jubilee year, the Middletown students took an official excursion to Washington's Mount Vernon estate at the invitation of the former president's heir, Bushrod Washington. The boys recalled that their host opened the vault in which President Washington was buried, permitting each cadet to "view the interior of the place that contained the mouldering remains of the greatest and best of men." One by one, the youths "approached and placed our hands on his coffin tenement—it was like the touch of a sainted spirit—the thrilling, ethereal influence sped back upon the heart," and "the swelling bosom sent forth in silence its fervent aspirations to Heaven, that, like Washington, we might possess and practice his stern republican virtues, although we might never expect to rank his equal in the annals of fame." Then, "Each withdrew in solemn stillness from the vault, fearful that the lightest tread of footsteps might disturb the calm, peaceful slumbers of the virtuous dead."

Next, the boys were conducted into the room that had been the general's private library. There, they beheld Houdon's bust of Washington. "This was, indeed, very interesting," the cadets recollected, "as we could here look with certainty on the exact features of Washington." Doing so, they perceived "a striking difference between this accurate resemblance and those imitations which we frequently meet with in different parts of the country." For example, "the hair was laid with more grace about the temples, giving more elevation and command to the forehead" than in other renderings. Apparently influenced by phrenology, or by one of the other contemporaneous popular physiognomic theories that held that character was physically legible, the cadets, by gaining such insights into Washington's bodily appearance from the mask, were able to "confirm our opinion of his exalted character."[16] Months later, when students at the academy took up a subscription for Achmet, perhaps their charity was at least partially inspired by a confidence that Achmet's Washington relics were genuine material proofs that he had enjoyed friendship with the man to whom they themselves had recently paid homage. In any case, by recalling Washington through physical objects, Achmet was tapping into a popular impulse not unknown in Middletown.

Washington himself realized well before his 1799 death that ordinary objects associated with him were becoming invested by his admirers with extraordinary significance. At the close of the Revolution, he thus presented his corresponding secretary Richard Varrick with the camp bed in which he had slept at Valley Forge—a memento that Varrick's progeny reverently preserved for generations.[17] By the mid-1820s, another relic, an old military field tent, retained by Washington heir George Washington Parke Custis, was being celebrated in the press as "THE TENT OF WASHINGTON."[18] Its postwar career was variegated: it was used to shelter Lafayette during his memory tour, for the funeral of a murdered Federalist, General James Lingan, and as a venue for the "the distribution of the first prizes given in America for the best specimens of sheep."[19] On one occasion, prominent Yale University chemistry professor Benjamin Silliman, a devoted Protestant evangelical, who as such might have been expected to regard relics as "popish," was permitted by Custis to see "the *material*" remains of the tent.[20] "Not content with" the "gratifications of sight and touch" that Custis meant to allow, the professor earnestly "insisted on being completely enveloped in the canvass, which was accordingly done."[21]

When even Washington's field tent could evoke such devotional behavior, the Washington relics that Achmet brandished could hardly fail to gain attention. As Bushrod Washington noted in 1811, by being "attached to the person of Genl. Washington" any object "however valueless in itself" could easily become a treasured Washington relic.[22] Relics of George Washington that Achmet possessed—the general's putative sword, waistcoat, and hair locks—could each have been assumed prima facie to have met such a test of bodily contact with Washington. When Achmet held Washington's monogrammed sword in his own hand, viewers could easily have imagined that decades before it was grasped by Washington's hand, or worn proudly upon the general's person, perhaps along with the very waistcoat that he had worn before its gifting as a memento to Achmet.[23] Still more thrilling to Middletown's residents must have been Achmet's exhibition of an actual bodily fragment of George Washington, the lock that the Black veteran claimed to possess of the good general's hair.

Hirsute Memory of Washington

By the 1820s, interest in hair reliquary was intense—though enthusiasm for collecting samples of Washington's tresses went back even further. In March of 1778, one of the general's aides forwarded a lock of his hair from Valley Forge to a female admirer.[24] Five years later, Washington concluded a letter to Andrew Billings—a Poughkeepsie, New York, watchmaker and the general's sometime dentist: "Mrs. Washington sends a lock of both our hair (Inclosed)."[25] On 17 December 1799, three days after Washington had died, his former assistant, Tobias Lear, recorded in his diary: "The body was laid in the Coffin—at which time I cut off some of the hair."[26] Less than a month later, members of the Grand Lodge of Masons of Massachusetts, which, like Hamet Achmet in the 1830s, possessed a sword of Washington's and clothing that he had once worn, wrote to Martha Washington, informing her that "a *Golden Urn*" would soon "be prepared" by the Lodge "as a deposit for a lock of hair, *an invaluable relique* of the Hero and the Patriot, whom their wishes would immortalize, and that" should the "favour [of a gift of a bit of the dead general's hair] be granted, Madam, it will be cherished as the most precious jewel in the cabinet of the Lodge." At Martha Washington's direction, Tobias Lear forwarded "a *lock* of her deceased Husband's *hair*" to the lodge, members of which subsequently held a mock funeral in which they bent "with anguish over the urn" into which they had placed the first president's tresses.[27]

Later, in 1824, a Washington heir wrote to a friend in Philadelphia, requesting that a breastpin be made to hold entwined strands of his famous forebearers. Designed as a gift for George Washington Lafayette, the marquis's son, it was to have the enclosed hair of George and Martha Washington affixed in its center and surrounded "with good pearls" set "in the best manner." On the provenance of the pile, the letter explained: "The General's hair was cut off in '76 . . . ," and advised, "It will be as well not to say, perhaps, . . . *whose* hair it is[,] as it is now so *scarce* an article."[28] One year later, in 1825, while taking a political swipe at John Quincy Adams for purportedly stealing the presidency from Andrew Jackson in a "corrupt" electoral "bargain," a news account alluded to Jackson's possession of a ring "With . . . the hair of Washington 'of the colour it was when he led our armies to Victory.'" How, the newspaper asked, could Jackson regret his loss in a presidential contest so notoriously stained by Adams's use of "'Bargain and Barter'"?[29] In 1826, the *Middlesex Gazette*—published in Middletown, Connecticut, where Achmet resided—reported enthusiastically on George Washington Parke Custis's gift of a lock of his namesake's hair to Simón Bolívar, the "George Washington of South America."[30]

Three years later, in 1829, John Pierre—who would soon provide John Fanning Watson with Washington locks—donated a shock of the general's hair to the Library Company of Philadelphia. Subsequently, that institution—possibly with Watson's encouragement—displayed the tresses in a frame made of wood from Washington's home at Mount Vernon; wood from a tree that Washington planted, and another that Lafayette planted; as well as fragments from Independence Hall, General Anthony Wayne's home, the frigates *Constitution* and *Alliance*, and Washington's pew at Christ's Church.[31] The symbolic exhibit, literally locating a part of Washington's body amid physical reminders of that Founder's material effects, relied concretely upon what an essayist had argued in principle in *The Polyanthos* in 1807: humans tended to remember something most clearly when it was associated mentally with a particular "locality" or "spot," and that principle was so "extensive in its influence" that it held even for portable loci, such as "a lock of hair."[32]

In this increasingly physicalized, biologized memory culture, Achmet's hirsute relic had a scientistic aura. Illustrating the diffusion of "scientific" claims about hair analysis into popular memory culture, an 1835 item in the *American Ladies' Magazine* on "Animal Magnetism" reported: "we are told that persons under the influence of animal magnetism . . . by being brought into contact with . . . a lock of hair" were "able to tell . . . what has happened years before . . . [even] to those whom" they have never "seen or heard of before."[33]

Finally, going just beyond the lifetime of Hamet Achmet, who died in 1842, Philadelphian P. A. Browne, of the Academy of Natural Sciences, began, by the late 1840s, to amass a collection of hair of leading U.S. founders and statesmen that eventually included samples from the first fifteen U.S. presidents, as well as Benjamin Rush, Charles Carroll, Charles Willson Peale, and many others. Simultaneously, Browne collected the filaments of other extraordinary personages—such as

"Gen[eral] George Washington's Hair Given to Mrs. S. A. Hart in 1840 by his servant-Hammet Achmet." (Middlesex County Historical Society, Middletown, CT)

insane-asylum inmates—believing that comparative analysis of human hair was a key aspect of "the philiological" and racial "science of man."[34] Lecturing seven years after Achmet's death, Browne announced that juxtaposing a lock of hair from the head of "his Excellency George Washington" alongside tresses from a "pure Negro" left him with "no hesitancy" in judging that "the white man" and "the negro" were "two distinct species."[35]

Taking Race by the Hair

Browne's ethnographic perspectives on hair, including Washington's, raise questions: was Achmet's display of the general's locks racially provocative? While the Black veteran was showing off Washington's hair, might his audience have been noticing Achmet's "African" hair, and comparing it with Washington's "European" hair? Did Achmet himself *intend* to provoke such comparison?

Surely, Achmet—who invoked his connection to George Washington to sell drums, and whose pension application argued from Revolutionary relics—could have empathized with Washington heir Elizabeth Parke Custis when the latter confessed to a correspondent that she hoped that "enclosed relics of the Immortal Father of Our Country" would evoke remembrance not only of Washington but of herself as well: "When I am gone & you can see me no more," wrote Custis, "look upon" the relics, "& when you think of General Washington, remember [me as] his best loved Child."[36] Similarly, Achmet, advertising himself "as George Washington's waiter," used his own Washington relics to draw attention not merely to the *general's* memory, but also to *himself*, as both a beloved servant of the general and his companion in arms.

Other evidence suggests that Achmet particularly delighted in garnering attention with his own hair, a predilection that apparently produced marital problems for the Black veteran. To obscure bodily evidence of their racially mixed union, Achmet's second wife, a White woman, once tried to dye her skin by "bathing in a decoction of mahogany chips." On another occasion, quite possibly because she considered his hair to be too flamboyantly African in appearance, while Achmet slept, she, so the story goes, surreptitiously shaved from his head long locks that were Achmet's "especial pride," but the wily Achmet only hid from her until they grew back.[37] The story, to be sure, seems apocryphal. It is hard to imagine that Achmet hid from his wife long enough for his hair to grow back.

Perhaps the tale was a trope applied symbolically to Achmet and not meant to be taken literally. In the 1830s, when Achmet was gaining fame telling his war stories, the "Old Testament," as Perry Miller once observed, was "so omnipresent in . . . American culture . . . that historians have as much difficulty taking cognizance of it as of the air the people breathed."[38] In such a world, Achmet's flamboyantly long hair and his marriage to a White woman would easily have brought to mind the Old Testament tale of Samson and Delilah in which mighty Samson's long hair is the source of his physical strength, but Delilah, his lover of another race, duplicitously shaves it off.[39] Very probably, then, the legend of Achmet's hair, as recorded several decades after his death, preserved a core historical truth: Achmet and his audience probably both recognized that he was effectively deploying his hair as a semiotic asset in a discourse that was fundamentally about race. Achmet likely knew that his own tresses, not merely his possession of some of Washington's hair, made him memorable and drove home the point that he was a *Black* veteran. In any case, half a century after his death, author Emile Stedman found persons who still vividly recalled Achmet's hair, describing in racialized terms as the veteran's "sooty wool," which "long manipulation had converted into pipe-stem curls" that "waved about his face in the most comical way imaginable."[40]

In Achmet's era, "sooty wool" was interpreted by many people, not just by P. A. Browne, as a significant racial marker. In several states, the so-called "wooly" hair of African Americans was read by jurists as presumptively excluding its possessors from full privileges of citizenship.[41] In 1763, in *The Rights of the British Colonies Asserted and Proved*, proto-Patriot James Otis had bristled at the suggestion that "any logical inference in the favor of slavery" could be drawn from someone having "short curled hair like wool, instead of Christian hair."[42] However, forty-three years later, in *Hudgins v. Wrights*, in his seriatim opinion for the Virginia Supreme Court, St. George Tucker explicitly maintained that among the "characteristic marks" with which "Nature has stampt [*sic*] . . . the African and his descendants," was "wooly hair," and the "burthen of proof" in Virginia was upon anyone wishing to argue that a given individual with a "wooly head" was not properly a slave.[43] Explicitly countering the claim of a signer of the Declaration of Independence, George Wythe, that all African Americans—the wooly-headed in Tucker's taxonomy—were entitled to natural-law human rights of the sort for which the American Revolution had purportedly been fought, Tucker insisted that Blacks who were not then legally freedmen had "no concern, agency, or interest" in the Revolution.[44]

Hamet Achmet was a living challenge to Tucker's memory of the Revolution. Achmet claimed to have effected his own revolution, fleeing the bonds of his enslavement to George and Martha Washington. Far from lacking "concern, agency, or interest" in the national Revolution, Achmet joined other African American Patriots of his generation in the fighting—including a number of slaves from Tucker's Virginia who battled in their masters' stead. Years later, rather than reading his own hair as indicating inferiority, Achmet took pride in his tresses, drawing an extant sketch of himself that emphasized his "wooly" locks.[45] Analysis of slave runaway advertisements from the period suggests that other African Americans in Hamet Achmet's era similarly delighted in displaying their hair, and—consistent with uniquely African semiotic traditions—used their hairstyles to convey messages about their own worth, status, and Africanness.[46]

It is possible that Achmet thought of his relic of Washington's hair in light of African or African American folk beliefs about how such

Hamet Achmet, pension-fund transaction note with sketched self-portraiture. (Middlesex County Historical Society, Middletown, CT)

locks could be used by a conjurer to gain mystical power over another person. In his autobiography, published in 1849, Henry Bibbs remembered that, while enslaved in Kentucky, he was told by an "old slave in that neighborhood, who professed to understand all about conjuration" that if he wanted to gain sway over his master, he should go "to the cow-pen after night, and get some fresh cow manure, and mix it with red pepper and white people's hair, all to be put into a pot over the fire, and scorched until it could be ground into snuff" then "to sprinkle it about . . . master's bedroom, in his hat and boots, and it would prevent him from ever abusing me in any way." After Bibbs "got it all . . . prepared, the smallest pinch of it scattered over a room, was enough to make a horse sneeze from the strength of it," but, to Bibbs's chagrin, the admixture "did no good," and he was "treated no better for it."[47] Quite possibly, Hamet Achmet—remembered not only for possessing locks from Washington's head, but also for his own hair—was doing similarly: drawing upon African sensibilities about hair that had transited the Atlantic with him.[48]

Their Bodies, Their Selves

Whatever he thought of the tuft of hair he possessed that he said came from George Washington's scalp, Achmet regarded his own body—not merely his possession of a relic from Washington's body, or of other artifacts external to himself—as evidence of his patriotic service and of his entitlement to federal compensation. His Revolutionary War pension application stressed: "I discharge Blood, and am unable to Labour much in consequence of a Wound Received at the Battle of Germantown."[49] Thus arguing from his own flesh, Achmet paralleled other Revolutionary War veterans in the new nation—including other Black veterans, such as Samuel Sutphen, Lewis Ambrose, and Sipeo Watson—who similarly stressed corporeal proofs of their patriotic sacrifices.

Beginning in 1832, African American Samuel Sutphen applied repeatedly to the federal government for a Revolutionary War service pension. Time after time, Sutphen's application was rejected—primarily because, as an enslaved man, he had fought as a substitute for his master. Thus, the War Department did not view the Black man's military services as his own. Still, Sutphen and White allies in his home state of New Jersey fought on, hoping that federal bureaucrats would finally be moved by the aged Black veteran's plea for "the pittance which I believe I have faithfully & honestly earned by my Militia services in the war[,] fighting for the white man's freedom."[50] Between 1832 and 1834, as the argument for Sutphen's cause evolved, it became increasingly physicalist and bodily in its epistemic emphases, conforming more and more closely to the contemporaneous physicalist turn in American memory culture. In 1832, Sutphen acknowledged that he could offer "no documentary evidence of his services in the war," but—not unlike Hamet Achmet—corroborated his story with a relic. For taking a British soldier prisoner at the Battle of Millstone, explained Samuel Sutphen, "general Dickinson Presented him with a Gun, which he still Possesses."[51]

Two years later, in another of Sutphen's pension applications, deponent Nicolas C. Jobs juxtaposed evidence from Sutphen's oral accounts, the physical confirmation of the surviving gun, and physical support from Sutphen's own body: "I have often heard him tell parts of his story which coincide with the facts stated in this application," Jobs declared. "One circumstance, I believe is not contained in his statement, which he has often related to me, that is he has often showed me a musket presented to him . . . long before the late law under which his claims were [made] passed[,] or he had any expectation of applying for a pension," and Jobs had personally "seen" bodily evidence, the "scars of the wounds" that Samuel Sutphen "says that he . . . received" fighting in the Revolution.[52] In documents produced only months later, for Sutphen's May 1835 bid for a pension, the bodily argument became more detailed. Sutphen described serving as a Patriot sentry at West Point, when his position was attacked by "a party of Hessians or Highlanders." As a result, deposed Sutphen, "I rec'd a bullet upon the button of the gaiter of my right leg, & both ball & button were driven into the leg, just above the outer ancle bone." In the "same affair," he continued, "I rec'd a wound just above the heel as high as the ancle, which appeared to be a cut almost dividing the legs cord behind the ancle, in the same leg." What is more, "Both these wounds and scars," he explained, "are yet plain to be seen and felt."[53] Supporting Sutphen's argument from his body, a physician and former congressman from New Jersey, Lewis Condict, offered medical testimony: "at the request of Samuel Sutphin, the coloured man within named who claims a pension, I examined his right leg & foot, alleged by him to have been wounded in an engagement with the enemy in the night, upon the Hudson river." Doing so, Condict discovered a "hard, knotty scar" that "is seen & felt inside the large tendon called by anatomists 'tendo Achilles,'" and judged that the wound was "the cause of a palpable and visible lameness, which yet afflicts Sutphen at this day." On the "same leg, about three inches above the ancle," explained the physician and politico, "is another scar, somewhat depressed, the size of a half dollar," and "I should think that the small bone of this leg (the *fibula*) must have been shattered, as the cover-membrane (priostrum) has been destroyed—the tendons & integements, being now all firmly fast to the bone & the motions of the ancle joint are greatly impaired, when contrasted with the other limb."[54]

Condict's bodily inspection of Sutphen could readily have called to mind other investigations in the early nineteenth century of Blacks' bodies by Whites. There was, for example, national interest in the late eighteenth and early nineteenth centuries in the physiognomy of Henry Moss, a Revolutionary War veteran of African descent who took advantage of his having had what today would probably be diagnosed as vitiligo, a disease which causes skin discoloration, to market himself as a curiosity whom onlookers excitedly interpreted as a Black man becoming a White man, inspiring hopes in some that, from the example of Moss, the American public would soon infer that being Black was an insubstantial, contingent, malleable matter of environment or of curable disease; problems of racial conflict in the United States might then benignantly pass into oblivion, as race was taken to be impermanent, and as techniques, developed from close observation of the "spontaneous cure" of Moss's Blackness, were perfected to, at will, similarly transform other Blacks into Whites. So great was the excitement that, for a time, as phrenologist Charles Caldwell remembered decades later, Black Revolutionary War veteran Henry Moss was "almost as familiar to readers of newspapers and other periodicals" as "John Adams, Thomas Jefferson, or James Madison." Yet, interest in Moss receded as racist attitudes in the United States progressively hardened in the late teens and early twenties of the nineteenth century. By then, innumerable White notables, from Benjamin Rush to Thomas Jefferson and George Washington, had already indulged their curiosity about the transformation of the once "very black" man who in "the late war . . . enlisted . . . in the continental army" as a private "and behaved himself very well as such." They had poked, prodded, pinched, and otherwise surveyed Henry Moss head to toe, excitedly commenting upon his complexion, his skin, his hair, his lips, his limbs, even his anus.[55]

Condict's 1835 explication of Sutphen's body might have evoked not only the notorious case of Henry Moss, but also personal testimonials by Blacks who had known slavery, such as Solomon Northrup's antebellum recollection of being inspected during a slave auction in the 1840s. Northrup remembered that he and other Blacks were obliged to "hold up our heads, walk briskly back and forth, while customers would feel our hands and arms and bodies, turn us about, ask us what we could do, make us open our mouths and show our teeth, precisely as a jockey examines a horse which he is to barter for a purchase." Some of the human chattel were "stripped and inspected more minutely." Whenever scars were discovered "upon a slave's back, they were considered as evidence of a rebellious or unruly spirit," making the slave less marketable.[56] Like Northrup and his fellow slaves, Sutphen was "minutely" inspected by a White man intent on finding scars. Yet the two investigatory regimes differed markedly. Sutphen, rather like the profiteering Moss, was examined at his own behest, not under the duress that Northrup experienced. Scars found on Northrup would have been read as indicating an offensive character, and literally be held to diminish his worth, but Sutphen stood to gain financially from Condict's verification of his wounds. Disfigurements could be read as evidence of the elderly African American's authenticity as a Revolutionary veteran and, thus, of his entitlement to a federal pension.

Whether in his own thinking Samuel Sutphen ever compared and contrasted Condict's inspection of him to the widely reported ogling of Samuel Moss decades earlier, or to contemporaneous bodily inspections of enslaved men, women, and children at auction, surviving sources do not reveal. Yet, as a longtime slave who only became free after purchasing himself after the Revolution, it is particularly possible that the latter comparison entered Sutphen's mind. More generally, his and Achmet's decisions to draw attention to marks of war upon their persons, like Moss's earlier self-marketing, could well have been informed by an awareness that Whites were apt to regard Black bodies as curiosities, as well as by the evident fact that by the 1830s Revolutionary War veterans in general were coming to be prized as scarce living embodiments of the glorious War for Independence.[57]

Like Sutphen and Achmet, African American Andrew Ferguson also used bodily evidence of his service in the Revolution to contend for a federal pension. Appearing in an Indiana courtroom in August of 1838, Ferguson described himself as "a colored man," born in "Dinwiddie County, Virginia," in 1765, and drafted into the Patriot forces "soon after the Declaration of Independence, the date not remembered." Fighting at "the Battle at Camden," he had been "Wounded . . . in his legg, which is still sore." Still more severe had been a combat injury to his head "in the Battle at Guilford." As a result of the head wound, testified Ferguson, "I . . . stayed about a month at the iron masks." Later, "a silver plate was placed on the fracture by Doct[or] John Sidney who attended him in the hospital; and still remains as evidence of the fact." In subsequent affidavits, Ferguson complained that the pain from his leg and head injuries had only grown more incapacitating, and supporters swore that while closely examining "the person of Andrew Andre Ferguson identified in the foregoing deposition as a revolutionary soldier," they had seen "apparent wounds and injuries which he states to have been inflicted while he was actually in the service of the revolution and in the line of his duty."[58]

While Sutphen's and Ferguson's pension applications both deployed sworn affidavits by White allies who formally inspected the old Black men's bodies for physical wounds from the Revolution, the pension application of Judah Watson, widow of African American Sipeo Watson, who had lived in Connecticut at the same time as Hamet Achmet, featured an equivalent bodily argument from a Black veteran's informal exhibition of his scars. Insisting that Watson's widow deserved a posthumous pension for his combat in the war, Zebulon Parkis put his mark to a deposition which asserted: "The said Sipeo and Judah were[,] when living in Plainfield[,] near neighbors to me[.] That Sipeo Watson was wounded in the Revolutionary war, and I have felt the Ball in his leg which he said was Shot in there when in an engagement."[59] In a revealing way, the touching of Watson's scars paralleled what happened to other Revolutionary veterans in Connecticut in 1817, when President James Monroe, on a visit to Fort Griswold at Groton, Connecticut, came upon two old veterans of the battle, "Mr. Park . . . and his brother Mr. Ebenezer," whose scars were too conspicuous to permit them to escape his "kind notice." Under "the impulse of the moment," Monroe reverently "laid his hands on the traces of their wounds."[60] Sipeo Watson and other reminiscing Black veterans who argued from their own bodies might thus be understood as using semiotics that reflected the contemporaneous bodily turn in American memory culture writ large.

Orality as Bodily Engagement

Robert J. Rude, whose family owned a farm on which Sipeo Watson lived and worked for nearly two decades, had his own memories of Watson telling war stories. Rude recalled that the Black man "who was lame in his leg . . . used to say that he was wounded while in an engagement with the enemy in the Revolutionary war and the wound on the leg was a running sore most of the time until . . . his Death," in the spring of 1815, when he was finally "buried on my Farm."[61] Thus, Rude, like Zebulon Parkis, remembered Sipeo for drawing attention to his Revolutionary services not only with the bodily evidence of his war wounds but also with autobiographical oral testimony.

While arguments from their bodies were prominent in reminiscences of many Black veterans, orally recounting their memories was an even more conspicuous means by which African American veterans throughout the young nation identified themselves as living links to the United States' founding epoch. Thus, Massachusetts resident Benjamin Richards, who, like Robert Rude, grew up on his White family's farm in the company of a Black veteran who worked it, recounted in 1833 that "between thirty and forty years past," African American "Quork Martrick . . . Laboured on the Farm owned by my father in Staughton." In his youth, explained Richards, he "often heard" friendly banter between the Black man and two others "who frequently labored on the Farm with Martrick," David Bunell and Jacob Goldthwait. The three "frequently conversed" together "relitive to the War of the revolution, as they were all revolutionary soldiers," reminiscing "about the stations they were placed" at during the conflict, "New York, New Jersey, West Point, &c, &c," and many other "particular places." Years later, Richards could "well remember hearing Bunell and Goldthwait state" that they were in the artillery, and Martrick was in the infantry, and from "the conversation those revolutionary soldiers" had, as well as from his personal experience of Martrick as "a person of truth," Richards was convinced of the veracity of Martrick's stories. Besides, he could not imagine how a poor African American, such as Martrick, presumably illiterate, and thus, Richards appears to have further supposed, limited to oral communication alone, could have fabricated tales so rich in incidental historical detail. Martrick, exclaimed Richards, was "African born," and so had "means of information" too "small" for him to have simply invented his narrations. Yet, he "has always been reputed to be a revolutionary soldier by the aged People in my neighborhood," and "I have always resided[,] since he came to live in the bounds of Staughton[,] within about a mile of him."[62] Orality was thus clearly effective for Martrick in conveying memories of his Revolutionary services, even if—as Richards apparently meant to imply—print culture was inaccessible to that "African born" serviceman.[63]

Significantly, Matrick may not even have valued literacy over orality. Quite possibly, he *preferred* orality. Whether or not he was exposed to reading or writing as a child in Africa, Martick had almost certainly been acculturated there to respect oral communication as an artful semiotic strategy of first choice. Scholars have often noted a penchant for orality in African and African American cultures antedating the era in which the African-born Martrick lived, and extending through the present day.[64] It is only reasonable to suppose that as Hamet Achmet, Sipeo Watson, and other African Americans voiced memories connecting themselves to the United States' nativity, they may often have been at least partially influenced in doing so by traditional African and African American emphases upon orality as a primary means of conveying memories.

If orality was indeed an African "survival" in the memory culture of the late early republic or early antebellum African American communities, how did Black veterans' oral performances of memory relate culturally to the frequent arguments from bodies and artifacts? Given prominent physicalist themes in the dominant American memory culture of the day, it might be tempting to assume that arguments from their scars and from relics in pension applications by Hamet Achmet, Samuel Sutphen, Lewis Ambrose, Sipeo Watson, and other African Americans *simply* reflected their assimilation of semiotic influences of the dominant U.S. culture, while oral communications reported in, or transcribed into, their own or other African American veterans' applications *simply* reflected "African" roots. Such a starkly bifurcated view, neatly dividing the "African" from the "American" in African Americans' practices of memory, would, undoubtedly, be too simplistic. Such orality as U.S. Revolutionary War veterans stood to inherit from Africa was what has been termed "primary orality," and as the late literary critic Walter J. Ong observed, such orality "always engages the body."[65] In primarily oral cultures, communication is *performative* utterance; bodily gestures, bodily deportment, hence the body itself, are inseparable from acts of oral communication and carry semiotic weight jointly, a point that may easily be overlooked by persons in a primarily literate culture, who may be acculturated to think of words as separable from the bodily presence of a speaker, as capable of existing with identical meanings apart from the speaker, as in a written script or transcript.[66]

Consider the characterization in a mid-nineteenth-century letter to the editor of the *Boston Journal* of the performativity of an African American Revolutionary War veteran, "Prince": "Many of the older portions of our town's folks have frequently heard" Prince tell "the story of" his own role in the surprise "capture of General Prescott" during the Revolution. Prince, "a native African belonging to the Goodwin family of this town" would be "all of a quaver [*sic*] in telling" the story, explaining that he had broken in the door of the room where Prescott had been hiding, by butting it "with his head." As he related his tale, Prince would make up the "defects of language by acting over again the incidents of the surprise."[67] Thus, the letter writer, as a literate person, assumed that Prince primarily used gestures to substitute for words, the meanings or pronunciations of which were unknown to him as a native African. However, as someone quite probably steeped in the body-incorporating semiotics of African orality, it is possible that the old Black war veteran, had he reflected upon them, would have considered his gestures as *essential* to his storytelling, not merely as countersigns for English words that could as accurately be understood as a written text separate from a physical performance.[68]

Perhaps it was thus for Achmet. Perhaps the African-born storyteller assumed that it was essential for his audience to understand his tales of Washington and the Revolution by reading his performing body, not just by listening to his words as abstract signifiers. Achmet's allusions to his visible war wounds might thus be understood as exemplifying, or amplifying, his already body-centered semantics. If, in the course of his performance, he went on to brandish a lock of Washington's hair, as his "curls . . . waved about his face," the juxtaposition of bodies—of Achmet's and of a keepsake fragment from Washington's—may have been more deliberate and more emphatic than those for whom literacy, not body-conscious orality, is primary are apt to assume.[69]

While semiotics of African-derived primary orality may thus have influenced Achmet's personal interpretation of the valences of his arguments from props and from his body, the general turn toward physicalism and bodies as legible objects in the broader American memory culture may also have influenced him, and other African Americans, to conspicuously deploy concretized and bodily arguments. Intent on persuading others to believe his reminiscences, Achmet could hardly have failed to learn—if only by trial and error—what appealed to his audience and adjusted his presentation accordingly. By the evidence of powerful White patrons' affidavits in his pension application, and from the generosity shown toward him by cadets of the American Literary, Scientific, and Military Academy, it is apparent that Achmet's reminiscing had a general appeal that resonated across the racial line in Middletown.

Pension applications of other Black veterans show that they too voiced, not only within their racial community, but also to Whites, memories of their own patriotic services. Indeed, every Black veteran who applied for a Revolutionary War pension needed to sensitively articulate his memories to a judge who would certainly be Caucasian. Such rememberers may have been acculturated to primarily rely upon African-style orality to convey memories, but as African *Americans* they could also be expected to, and needed to, argue with fluency in the semiotics of the dominant American memory culture.

Verbalizing Bodily Proximity or Physical Connectedness

African American veterans in the early nineteenth century appear to have simultaneously met requisites of African orality and comported with an increasingly physicalist contemporaneous American memory culture as they narrated tales of their own physical proximity, or material connection, to the Founders. Thus, Hamet Achmet could allude to, or display, his Washington memorabilia while telling "long stories" connecting himself to the general.[70] Quork Martick's pension application indicated that, while he could not remember the names of his immediate commanding officers in the Revolution, Washington had been known to him personally.[71] Charles Barnett's 1833 application emphasized that: "At York this declarant saw Genl. Washington, Steuben, Lincoln, and Lafayette and other field officers."[72] African American Primus Babcock, also of Connecticut, who frequently told tales about his personal involvement in the Revolution, delighted "for many years" in supplementing his narration by showing those who listened that his military discharge certificate was personally signed by George Washington[73] Judge Calvin Goddard, who claimed to have helped nineteen Black veterans to secure federal pensions, later declared that he could not "refrain mentioning" how "Primus Babcock . . . proudly presented to me an honorable discharge from service during the war, dated at the close of it, wholly in the handwriting of George Washington. Nor can I forget the expression of his feelings, when informed, after his discharge had been sent to the War Department, that it could not be returned. At his request, it was written for, as he seemed inclined to spurn the pension and reclaim the discharge."[74]

Similarly, an African American veteran from New Jersey, Oliver Cromwell, delighted in pointing out that his discharge certificate had Washington's signature upon it. After Cromwell's certificate, like Babcock's, was sent away to the War Department as part of the pension application process, a newspaper reported of Cromwell, "He mourns . . . much" that he no longer has the certificate, "and always speaks of it being taken from him with tearful eye."[75] That Goddard and Cromwell so treasured their discharge certificates for the material traces of Washington that the latter bore in the form of the vaunted figure's handwriting is not surprising when one considers that Washington autographs had, by then, become so highly prized generally that, in 1828, a Washington heir, betraying no sense of irony, honored one friend with a gift of the words "the post office" pared from a letter that Washington had written years before, and gave to another friend a fragment consisting only of: "The words 'that it[,]' written by his hand."[76]

In testimony supporting his own federal pension application, William Coff, a Black Virginian, highlighted his own bodily connection to a Revolutionary officer, albeit deceased, by stressing his wartime physical proximity to the latter, noting that he "well recollects . . . when Col. Malmody[,] a French man and a continental officer'[,] was killed in a duel . . . and that" he "and three others . . . buried the body of . . . Col. Malmody."[77] Similarly, Black veteran Primus Hall distinctly recollected "the death of Captain Samuel Flint . . . that he was standing near his Captain when he received his mortal wound, and caught him in his arms to prevent his falling." In the same 1838 affidavit, the African American stressed his close personal contact with Washington during the war: not only had Washington personally discharged him; Hall had joined the Patriot forces "at the earnest solicitation of General Washington" and reenlisted "at the earnest request of the General."[78] Though he omitted the tale from his deposition, Hall, who became a wealthy Boston soap maker after the war, "used to entertain the social circle" in that city with an even more striking tale of having been physically close to the general, a truly unique variant of the "Washington slept here" trope. During the Revolution, explained Hall, he found himself one night "in the possession of a blanket, at a time when such a luxury had become scarce." Presently, "Gen. Washington," who had kindly given his own bedding to "worn out soldiers," entered the tent. Out of respect, "Hall immediately tendered his blanket to the General, who replied that he preferred sharing the privations with his fellow soldiers, and accordingly Gen. Washington and Primus Hall reposed for the night together."[79]

Remembering Proximity in Slavery

Achmet, so far as surviving sources indicate, neither claimed to have slept next to George Washington nor to have had noteworthy personal contact with him as a soldier *during* the Revolution. Yet, he did claim unique knowledge of Washington as a former slave at Mount Vernon. Other Blacks in the young nation, sometimes publicly, sometimes privately, also claimed special insight on the basis of their having been physically proximate through the "peculiar institution" of slavery to the champions of the nation's liberty. Paul Jennings, for example, born enslaved to James Madison in 1799, gained notoriety in his later life as Madison's former "body servant," proudly verbalizing into the Civil War era the bodily intimacy with which he had known "the Father of the Constitution": "I was always with Mr. Madison until he died, and shaved him every other day for sixteen years."[80] For her part, Sally Hemings, enslaved by and longtime concubine of Madison's neighbor and political ally Thomas Jefferson, apparently taught her children, whom her master, the author of the Declaration of Independence, had sired, the truth about their physical parentage, though Jefferson, so far as is known, never publicly acknowledged paternity.[81] Such a connection to a Founder, invoking not only the glory of the nation's beginning, but also the indignities of its slave system, was apt to be bittersweet. Jefferson's son, Madison Hemings, born into slavery at Monticello in 1805, in a newspaper interview decades later, signaled his pride in being a son of someone who "was considered as a foremost man in the land, and held many important trusts, including that of President," but remembered too that Jefferson had never been "in the habit" of showing the sort of affection toward his illegitimate mixed-race enslaved children that he demonstrated toward his legitimate White grandchildren.[82]

Hemings's descendants made varying choices about how to handle their conflicted family heritage. As Madison Hemings acknowledged late in his life, several of his light-skinned relatives sought to escape the pressures of racial prejudice by "passing" into the dominant White culture.[83] Doing so successfully would have entailed guarding closely, perhaps even choosing not to share with one's offspring, the family's memories of their physical connection to Jefferson through an enslaved forebearer. Nonetheless, many Hemings relatives took pains to carefully preserve within their families the story of the Hemings-Jefferson affair. Numerous descendants of Sally Hemings are *still* passing on vibrant, apparently unbroken traditions of their Jefferson ancestry, and other families descendant from Monticello slaves likewise have inherited knowledge of their progenitor's bondage to Thomas Jefferson.[84] Generally, the means of transmitting memory of their bodily connection to Jefferson in these families has been orality of a sort that African-born Hamet Achmet could have appreciated. In addition, as Achmet did when showing off his souvenirs from George Washington, the Hemings heirs have also used heirlooms putatively associated with their Monticello master to corroborate their tales.[85]

Shocking as it may seem by current mores, many of Jefferson's slaves who survived him were evidently purchased as living souvenirs of Monticello and its famous proprietor. In 1826, when word spread that two of the men most associated with the Declaration of Independence, Thomas Jefferson and John Adams, had died on the very day of the much anticipated jubilee of American independence, July Fourth, the conjunction of their deaths was widely interpreted as an omen of God's favor toward the United States. Thus, the two Founders became even more celebrated in the immediate aftermath of their deaths—and certainly less controversial—than during their long lives.[86] Six months later, on 15 January 1827, when many of Jefferson's enslaved men, women, and children—having been advertised in the local newspaper along with such Monticello memorabilia as the "household furniture, many valuable historical and portrait paintings, busts of marble and plaster of distinguished individuals, one of marble of Thomas Jefferson," and "a polygraph or copying instrument used by Thomas Jefferson"—were sold at auction, it is perhaps unsurprising that they generally fetched prices well above their appraised market value, suggesting that they were being valued as relics, living remembrancers of their deceased master.[87]

Part of their attraction may have been that they could tell stories of their firsthand dealings with Thomas Jefferson, as Isaac Jefferson did. In about 1847, Isaac, who adopted his enslaver's surname, recounted to a White man, the Rev. Charles Campbell, his remembrances of Thomas Jefferson, who, the Black Jefferson said, "used to talk to me mighty free." Isaac especially remembered his master's physique. Thomas Jefferson had been "a tall strait-bodied man as ever you see, right square-shouldered, well-proportioned," not a "man in this town walked so strait, as my old master; neat as built man as ever was seen in Vaginny, I reckon[,] or any place—a straight-up man; long face, high nose." The old Black man considered himself to be enough of an authority on Thomas Jefferson's physiognomy, as well as that of Washington, to declaim that a published depiction of Thomas Jefferson was incorrect. "Old master never dat handsome in dis world," Isaac Jefferson told Campbell after seeing the image in question; "dat likeness right between old master & General Washington."[88] Thus, Isaac Jefferson, as Thomas Jefferson's former slave, in a period when portraiture was thought to reveal character, implicitly argued from his former physical proximity to the more famous Jefferson that he, Isaac Jefferson, had special knowledge of Thomas Jefferson's true physiognomy, and how it compared unfavorably to George Washington's.[89]

In the 1830s, Hamet Achmet too wanted to be remembered as the former slave of a now-dead Founder. He was creating and capitalizing upon his own celebrity as he walked Middletown's streets, advertising toy drums that he had made in his cottage as productions of a former "waiter of Washington."[90] Bona fide or not, Achmet's claim to have been a slave of Washington's was likely to have had different significance than claiming to have been held in slavery by any other Founder. First, Washington was the dominant figure in nationalistic memory; no name had more cachet than his. Secondly, George Washington, unlike any other Founding Father, could be recalled as an actual liberator of his Black slaves, not merely as someone who had held them in servitude. By the terms of his will, executed after his death in 1799, George Washington freed all slaves "which I own in my own right."[91] To identify one's self as a former slave of George Washington, then, might conjure not only enslavement but also manumission by the most revered Founder of all.[92]

Whether such calculations entered into Achmet's decision to publicly portray himself as Washington's former property, he was not the only African American to gain attention as one of Washington's supposed enslaved attendants.[93] The most famous contemporaneous example was Joice Heth, shamelessly exhibited by showman P. T. Barnum as the over-one-hundred-year-old wet nurse of baby George Washington. For a period in the 1830s, Barnum made a good living off of Heth, as the Black woman, whom he purchased as a slave, traveled with him about the country, entertaining crowds eager to believe that they were personally seeing, and listening to, someone who had nursed the long-dead father of their country in his infancy.[94] Whether Achmet too had only a fraudulent connection to Washington, the Black veteran's stories and artifacts—indeed, his entire nostalgic performance—could similarly appeal to a broad audience. Apparently recognizing this, Barnum made an unsuccessful effort to persuade Achmet to become one of his traveling curiosities.[95]

Remembering amid Interracial Politics

What appears to have impressed Barnum about Achmet—the African American's conspicuous success at evoking widespread interest and sympathy with his reminiscences—is especially striking given the divisive politics of race in Achmet's era and locale. Though by the 1820s few of its Black residents were legally enslaved, African Americans in Connecticut, Samuel J. May remembered, were a "proscribed, despised class," liable to retaliation for any conspicuous effort to assert themselves socially or politically.[96] A series of incidents in the 1830s in the village of Canterbury, some thirty miles from Middletown, became emblematic of contemporary popular prejudice against Blacks in the state, even while inspiring recollections of the sacrifices of Black Revolutionary War soldiers from Connecticut.

Prudence Crandall, headmistress of a school for young ladies, which she operated out of her home, was approached in 1832 by Sarah Harris, then about seventeen years old and of African and Indigenous descent. Sarah asked if she might be admitted as one of Crandall's pupils, so "that she might go forth qualified to be a teacher of the colored people of our country, to whose wrongs and oppression she had become very sensitive."[97] Crandall, at first, hesitated. Many of the parents of her current students were openly in sympathy with the American Colonization Society.[98] From its founding in 1816, the ACS sought to remove free Blacks from the United States to Africa, voluntarily if possible, by coercion if necessary. The society enjoyed widespread support among

Whites in both the North and the South, including in Connecticut, where the state legislature formally endorsed colonization.[99] Wanting to encourage free Blacks to emigrate to Africa, many colonizationists opposed any measure that might make African Americans feel more comfortable or successful in the United States. Crandall therefore expected that there would be intense opposition from procoloniza-tionists to admitting Sarah into her girls' school, yet agreed to Harris's request. For a time, all went well, and the young Black woman pursued her studies unmolested. Soon, however, parents of Crandall's other pupils began to complain strenuously of race mixing in the school, just as the schoolmistress had anticipated. Rather than dismissing Harris, Crandall, whose personality was by all accounts adamant, instead dismissed all of her White pupils and advertised that henceforth her school would admit "young ladies and little misses of color."[100]

Reaction was frenzied.[101] In Middletown, Connecticut, where a Black man, on the basis of his race, had only recently been denied admission to Wesleyan University, Jehiel C. Beman, an African Methodist Episcopal Zion Church clergyman, and the son of African American Revolutionary War veteran Cesar Beman, worked to recruit Black students for Crandall's school.[102] Enraged Whites in Canterbury had other ideas. They were determined, as one newspaper explained, that "a school to teach girls with black skins, wooly heads, and flat noses, the same thing that white girls are taught" should not "be endured," and Crandall's opponents employed means both legal and extralegal to drive the schoolmistress and her Black pupils out.[103] Manure was smeared on the school's front steps. Local boys followed Crandall's Black students about town, beating drums, perhaps to evoke stereotypes of drum-beating Africans. In a midnight raid, vandals smashed ninety panes of glass out of the boarding school's windows.[104] Responding to angry petitions from White citizens, Connecticut's legislature, in May of 1833, passed a "Black Law" aimed at closing down Crandall's academy, and preempting any similar undertakings in the state.[105]

Hanging over the court battles that ensued was memory of the Revolution and questions about what rights, if any, Black Patriots' military services in that conflict had or had not merited for African Americans as a race. Crandall's counsel noted that she was on trial "within a stone's throw of the house where lived and died General Israel Putnam, who, with his compatriots of 1776 periled his life in defence of the self-evident truth that 'all men were created *equal*, and endowed by their Creator with the inalienable right to life, liberty, and the pursuit of happiness.'"[106] At trial, the state of Connecticut argued that since Blacks were legally barred from voting in Connecticut, African Americans residing within its jurisdiction, including Crandall's pupils, were legally citizens of neither Connecticut nor the United States, and so were not within the purview of the federal Constitution's "equal protection" clause. Thus, Connecticut could deprive Blacks of rights of assembly, including for purposes of education. Crandall's attorney, William Wolcott Ellsworth, son of Oliver Ellsworth, who had been chief justice of the United States Supreme Court, countered that, as a race, African Americans from Connecticut had effectively won citizenship by the sacrifices of Black Patriot soldiers in the Revolution.[107]

Later, when Crandall's conviction was appealed to the state's Supreme Court of Errors, Andrew Judson argued on behalf of the state that Prudence Crandall's conviction must be upheld, and Connecticut allowed to deny citizenship privileges to Blacks, or "this *American Nation*—this nation of white men," might "be taken from us, and given to the African race!"[108] "America," Judson declaimed, "is ours—it belongs to a race of white men" whose "fathers" purchased it by their "blood."[109] Representing Crandall, William Ellsworth answered that the federal military pensions given to Black veterans of the Revolution were a "testimonial" that African Americans "had a country" in the United States and "had bled for it."[110] "We come," declaimed another of Crandall's attorneys, Calvin Goddard, "in behalf of those and the children of those who fought and shed their blood with our fathers to secure these blessings—we come to ask *to pursue* that happiness for which they fought, and to enjoy that life and liberty which they then secured."[111] Goddard recalled that some years before, when "clothed" as a Connecticut judge "with authority to examine the qualifications of applicants" for federal Revolutionary War pensions, he had "found within the little circle of my residence, nineteen colored persons whose claims, I believe, were well founded" for such a pension. Dramatically, the Connecticut jurisprude invoked his memories of Primus Hall, and of how that African American veteran had treasured his discharge paper, because it bore George Washington's signature. "Was not Primus a citizen? 'an illustrious citizen?'" asked Goddard, and, at the close of the Revolution, when the Continental Congress set aside 18 October 1783 as a day for *"the citizens of these United States"* to render "praise and gratitude to the God of their salvation," had "the colored people, who had fought, and bled, and suffered to obtain these rights of 'human nature,' no part nor lot in this matter? Had they no cause for gratitude? Or were they turned out of the human family, not even 'fragments of citizens'? Did Primus keep this thanksgiving?" How, Goddard wondered, could the court suppose that citizenship in the United States may be limited to Whites alone, when the Constitution of the United States, was "adopted" only "about six years after the peace," and written by "leading men of the old Congress," in whom "memories" of Black Revolutionary War service simply could not have "faded" so soon.[112]

In the end, the Connecticut Supreme Court of Errors evaded Goddard's implicit challenge to rule on the integrity of the United States' Founders, vacating the charge against Crandall on grounds of "insufficient information" without resolving questions raised by Crandall's attorneys about whether the citizenship status of Connecticut's Black residents was affected by the Revolutionary War service of such African Americans residents of Connecticut as Primus Hall or Hamet Achmet.[113] Yet, those questions, and the charged racial politics surrounding them, could certainly have been on the minds of Achmet and his White admirers in Middletown, Connecticut, as the old Black man claimed to have fought in the Revolution and to have been Washington's beloved slave. By identifying himself as an actor in the nation's natal conflict and affiliating himself with its leading political icon, George Washington, Achmet could easily have been understood as signaling that he was a true American and no fit subject for removal to Africa, as the American Colonization Society—then active in Middletown—would have prescribed.[114]

If Achmet was, in fact, contending for his Americanness, a historicized perspective on the semiotics of his argument suggests that he did not do so at the cost of obscuring or abandoning his African heritage. On the one hand, Hamet Achmet exemplified the bodily and physicalist turn in the dominant memory culture by brandishing a lock of George Washington's hair, while, on the other hand, being proud of his own conspicuously African hair, which he may well have thought about in terms of African semiotic standards.[115] Similarly, while Achmet's "long stories" about his service to General

Washington were apparently for the purpose of highlighting Achmet's legitimacy as an American, such conspicuous orality might also
have been read as typically African. Thus, Achmet's performances of
memory were apparently neither merely "American" nor simply "African," but notably "African American."

Remembering amid Intraracial Politics

Tell-tale African survivals in their memory practices seem to have
bothered neither African born Hamet Achmet nor most other African
American Revolutionary War veterans, but they were off-putting to
some middle-class members of the rising generation of Blacks in the
urban North of the 1820s and 1830s. In an era when White American
nationalists such as Jeremy Belknap, John Pintard, Noah Webster, and
others were asserting the superiority of tangible, written history over
evanescent oral history, it is perhaps unsurprising that some young
urban Blacks, though demanding inclusion in the body politic because of their forebearers' participation in the Revolution, betrayed
discomfort with the orality by which the very memories from which
they were arguing had been handed down. A case in point was New
York's pioneering African American newspaper the *Colored American*. That publication—which sold particularly well in Middletown,
Connecticut—briefly lauded Hamet Achmet as the "last" living servant
of Washington and published written manifestos by Black activists demanding political rights because "[our] fathers fought by the side of
yours in the struggle which made us an independent republic." Yet, the
newspaper admitted, in "giving account of the services of colored men
in the American Revolution, we are compelled to a great extent to depend upon traditional, instead of written history." The same newspaper
routinely derided orality as inferior to literacy. It printed the maxim:
"Books are standing counsellors and preachers, always at hand, and
always disinterested; having this advantage over oral instructors, that
they are ready to repeat their lesson as often as we please." An essay it
printed railed against laws forbidding Blacks from being taught to read
as relying upon a false supposition: that "all the knowledge of our duty
toward God and our duty toward our neighbor, may be communicated
by oral instruction." The *Colored American* published too the epistolary complaint of "A COLORED BALTIMOREAN" that "if [a Black]

minister should . . . suffer to be seen in the pulpit, for the assistance of his memory, a small piece of paper, embracing the heads, &c. of his discourse, he is by some" ridiculed for depending upon "what they are pleased to call 'a little paper god,'" and it printed another letter arguing: "we cannot expect to accomplish much, without the powerful energies of the press" which "effected the American Revolution."[116]

Typifying the semiotic suppositions of the rising generation of self-consciously literate Black activists was African Methodist Episcopal Church bishop Daniel Alexander Payne. Payne was an antebellum-era affiliate of the founding editor of the *Colored American* and the grandson of a Black man who, Payne "was informed"—apparently through family tradition—fought in the American Revolution. Bishop Payne became embittered when "the General Conference of 1848 . . . appointed me to the position of historiographer of the A.M.E. Church, and I therefore resolved to request Bishop Quinn to release me from pastoral duties, that I might travel in search of the [documentary] materials necessary for such a history." Quinn refused, and, after indignantly resigning his ministerial post, Payne devoted himself to collecting documents from which to write a proper history of the AME church. He soon became frustrated, as he found that most of what could be known about the church's founding era could only be had by accrediting oral tradition. Out of necessity, Payne used oral testimony as a source for his written ecclesiastical history. Decades later, still abashed at having had to do so, Bishop Payne vented in print about the failure of the AME's founders to keep written records, reiterated that oral tradition was never as reliable as written historical evidence, and indicted as a group the generation of African Americans who were active in "the American Revolution," for having done little subsequently for the "elevation of" their "race" through "education," by which Bishop Payne clearly meant education in the forms of European-style literacy and away from un-lettered African orality.[117]

However embarrassed Payne and other young, elite, urban, literate Blacks in the early antebellum era may have been by widespread illiteracy and persistent African-style primary orality among elderly Black Revolutionary War veterans such as Hamet Achmet, they nonetheless owed much of their social and political confidence to inspiration drawn from memories, almost always communicated to them orally, of the Revolutionary War sacrifices of Black veterans. It was with some pride that Bishop Payne asserted early in his autobiography that he had been "informed" that his grandfather "was one of six brothers who served in the Revolution."[118]

Another Black clergyman of Payne's generation, Baptist minister Jeremiah Asher, likewise opened his printed memoirs by remembering how, as a child, he had "often listened with feelings of unmingled grief" as his grandfather, Gad Asher, who lived less than twenty miles from Middletown, Connecticut, described being captured and enslaved in Africa by "white men."[119] Asher's grandfather told him that later he "fought side by side with white men in two or three important battles of the American Revolution, including the memorable battle of Bunker Hill, where he lost his eyesight, which he never regained." For the elder Asher, the promise of freedom and participation in the Revolution had been linked inextricably. He had gone to war as his master's substitute on the latter's pledge of manumission in return, an agreement not honored at the conflict's end.[120] Thus, Jeremiah Asher's grandfather Gad orally communicated memories central to his identity—his African roots and his connection to the United States as an actor in its founding drama—with wounded eyes as bodily evidence of his sacrifices for a nation still dominated by men who, like his old master, wished to deny African Americans natural liberty of the sort for which Gad and others had fought in the Revolution. In effect, Gad Asher voiced to his grandson what the pioneering Black historian W. E. B. Du Bois would later call a "two-ness" experienced by African Americans, a sense of being *both* African and American, with all of the social and cultural complications attending such a dual identity.[121]

In the late republic and early antebellum eras, Black veterans and Blacks who had once been enslaved by a Founder reflected hybrid African and American identities, not only by *what* they remembered, but also by *how* they remembered. Telling stories linking themselves to the United States' founding epochs and statesmen, they employed memory strategies that had notable affinities with prevailing vectors in both the dominant American memory culture *and* with "surviving" African semiotic traditions. In an era when many colonizationists thought of Blacks in the United States merely as out-of-place Africans, and in which some self-consciously literate, elite Black assimilationists cherished a hope that Americans of African lineage would purge themselves of every trace of African influence, including reliance upon orality, the thoroughgoing cultural "two-ness," apparent in performances of memory by Gad Asher, Hamet Achmet, and other reminiscing Black veterans and former slaves of the American Founders put the lie to simplistic assumptions by assimilationists and colonizationists alike. Both by *what* they remembered, and by *how* they remembered it, Hamet Achmet and his contemporaries conveyed that they had blood-bought rights to participate fully in American life, and that they would do so without abandoning their hybrid African American identities.

Growing up not far from Middletown, Connecticut, young Jeremiah Asher was listening closely. In 1862, he vividly remembered the "colored soldiers of the Revolution" in Connecticut who were "accustomed to talk over the motives which prompted them to 'endure hardness.'" Asher had listened to them "talk, until I almost fancied myself that I had more rights than any white man in the town." It was from hearing those "old veterans and champions of liberty" tell tales about their own participation in "never-to-be-forgotten battle for American Liberty," that he developed his "first ideas of the right of the colored man to life, liberty, and the pursuit of happiness," and began acting upon them: "I confess that the result of their teachings gave my parents much trouble, for whenever I was insulted, I would always resist it. Neither my father nor my mother could persuade me that white boys were allowed to insult me because I was colored. I invariably felt justified in defending myself."[122]

As Jeremiah Asher thus appertained in his youth, there was an implication of militancy in the old Black veterans' reminiscing.[123] Yet, perhaps reflecting firsthand awareness as combat veterans of what a pitched fight could cost in broken lives, elderly African American servicemen, including Hamet Achmet, seem not to have been carelessly provocative when telling their stories. Instead, determinedly communicating their politically charged memories of their Revolutionary service to Whites and Blacks alike, they labored to woo audiences, employing both prevalent American *and* traditional African memory strategies. The "old colored veterans of the Revolution" thus showed semiotic savvy, even as they remained faithful to their complex identities as American warriors of African descent.

To Emile Stedman, describing him years later primarily on the basis of oral history in Middletown, Hamet Achmet had been a "harmless, kind old man" who was "very short and thick set," was noted for dressing up in "quaint regimentals," and insisted on being buried with many of his relics of Washington and of the Revolution, fearing that someone would "rob him of his treasures so carefully guarded during his long life."[124] Yet, "for all his ignorance," to borrow a phrase that Stedman used, the "little black drummer" garnering attention in Middletown Connecticut, and beyond in the 1830s, with his long locks, his George Washington relics, toy instruments, and ready tales, was no fool.[125] Contemporaneous newspaper accounts divulged that he "converses freely in three or four different languages—the French, Spanish, and German—besides his native African tongue," suggesting that early in his life Achmet was what the late historian of slavery Ira Berlin dubbed an "African Creole," a cultural polymath, a native of Africa who deftly learned to speak the native languages of European slave-trading powers that had encroached on that continent, yet nonetheless fell victim to their rapacious trafficking in human flesh.[126] Ultimately, however, Hamet Achmet was irrepressible, a survivor, a virtuoso of oral and material memory, one of *many* African Americans in the early republic artfully remembering themselves as the United States' forgotten Founders.

4

THE EVANGELICAL

In 1840, Charles Downey, a student at Methodist Wesleyan University in Middletown, Connecticut, called out to Hamet Achmet, whom he knew as an "old negro man" who "lived near the college buildings." "I jokingly offered," Downey later recalled, "to throw a piece of furniture from an upper window into the yard," saying that "if he would catch it[,] he might have it." Achmet "became much excited. . . . He was too old to walk upstairs, wanted me to bring the piece down," and "as the strongest temptation he could command," declared: "I give you—O'—I give you six [of] Massa Washington's hair[s]."[1]

One might assume that Christian evangelicals, including Methodists such as Downey, would have opposed, or at least not readily joined, the turn to relics in the new nation's patriotic memory culture.[2] Protestant evangelicals notoriously mocked Catholics for venerating relics, and British Methodist founder John Wesley's well-known opposition to the American Revolution left that denomination's reputation vis-á-vis the Revolution fraught. Yet, when confronted with Achmet's offer of six of George Washington's hairs, Charles Downey hesitated not a moment to accept and later noted that no less a Methodist than Wesleyan University president Willbur Fisk had been sufficiently impressed with Achmet's cache of the founder's filaments that, when the latter was persuaded "to sell" but "a small portion" of his Washington stash, Achmet earned the "remonstrance of Dr. Fisk and others." Thereafter, he "could not be induced to sell any more" and he kept the rest of the hair "securely preserved." To Downey's happy surprise, however, "the bargain" between himself and the savvy old man was speedily "closed and executed." In the wake of their deal, the young student wrote an enthusiastic record of their exchange, to which he sewed the hair itself, concluding triumphantly: "this is the hair."[3] Downey's stitched-together micro essay and hair relic would be treasured and passed down through generations of his family, until, in 2018, the heirs to the hairs deposited them for safekeeping in the archives of De Pauw University in Indiana, where Downey had been a professor.[4]

Nearly a thousand miles away, at the Strawbery Banke Museum in New Hampshire, another extant artifact similarly evidences comingling in patriotic early American memory culture of word and flesh, fetish and faith. Crafted by the niece of George Washington's private secretary, Tobias Lear, soon after the ex-president's death, it spells out in bodily *fragmentum*, in hair taken from George and Martha Washington's heads and then stitched onto paper backing, a tribute poem composed by Tobias's mother:[5]

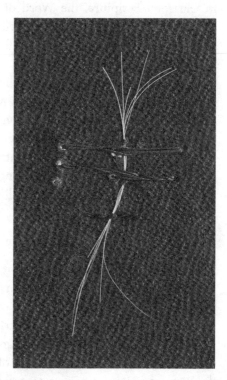

Six strands of hair given to Charles Downey by Hamet Achmet in 1840. (De Pauw University)

This is work'd with our illustrious and beloved General
GEORGE WASHINGTON'S hair:
Which covered his exalted head;
But now enroll'd among the dead.
Yet wears a crown above the skies,
In realms of bliss which never dies.

This is work'd with Lady
MARTHA WASHINGTON'S hair,
Relict of our beloved General.
I pray her honor'd head.
May long survive the dead;
And when she doth her breath resign,
May she in heaven her consort join.

This hair was sent to Mrs. Lear,
By her good friend, Lady Washington.

In Christian Scripture, the Word of God "became flesh and dwelt among us." Scripture was instantiated as the incarnate Christ.[6] In the Lears' relic, the flesh—or, at least, the hair—of George and Martha Washington was transmogrified into a document articulating faith in the heavenward destinies of the Washingtons. Between that hairwork's creation and Downey's purchase in Middletown of a part of Hamet Achmet's hank of George Washington's hair four decades later, American evangelicals had been tacking back and forth between, and at other times revealingly juxtaposing and interweaving, relics and words, artifacts and preachment, while laboring to annex patriotic memories of America's nativity to their earnest religious cause.

Fisk and Reliquary

To begin to understand what it meant, and what it took, for putatively relic-averse Protestant evangelicals in the young nation unabashedly to prize patriotic relics, we might look more closely at Downey's apparent mentor in both theology and patriotic reliquary, Dr. Willbur Fisk, who, as Downey noted, rebuked Hamet Achmet for not being a discriminating enough keeper of relics of Washington. In the late 1830s, the Wesleyan University president spent months traveling throughout

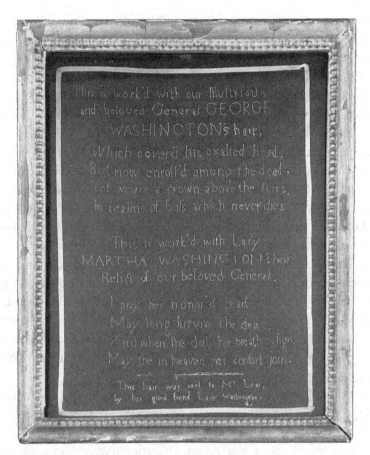

The Lears' embroidery of George and Martha Washington's hair. (Carter Collections Center, Strawbery Banke Museum, Portsmouth, NH)

Western Europe on business for his university and denomination. His published travelogue of that journey can be read as an extended meditation on both the theological perils and the practical promise of relying upon relics to buttress personal and collective memory. Recapping the Italian leg of his tour, President Fisk expressed dismay that the corpse of the late sculptor Antonio Canova had been parceled out for incorporation and internment in monuments to the artist's memory: "This cutting up the body of a great man, to scatter it among his admirers is a revolting barbarity, and species of *superstitious materialism* that ill becomes a rational believer in the immateriality and immortality of the soul." It was, however, "in perfect accordance" with the "rage for relics . . . in Catholic countries," that in "the religionist" may "be vented upon a toe of a saint," but, in the soldier was "called into action by the relic of a general or hero."[7]

Though Willbur Fisk repeatedly condemned popular Catholic adoration of relics in his travelogue, he was enraptured by loci and objects evoking either patriotic American history or the history of Methodism. He boasted that in France, in the very "house where Lafayette, that 'patriot of two hemispheres' breathed his last, I had the pleasure of preaching." In England, Fisk was "most interested" when visiting a church where "the great Wesley preached, and here his mortal remains are deposited, as also several others of the most eminent Wesleyans of England," all marked rationally by "chaste and beautifully designed and executed monuments . . . with appropriate epitaphs." He was enamored with John Bunyan's "humble cottage, . . . still standing," and earnestly prevailed upon the "pious old couple" living there "to give us a chip from the beam of the house" as a relic. At Kingswood, he viewed "Mr. Wesley's gown, now almost hanging in shreds, which I had the curiosity to put on," and "the association was almost inspiring," though "I fear no permanent inspiration resulted from the temporary investiture."

Fisk could count on biblically literate readers of his book to mentally compare his donning of Wesley's gown with the scriptural tale of Elisha putting on the mantle of the ascended prophet Elijah and with it the prophet's gift of divine inspiration. Declaring that he had worn Wesley's physical clothing, but not thus expropriated the great man's metaphysical empowering by God, President Fisk leaned into a distinction popular among his coreligionists. "We do not worship relics," an article in a Methodist magazine conventionally explained years later, "yet, as Charles Wesley says in one of his Scripture hymns—alluding to Elijah's mantle, which he dropped . . . , and which Elisha caught and kept— 'We gather up with pious care'" that which "'pious saints have left behind,'" and "'dearly love and highly prize, the mantle for the wearer's sake.'" As a Methodist theologian, Fisk would always equate the "Catholic who believes in the virtue of" relics with "an ignorant African pagan" who "talks about the virtue of his *gree-gree*, and relies upon it for his protection." As an enlightened university professor, he might also have appreciated historical artifacts such as hairs from Washington's scalp as tangible loci for materially underwriting memory in agreeance with prevalent local memory theory that was then vectoring toward physicalism.[8]

Fisk died in early 1839. Three years later, Joseph Holdich's *The Life of Willbur Fisk* remembered its subject as both conversant in local memory theory and patriotic. Holdich lauded Fisk's published account of his European trip for offering "local descriptions," and impressive "allusions to the chief historic associations connected with . . . places through which" he passed. He also highlighted Fisk's well-documented reverence for icons of the United States' Founding, including Franklin and Lafayette, and he observed that 22 February was both the day of Willbur Fisk's passing and that of George Washington's birth. Declared Holdich: "Thus, may the names of Washington and Fisk" ever "blend in future unison, their happy spirits," having "long since greeted each other in the plains of the brighter world above." Later, in 1858, Methodist preacher J. B. Wakely defended enthusiasm for patriotic reliquary by citing Fisk's example: "I know there are some who pay too much veneration to relics," wrote Wakely, but "there are others who value relics of the past," such as "the late Dr. Fisk." Thus, the chair in which Washington used to sit, "the table on which he wrote are held in high estimation," and the "pen with which the 'Declaration of Independence was signed is preserved in the Massachusetts Historical Society." Even "tea is still preserved that lodged in the shoe of one who aided in throwing it overboard in Boston harbor at the Commencement of the Revolution." So if, in 1840, as he peered out the upper-floor window of his room overlooking the yard at Wesleyan University while entertaining Hamet Achmet's offer of six hairs from the head of George Washington, young Charles Downey did indeed think of President Fisk as someone whose personal example afforded precedent for a Methodist to appreciate patriotic relics—if not also their sale or religious veneration—he was not the last Methodist to make that argument.[9]

Nathan Bangs and the *Advocate*

After Fisk's death, his soon-biographer, Joseph Holdich, a preacher and professor of philosophy and literature at Wesleyan University, pled at a memorial convocation for someone to take up the mantle of Willbur Fisk. Now, our "prophet," President Fisk, Holdich intoned, "is translated," like Elijah of old, but "where," he asked, "are the Elishas who have caught the falling mantle of our ascended Elijah?"[10] Eventually, Willbur Fisk's office at Wesleyan University, if not his mantle, was taken up by the university's second president, the Reverend Nathan Bangs, who had served on the school's board of visitors for years, chairing it from 1833 until the beginning of his presidency in February of 1841. In August of 1842, however, only a year and half into his presidency, following complaints by students that he lacked administrative and scholarly acumen, Bangs resigned the office.[11]

Nevertheless, as someone who regularly visited the Middletown campus in the 1830s, and for a time was there in residence, Bangs likely knew, and almost certainly knew of, that African-born self-proclaimed living link to the American Revolution, former slave of Washington, and keeper of Washington's hair relics, Hamet Achmet. Heman Bangs, Nathan's brother, and also a Methodist minister, officiated at Achmet's marriage to his second wife, a White woman, in 1827.[12] By the time Nathan Bangs became the university's president, the Achmets were living "on an eminence at a short distance in the rear ground of the Wesleyan University" and, like Hamet Achmet himself, his cottage was hard to overlook: "surmounted," as it was, at each corner of its "roof with an American eagle," and sporting a "small American flag" that could be "seen streaming from the 'topmost top' of a flag-staff planted before" the old Black veteran's door. "Former and present students of [Wesleyan University], the professors, and others connected with" that school, declared a newspaper article after Achmet's death in 1842, would never forget Hamet Achmet for multiple reasons: his marriage to "a white woman 40 or 50 years younger than himself," his "frequent" recounting of his memories of General Washington, his habit of wearing "a blue cloth . . . coat . . . cut *a la militaire* and trimmed with a sort of an epaulette and a gilt eagle on his left breast," his "gasconading voice," his "comic air and buffoon trick," the "rat-tat-tat" of his "busy drum," the "smirk of" his "ever-twitching, India rubber phiz," that is, his face, and his frequent visits to the campus, "always attended with drafts upon their small-change or cast-off wardrobe," or, in Downey's case, furniture.[13]

Whether or not Nathan Bangs ever personally took notice of Hamet Achmet as a living relic of the Revolution, a keeper of relics of Washington, or a virtuoso of oral-history performance, Bangs himself exemplified and affected American evangelical, and especially American Methodist, engagement with patriotic memory in an era of unprecedented growth for those fellowships. Aiding in and emblematic of the ascendancy of evangelicalism generally, and of Methodism specifically, was the *Christian Advocate and Zion's Herald*, a weekly newspaper, which Bangs helped to found in 1826 under the auspices of The Book Concern, the publishing house of the Methodist Episcopal Church.[14] With Reverend Bangs as its editor, that paper's "circulation, in the course of one year from its commencement," he later accurately recalled, "by far exceeded every other paper, religious or secular, published in the United States."[15] By 1828, the *Advocate* had 25,000 subscribers at a time when leading European newspapers, such as the *London Times* and the *Berlin Gazette*, sold only half as many copies, and no secular American periodical had a circulation as high as 5,000.[16] Only five years after it began, the *Advocate* was hailed for having "the largest subscription in the world."[17] The size of its readership was even greater. Consumers of periodicals in the early nineteenth century routinely shared subscriptions, with multiple families often reading a single newspaper.[18] Bangs assumed that in an average week the *Christian Advocate* was "probably read by more than one hundred and twenty thousand persons young and old."[19] As George Bancroft recognized in 1834, the *Advocate* was especially popular with "the common man" who "is the representative of [public] opinion."[20] In the words of one leading reference work on American religious periodicals, it soon had "no real rival as the prime source of information for the American mind."[21] Published in New York State, notorious for its "Burned-over District," in which the flames of evangelical revivalism had been particularly scorching, the *Christian Advocate*, from the late 1820s through the 1830s, affords ready entrée into the epicenter of what historian Jon Butler has termed antebellum America's "spiritual hothouse," and telling evidence of how evangelicals then understood the faculty of memory itself, even as they endeavored to shape and enlist popular patriotic memory in support of their cause.[22]

Revealed in the *Advocate* of the 1820s and 1830s, American evangelicals' understandings of memory were teleological (specifically, millennialist), moralistic, appreciative of accessible print culture, and predicated upon an anthropology of mind-body dualism. The teleological quality in evangelicals' assay of memory was their Christian faith that history was not simply pushed by antecedent causes that produce future effects, but ultimately drawn by Divine Providence, by God Himself, toward the realization of His own final ends. Concomitantly, the evangelical subculture regarded memory as a forward-pointing faculty, a recollection of the past meant by God to serve His own ultimate purposes, including, many evangelicals inferred, rendering a just and final moral judgment of every person. An essay on "Memory" in the *Advocate* in 1836 reminded readers: "It has been supposed that no impression made on the memory is ever entirely effaced or forgotten," and the "very solemn thought" has "been suggested that . . . revived memory" after death "may be the record in which all our thoughts, words, and deeds, will be distinctly read in the day of final retribution."[23]

The April 1838 issue of the *Methodist Magazine*, a periodical that Bangs had edited in an earlier period, carried a sermon on the nature of memory by "the Rev. James Floy, of the New-York Conference." The preacher's text was Revelation 20:12: "I saw the dead, small and great, stand before God: and the books were opened:—and the dead were judged out of those things which were written in their books, according to their works."[24] From this prophecy of the Last Judgment, Floy argued that the human capacity for memory is God's provision of a "Judgment Register," a "perfectly correct," complete record of what an individual has done, stored up "for that day" of final reckoning foretold in Scripture. The minister observed that even "after the lapse, it may be, [of] half a century," incidental happenings, such as "the sight of a particular, tree, house" or stream can still stir childhood memories in the aged "that seem to have been blotted out to make room for others." Evidently, "Memory is indestructible." Indeed, for theological reasons, it must be so. According to Floy's sermon, memory was essential to individual human identity and hence accountability, and Scripture was clear that God held individual humans morally accountable after death. "Every secret thing" that one did while living on earth was "remembered" at the Last Judgment and "taken into account" by the Divine Judge. In this life, then, preached Reverend Floy, humans ought to live in remembrance of that future day when "they must stand before God"; and the books of memory "shall be opened, to be shut no more forever."[25] Intimately affiliated with memory in the evangelical understanding, then, was the specter of end-times judgment by God and the inescapable implication that the wise ought ever to try to learn from the remembered past and to amend their ways in the here and now. Evangelicals' beliefs about memory itself thus encouraged them to prize, and to deploy injunctively in the present, morality-encouraging "memories" of the past.

Consistent with that imperative, Bangs acknowledged in 1828 that his popular newspaper had an editorial bias: it gave special attention to the "remarkable," particularly to whatever "may be held up" as a positive "example" from which to advocate for the evangelical world-view.[26] It is hardly surprising, then, that allusions to the United States' natal past in the *Advocate*, as in the evangelical press generally, disproportionately recalled incidents and characters that evangelicals could commend, consistent with the scriptural verse beneath which that newspaper printed obituaries: "The righteous shall be had in everlasting remembrance," Psalm 112:6.[27] Thus in 1839, after a motion was introduced in the United States Congress that would in effect have ended "the . . . practice of employing chaplains" in the national legislature, and a godly member objected that the proposal denied "the faith of our fathers," specifically Benjamin Franklin's call for clergy-led prayer at the 1787 Constitutional Convention, the *Advocate* urged that the pious example of faith at the nation's Founding referenced in the congressman's apologia be "treasured up in the memory against the coming day."[28]

Such fervent teleological, didactic, forward-looking invocations of patriotic memory were often underwritten by an expectation, popular among patriotic American evangelicals in the new nation, that the United States would have a privileged role in God's end-times economy, His providential plan to finally reconcile the world to Himself and to set all things right in a coming millennium. Roots of such nationalist "millennialism" stretched back to Elizabethan-era confidence among British Protestants that there was a divinely appointed Anglo-Saxon eschatological mission, and the New England Puritans' sense that they were on an errand for God is well known.[29] American clergyman responded to the Seven Years' War by envisioning America as central in the end-times drama. The American Revolution transferred that divine mission to the new nation, rather than to Britain, so that God was finally seen as explicitly favoring the United States.[30] By 1835, the prominent New England clergyman Lyman Beecher was confident the millennium would begin in America, and preacher Beecher declared that the United States of America was evidently God's chosen instrument for overturning "the existing civil organization of the nations" and effecting a "rapid and universal extension of civil and religious liberty introductory to" millennial "triumphs of universal Christianity."[31]

In the 1820s and 1830s, driven by patriotic visions of "our American Israel" being teleologically drawn toward millennial greatness,[32] American evangelicals were inspired to "remember" natal American events and leaders as schematically situated on a historical plotline that would culminate in realization of their nation's God-appointed, glorious destiny. For example, more than a few White American evangelicals in those years interleaved popular patriotic memory and millennialism when advocating for efforts of the American Colonization Society—"God's Society" Lyman Beecher called it—to end racial tension and injustice in the United States by "returning" millions of African Americans "back" to Africa, even though most African Americans were at least one generation removed from that continent, and thousands, such as Hamet Achmet, had fought in the Revolution as Patriot soldiers.[33]

In an 1829 July Fourth address published in the *Advocate*, Methodist newspaperman G. V. H. Forbes took up his "prophet pencil" to sketch "three views taken on different continents, at periods distant from each other, diverse in outward form, but bound together" in the divine plan. Historically central was the 1776 U.S. Continental Congress declaring independence from Britain, an "illuminated page," in Forbes's telling, on the judgment "register of the earth's doings, throwing its light backwards on the heavy glooms of antiquity, and forward on the coming shadows of the world's history." In his mind's eye, Forbes could see "the committee room" in the Pennsylvania State House, located in "the peaceful city of Penn . . . above the confluent waters of the Delaware and the Schuylkill." There, it was "morning," and a "momentous, but as yet secret movement" was teleologically "hastening on to its maturity." Forbes glanced about, sizing up the Continental Congress. In the "eye of Jefferson" he spotted an "uncommon fire" that seemed "to throw around the . . . room" the "anticipated glory of the parchment over which his pen is drawing the characters of independence." Forbes could see "Hancock, Adams, and Carroll . . . there," and hear "the spirit-stirring voice of John Adams" as it "summons to the deed of immortal remembrance."

At last, Forbes reported back to his present-day audience, "It is done," an event of global epochal and eschatological importance. "The church that . . . has fled to this western wilderness to escape the dragon flood of persecution now breathes free" as the "tyrants of the earth tremble." Even as he thus ahistorically remembered the Founders' 1776 move to separate from Britain, the evangelical orator encouraged his audience to join him in mentally picturing the scene on a longer prophetic timeline between two events that Forbes viewed as providentially connected to the Founders' history: the Passion of Christ—His death and resurrection, which Forbes characterized in language evoking republicanism as "a death blow to the heart of spiritual tyranny"—and a future epoch, a utopian day, clearly visible to the Methodist preacher, when, with the help of "your contributions . . . in accordance with the great principles of Christian benevolence," the goals of the American Colonization Society will at last be achieved.[34]

As the translation of Forbes's address into columns of newsprint in the pages of the *Advocate* exemplified, the evangelical subculture was significantly a print culture, privileging the written word and prioritizing its dissemination to the masses. Evangelical leaders such as Bangs, whom Wesleyan students would judge as lacking intellectual heft, were popularizers. Not many were given to reading or writing complex, rarified academic treatises, except perhaps in theology. Yet, both by conviction and heritage, they were "people of the book," a Bible-centered fellowship, used to closely reading, citing, and debating texts, and hoping to see the realization of John Wycliffe's fourteenth-century dream that such habits would finally extend to people of every class, including every "plowboy" in the land.[35] Bangs and his fellow evangelicals in the new republic were thus inclined to favor written evidence and argumentation, which they hoped would crucially shape their own and America's practices of memory, including performances of patriotic memory. The *Advocate* routinely summarized books for its mass audience, including patriotic works.

In 1840, a correspondent celebrating a new set of biographies for children, including one of George Washington, cited John Wesley's positive example of "condensing the matter and cheapening the price of valuable works, in order that the poor, and those who had little time for reading might be benefited by the means of instruction."[36] The newspaper had carried Gabriel Disoway's 1829 Fourth of July Address in which the preacher asserted that the "immortal declaration of independence . . . should be read on this day, next to our Bible, with deep attention and holy gratitude. And to use the language of inspiration, 'When thy son asketh thee in time to come, What is this? thou shalt say unto him, By strength of hand the Lord brought us out of Egypt from the house of bondage.'"[37] As volumes of the letters of George Washington or of Benjamin Franklin—both series edited by Jared Sparks—were published, the *Christian Advocate* took notice and its articles sometimes cited details from those collections.[38] In 1827, for example, evoking three of its favorite themes at once—the U.S. Founders, church praxis, and print culture—the *Advocate* reprinted Benjamin Franklin's 1785 assertion that, for a church, a library would be a better use of funds than a steeple.[39]

In 1839 and 1840, reiterating the importance of the written word in anchoring memory, the newspaper lauded the formation of Methodist and state historical societies to conserve primary-source documents, without which essential facts of history would be lost. Fireside memories of their own religious fellowship's roots, the *Christian Advocate* acknowledged, might still be heard in some subscribers' homes, when, with his family "surrounding some sparkling fire, a 'father in Israel' is perhaps reminded of his early history, and by the simple relation of some moving incidents, holds you for hours in raptures, in joy, and in tears." Yet, there are "a number of documents already decaying with antiquity that contain many facts of a more weighty character" that ought to be "collected and carefully preserved in the archives of" historical societies, and before the aging eyewitnesses fight their last "battles" with death, their oral recollections should be "written down" consistent with the mnemonic imperative of locality, "on the spot where the incidents occurred."[40] Finally, newspapers, such as the *Christian Advocate*, should be preserved, for a "volume of newspapers is a book unbound," which if "wantonly destroyed" will deprive "future generations" of "nearly all knowledge of our doings, but what shall be contained in the records of the nation, or handed down to them in the uncertain stories of [oral] tradition."[41] Bangs himself would repeatedly cite the *Advocate* as an authoritative source in his epic *History of the Methodist Episcopal Church*.[42]

Memory, as Protestant American evangelicals in the 1830s understood it, was thus properly teleological (particularly, millennial), moralistic, and centered around popular print culture, but what were spiritually minded evangelicals to make of the contemporaneous turn in memory culture to material relics and other physical remembrancers? Could they follow it without descending into rank "materialism," of the sort that Willbur Fisk—who, in practice, could appreciate a good historical relic himself—had highlighted and condemned in relic-venerating Catholic memory culture in Europe?

Protestant evangelical theology as seen in the *Advocate*—and traditional Catholic theology as well—generally accepted mind-body dualism: believing that there was a real and necessary interaction of body and soul, of material physics and immaterial spirit, in performances of memory and other conscious human activities.[43] Accurate understandings and acts of memory in that dualist view had to give due ontological and epistemological weight to both body and spirit, to the material and the immaterial. They had to be well-balanced. In the preferred parlance of nineteenth-century Protestant evangelical moral rhetoric, they ought to be "temperate." An 1835 essay reprinted in the *Advocate* therefore argued that while memory was designed by God to be a higher moral faculty of the mind serving the needs and cultivation of one's spirit, physically intemperate actions might create physical disruptions and distractions that would "clog" the faculties. Thus, the body of one who serves Satan by "gorging himself at dinner," might have to "allow so much of the nervous energy to expend itself upon the digestive functions during the next three or four hours, that thought, which demands the same power to be at command in the brain" would, for that period of time, be "quite destitute of life," being "forced to wait for the requisite physical aid." Any "uneasiness of the body caused by some form of intemperance, as it irresistibly fixes some portion of the attention, subtracts its part from the force that might serve the judgment or memory."[44] More broadly, whether evangelicals, who did not deny that embodied human memory had material requirements, could temperately appreciate material supports of historical memory, such as historical artifacts, without venerating them intemperately as relics, as Protestant evangelicals accused Catholics of doing in the extreme, was an open question that, by the 1830s, hung not only over Fisk's fitful meditation on the status of material remembrancers in his travelogue, but also over patriotic, Protestant American evangelical memory culture writ large.

Godly Veterans

As evangelicals' performances of memory were shaped by their assumptions about the nature of memory, they were also affected by charged memories current in their own biographies, churches, and communities. Nathan Bangs, for example, never forgot that his father fought on the Patriot side during the Revolutionary War and enthusiastically told tales of his military exploits to young Nathan and his brothers.[45] Bangs could knowingly claim a Revolutionary pedigree. Yet, evangelicalism in general, and Methodism in particular, had a more problematic association with the nation's founding conflict. Nineteenth-century evangelicalism was a transatlantic phenomenon. American and British evangelical groups notoriously shared resources and personnel. American evangelicals' collaborations with Britons may have been theologically commendatory for recognizing the transnational universality of the body of Christ. But they were also politically provocative in a time when memories of British violence against Americans in the Revolution remained fresh. In 1817, when it became known that an emissary of the American Bible Society had met with counterparts in the British and Foreign Bible Society on friendly terms, an incredulous "Soldier of the American Revolution" responded in print with an embittering recollection of how, during the Revolution, British redcoats cold-bloodedly burned and shot to death an American preacher's wife. By determining its alliances on theological grounds, with no concern for nationalistic memory, argued the "Soldier," the American Bible Society exercised inexcusably poor judgment.[46]

If evangelicals in general risked running afoul of patriotic American memory, Methodists faced special danger. As the leading historian of American Methodist history, Nathan Bangs felt his denomination's burden acutely. His *History of the Methodist Episcopal Church* acknowledged a "spirit of persecution" in the era of the Revolution that had sanctioned harassment of Methodists for being denominationally linked to such British loyalists as John Wesley.[47] In his *History*, Bangs criticized Wesley for his well-known 1775 pamphlet opposing American independence. Wesley, Bangs judged, was guilty of "interfering in the political affairs of this country," increasing "the difficulties with which . . . [American Methodist] preachers had to contend."[48] Christine Leigh Heyrman has shown that southern Methodists of the early nineteenth century worked to overcome their denomination's lingering taint of Tory disloyalty by appropriating symbols and motifs from the Revolution.[49] The examples of Nathan Bangs and his *Christian Advocate* make it clear that northern Methodists, too, used such tactics.

In 1826, the *Advocate* printed a Fourth of July oration in which Abraham Brower, "one of the Patriots of the Revolution," imagined revivalist camp meetings as linear, teleological successors to Revolutionary military encampments.[50] As historian Dee Andrews notes, the ubiquitous term "camp," when applied to Methodist mass meetings, underscored their militarized ethos, and camp organizers appointed guards regimented like military units to protect attendees. "I have no doubt," recalled one sentinel, that many camp guards "thought themselves as highly honored as General Washington and his officers did, when they took command of the armies of the united colonies of the revolution," and a late nineteenth-century Methodist memoirist noted proudly that "the Methodist Episcopal Camp-meeting Society" in what later became Ossining, New York, had met on mnemonically evocative "ground containing the generous spring which supplies the meeting with water, and from which General Washington and his staff" in the Revolutionary War "once drank on their way from White Plains."[51]

In his *History*, Bangs similarly enlisted spread-eagled militarism and nostalgia for the Revolution. He referred to Methodist circuit riders with martial language and made much of the story of Joseph Everett—a Marylander, born in 1732—who "volunteered as a soldier in the militia of Maryland in defense of his country's rights in the time of the revolutionary war," converted "under the preaching of Mr. Asbury" to Methodism in 1778, and found a "new field for the exercise of his talents," becoming a Methodist itinerant. According to Bangs, it was this Revolutionary War veteran who "contributed largely to fix Methodism on that broad basis on which it has long since stood unshaken amid the storms and billows with which it had to contend."[52]

Bangs's evocation of Private Everett—probably first composed in the 1830s—came at a historical moment when ordinary veterans of the Revolution were garnering attention for reasons largely demographic. Recall that by the 1820s, a much higher percentage of the survivors of the Revolution were former enlisted men than that group's majority share of the original cohort of veterans.[53] As the number of veterans of the Revolution in a community neared zero, the last veterans were overwhelming likely to be privates, suddenly celebrated as living relics of the nation's natal past. By 1840, the Private Everetts of the war were far more likely than before to be noticed for their military service. Considered demographically, such veterans were almost certain to be disproportionately evangelical. Most were from lower-to-middling social classes that had been receptive to post-Revolution evangelical revivalism.[54] By the late 1820s, more than a few were simultaneously being feted as relics of the Revolution and as evangelical true believers. In Wilkes-Barre Pennsylvania, on July 4th, 1826, the jubilee of American independence, "remaining veterans of the Revolution" in the community, some "40 aged Heroes," honored as "relics of the revolution," processed through "a part of the borough" behind an honor guard of clergy, to the Presbyterian church, where the Declaration of Independence was read aloud, and, standing behind the sacred pulpit, "Rev. Mr. Bidlack, one of the aged veterans of the Revolution," gave an address reiterating from "actual knowledge and experience" the "fatigues and dangers" of the veterans' "early days, and endeavoring to enforce the necessity of practical religion upon his old comrades and the audience generally."[55]

In later years, as federal pension laws took effect, applications evidenced the interwoven identity of many veterans, especially of low-ranking veterans, as both evangelicals and embodied artifacts of the Revolutionary War. In Harlan County, Kentucky, Private James Hall deposed in 1832: "on the 8th day of September 1781 we fought the battle of the Eutaw Springs—I well remember this day for I received a wound in my right wrist which destroyed the Joint and has left me a cripple to this day," and "I am [now] known to every person in the surrounding country, having been engaged for 14 years . . . trying to preach the Gospel of Jesus," and as "my stiff wrist could but be observed by my audiences . . . I [have taken] pride in giving an account of those days which tried men's love of liberty."[56] John Anderson, "a private in the North Carolina Continental Line," declared in 1835 that: "the greatest Satisfaction I have in life except for my eternal Salvation is that I was one of the Instruments that [helped] to bring about the happy government we live under."[57] In Dover, Delaware, Patrick Connolly was respected by 1818 "both for his faithful revolutionary services (which are of public notoriety) and his unfeigned devotion to the cause of vital religion."[58] In Augusta County, Virginia, in 1849, John Crawford's family remembered him as almost unbalanced in his identity as a religious Patriot. His wife had "often seen the wounds which he received at the battle of Cowpens." His daughter, Nancy Newman, testified that the family retained a relic of Crawford's service, a sword he had used in the war, and remembered that her father's pastor, "Rev. Mr. Calhoun often visited with my father to converse with him on the subject of religion, and such was my father's love of liberty that he always mixed into the conversation some of the trials through which he passed while serving ... in the Revolutionary War." Indeed, "some thought he loved patriotism as much as religion."[59] James Riley of Elbert County, Georgia, would be identified in October of 1832 as "an old revolutionary soldier & an exhorter of the Methodist Episcopal church for twenty five years or more" who "still continues to be on[e]."[60] In a deposition years later, the sexton of the tomb in Washington, DC, in which one "Captain Benjamin Burch" had been buried related that Burch's tombstone recorded that he "served his country with fidelity and honor throughout the war of the Revolution," and was "a professor of the Religion of Christ."[61] When Josiah Cleveland died in 1843, newspapers carried the eulogy offered by his Episcopal clergyman, who argued from a juxtaposition of texts as relics: "We find among his papers, side by side with the muster roll of his company in the war of the Revolution, the roll of the communicants of St. Paul's Church, ... testifying that nearest his heart in life were the freedom of country and the freedom of his soul," and illustrating that "his dying aspirations, like his living faith, were 'for God and his country.'" The pastor declaimed: "Learn from the example of this Christian veteran, not only how to die, but how to live."[62]

From the second quarter of the nineteenth century, the prominence of godly veterans as such—most of whom had not been high-ranking in the war, and did not convert until *after* the Revolution—allowed Bangs's *Christian Advocate* and evangelicals generally to easily affiliate their religious cause with patriotic memory.[63] In 1828, under the heading "THE SOLDIER'S MITE," the *Advocate* printed the text of a letter to editor Bangs conveying an anonymous three-dollar donation in support of Methodist missionary outreach and to a fund for "worn out preachers," given by "one of our venerable, old revolutionary soldiers who fought and bled to achieve the inestimable rights which, by the blessing of Divine Providence, we enjoy." The letter noted that the old veteran "converted to God" in the wake of the War for Independence, yet seemed to enlist the unnamed everyman soldier as a pious exemplar of the Revolutionary generation as a whole.[64] Similarly, an 1833 item in the *Advocate* worked by synecdoche to interpret a lone, anonymous godly participant in the Founding as general evidence of piety among the Patriot Founders' generation. That piece was a fictionalized dialogue between a young boy, "William," and his uncle, "Duncan." On a visit to the U.S. Capitol building in Washington, DC, William expresses to Duncan excitement at being able to "inspect minutely the temple of liberty of this nation," prompting Duncan to declare: "Your grandfather was one of the early patriots who contributed largely to founding this noble republic; and I . . . may add, which you have often heard, that your grandfather was a *Christian-patriot*. . . . There was, it is to be feared, more of a spirit of religion which inspired our patriot fathers. . . . But more of this at some other time."[65]

In two popular books whose dates of publication bookended development of the trope of the godly veteran, flesh became word as the life stories of evangelical Revolutionary War enlisted veterans, sailor Andrew Sherburne and Private John Gray, were marketed to a mass audience. Sherburne's autobiography, first published in 1828, recounted that he went to sea as a Patriot at the age of thirteen, leaving Portsmouth, New Hampshire, on the eighteen-gun *Ranger*, a "continental ship of war." He endured hardships of combat, was captured and held in conditions of near starvation aboard the infamous British prison ship *Jersey*, converted to faith in Christ following the war, and became a Baptist preacher. After the first edition of his book was published, Sherburne spent months traveling up and down the eastern seaboard and into the Midwest, guest-preaching, peddling one-dollar copies of his memoirs from church to church, and collecting an impressive sheaf of written endorsements, published in the second edition of the book, from other evangelical preachers and laity, urging "the patriot and the Christian . . . alike" to buy Sherburne's edifying autobiography.[66]

Four decades later, the stereotype of the godly Revolutionary War veteran reached its denouement as James Dalzell's breathless 1868 biography of 104-year-old *John Gray, of Mount Vernon; The Last Soldier of the Revolution*. Dalzell revealed that Gray, the last surviving federal veteran Revolutionary War pensioner, had been a "common man," a devout Methodist evangelical who "lived and died" secure in his expressed belief that "Christ died for me, and that through him I hope for life eternal; and that makes me happy, and it is enough for me."[67] As a child Dalzel had met Gray, his Ohio neighbor, in the 1840s, and "looked upon him as preserved through four generations to show his children and his children's children what a noble type of men were our revolutionary fathers." Dalzell found it particularly noble that the aged Gray was "a Christian," a "consistent member of the Methodist Church," a "model of piety to his church," one whose life was "'a living epistle known and read by all men,'" pointing both to Jesus Christ and to George Washington. In God's remarkable, teleological providence, Dalzell argued, Gray, as "the last soldier of the Revolution," lived and died as a type of "the first soldier of the Revolution," Washington.[68] "Sixty-eight years ago[,] Washington died. John Gray died March 29, 1868." George "Washington was a patriot and a Christian; so was John Gray," who "folded his hands quietly over his patriotic heart[,] and fell asleep in Jesus."[69]

The parallels, in Dalzell's telling, went on and on: "Washington," for example, "was a Virginian," and "John Gray was a Virginian too." Washington had his "home at Mount Vernon," and "John Gray's birthplace was Mount Vernon," where he eventually was employed by Washington in felling trees. "It would seem as if this coincidence" of being born on George Washington's estate "worked a charm to preserve John Gray alive" until after every other Revolutionary War veteran had passed. "It would seem as if to be born at Mount Vernon were to inherit immortality. . . . It seemed as if born at Mount Vernon he could not die." "Hereafter," opined Dalzell, "whoever may . . . visit Mount Vernon" ought to be captivated by the power of local memory, by realizations that John Gray, "Washington's last soldier[,] was born upon its ample acres," was a "dear personal friend to Washington," and Washington's "hand crumbling to dust in that white coffin there has often pressed the hand of John Gray."[70]

The flesh-pressing bodily juxtaposition of Gray and Washington in Dalzell's mid-nineteenth-century biography partook of an American cultural pattern that had been strengthening for over half a century. An "exhaustive" memory of the nation's beginnings was simply too fatiguing for the rising generation to maintain.[71] Instead, as Dalzell's book, the *Christian Advocate,* and innumerable other contemporaneous sources illustrate, during the first half of the nineteenth century, the attention that Americans gave to their patriotic memory was, on the one hand, disproportionately lavished on long-dead top-tier Founders, such as George Washington and Benjamin Franklin—the only other Founder mentioned by John Gray in Dalzell's account—or, on the other hand, upon still-living or only-recently-deceased, low-ranking veterans of the Revolution, the John Grays of that war. During that same period, memory of those in the founding cohort who had been of middling rank, power, or prestige was increasingly neglected, and, on its face, such mnemonic winnowing might have frustrated any effort by evangelicals to reconcile patriotic natal American memory to their own proprietary, teleological view of the United States as a land chosen by God. As Mark Noll has noted, by the time of the Constitutional Convention, there were few if any evangelicals among the most elite Founders at the level of influence of a George Washington or a Benjamin Franklin. Such evangelicals as were in that group—Patrick Henry, Elias Boudinot, and John Jay, for example—were, Noll notes, comparatively second-tier in their influence and fame.[72] Thus, they were part of the very sub-cohort increasingly neglected in American memory culture during the first half of the nineteenth century.

How then did American evangelicals, during the country's evangelical surge of the 1790s to the 1840s, lay claim in the *Christian Advocate* and elsewhere to the nation's natal memory?[73] They primarily did so in ways consistent with this winnowing of American patriotic memory, and with the growing emphasis in contemporaneous American memory culture on using available physical props. They seized the teleological, material evidence at hand of local godly enlisted veterans of the Revolution in their own communities. Like much of the nation, they largely neglected memory of the second, or middling, tier of the founding cohort—in which, ironically, there had been significant evangelical representation—and they took the commanding heights of American patriotic memory, retrospectively, and sincerely, though often ahistorically, "remembering" as evangelicals, or, at least as proto-evangelicals, the most famous Founders, particularly Benjamin Franklin and George Washington.

Redeeming Franklin

At first blush, Franklin might seem to have been an unlikely candidate for evangelicals to promote as a positive model. He publicly divulged in his autobiography that at age fifteen he had embarked upon a spiritual journey that led to his becoming "a thorough Deist."[74] He enjoyed the friendship of Methodist revivalist George Whitefield but quipped that though the evangelist "us'd to indeed sometimes pray for my Conversion," he "never had the satisfaction of believing that his Prayers were heard."[75] In March 1790, little more than a month before dying, Franklin had rebuffed a plea from Ezra Stiles, president of Yale College, to the desperately ill Founder to trust for salvation in the sacrificial death of Jesus. "As to Jesus of Nazareth," Franklin answered, "I have . . . doubts as to his divinity; though it is a question I do not dogmatize upon, having never studied it, and I think it is needless to busy myself with it now, when I expect soon an opportunity of knowing the truth with less trouble."[76] Yet, notwithstanding his theological heterodoxy by evangelicals' standards, within a few years of his death, compositions for and by evangelicals were impressing Franklin's iconic status in American memory.

In 1819, former Anglican clergyman Mason Locke Weems, who had long been moving in the direction of evangelical revivalism, and particularly toward Methodism, published a *Life of Benjamin Franklin*, wherein Weems breezily allowed: "Because he was not gloomy, some well meaning people have doubted whether . . . Franklin was a Christian," but Christianity being "a system of repentance manifested by love and good works, there have been but few better Christians than doctor Franklin."[77] The ex-preacher artfully rewrote and excerpted Franklin's deathbed missive to Stiles, omitting Franklin's admission that he doubted Jesus's divinity and culminating in a defense of Poor Richard's religious bona fides in a scriptural style: "to those who will have it, after all, that doctor Franklin was only a good sort of deist, I shall answer pretty nearly in the spirit of St. Paul's prayer, before the unbelieving Agrippa: 'Would to God we had now among us some millions of, not only almost, but altogether[,] such men as doctor Franklin.'"[78]

For the most part, evangelicals in the new republic cultivated a memory of Franklin that was carefully crafted, as Weems wrote that his biography of Franklin would be, to "help to multiply" middle-class

"Virtues of Industry, Sobriety, Frugality, Honesty, Patriotism, Devotion to useful Science &c," of which all moralists would approve, and "for which Dr Franklin was so illustrious."[79] Such was the approach taken by a young Willbur Fisk in his 1813 manuscript, "Remarks on the Life of Franklin," subtitled "Practices and Principles Worthy of Imitation," and it would be the clear point of departure for most of the numerous references to Franklin in the *Christian Advocate* of the 1820s and 1830s.[80] In addition, memories of Benjamin Franklin sometimes served in evangelical polemics as a cultural and theological backstop, demarcating the outer limits of the Founders' theological unconventionality, and, by implication, boundaries of the acceptable in America. In 1828, for example, the *Advocate* reprinted an undated letter in which Benjamin Franklin warned an unnamed correspondent, whom the evangelical press including the *Advocate* assumed was Thomas Paine, against publishing a manuscript, which the *Advocate* and the evangelical press supposed was an early draft of *The Age of Reason,* Paine's attack on orthodox Christianity. In the letter, Franklin expressed concern that the manuscript threatened "all religion," and popular morality too. An implicit message conveyed in the *Advocate*'s piece was that if even Franklin, a Founder who, after all, had once been a deist, ultimately opposed "attacks on the Christian religion," such attacks must be regarded prima facie as violating America's foundational ideals.[81]

The *Advocate* also repeatedly printed versions of a tale about Franklin and the crafting of the federal Constitution. It was a story that American evangelicals of the 1820s and 1830s never tired of telling. In June 1787, went the uncontroversial portion, the Constitutional Convention was at an impasse. At issue were competing schemes for apportioning representation in the proposed national Congress. Tempers flared. Hopes for a new political union nearly evaporated. Then, Benjamin Franklin spoke. Lamenting the "small progress we have made after four or five weeks' continual reasonings with each other," the Convention's eldest statesman asked, "how has it happened ... that we have ... not once thought of humbly applying to the Father of lights to illuminate our understandings? . . . The longer I live, the more convincing proofs I see . . . that God governs in the affairs of men. . . . I . . . beg leave to move that, henceforth, prayers imploring the assistance of Heaven, and its blessings on our deliberations, be held in this assembly every morning before we proceed to business, and that . . . clergy . . .

be requested to officiate in that service."[82] Renditions of the tale carried in the *Advocate* in 1827 and 1830 ended the episode there. The 1827 offering, "Dr. Franklin on Prayer," was printed in a section of the magazine called "The Gatherer," under a subheader of text lifted from the Bible that, as repurposed out of context in the *Advocate*, allowed for literally fragmentary reportage in the interests of history and memory: "Gather up the fragments that nothing be lost."[83]

The similar 1830 report of the story in the *Advocate* featured an editorial preface, at once triumphalist and evidentialist, expressing "peculiar delight" in the story itself, and in the opportunity to "transfer the record to our columns as reflecting more decidedly and happily upon Dr. Franklin's religious character, than does any other act of his life with which we are acquainted."[84] In 1832 and 1836, the *Advocate* repeated the tale with an expanded chronology, one that revealed the Constitutional Convention's response to Franklin's motion. The 1832 version, meant to "be read with delight by every Christian and patriot, and preserved as an important document in the history of Franklin, Washington, and the Union," offered what it termed "the whole story" of how delegates reacted: when Franklin took his seat, "a silent admiration superseded for a moment, the expression of . . . assent . . . which was strongly marked on almost every countenance." A lone dissenter rose to counter that the Convention did not need the "foreign aid" of Divine Providence. George Washington fixed "his eye upon the speaker with a mixture of surprise and *indignation*," then looked "to ascertain" the response of the other delegates, who "did not leave him a moment to doubt." The "motion for appointing a chaplain was instantly seconded, and carried."[85] The 1836 iteration of the tale in the *Advocate* had a different ending: " 'The convention, except three or four persons thought prayers unnecessary!![*sic*]' These words . . . were written by Franklin himself." Franklin's still-surviving manuscript of his remarks does, in fact, bear that angry notation, and from other material evidence too, it is clear that the 1836 report that the Convention failed to enact Franklin's motion was correct, while the 1832 version, the one in which Franklin's motion was "instantly seconded and carried," was inaccurate. Yet, in 1836 the *Advocate* failed to note that it had offered an irreconcilably different, if more pious, version of the happening four years earlier, and now, even as it accurately acknowledged the Convention's rejection of Franklin's proposal, the newspaper reasoned by synecdoche that Franklin's lonely act of piety might be cited to refute any "charge of infidelity upon" the convention of "men whom we gratefully acknowledge as the founders of our happy republic."[86]

If memory of Benjamin Franklin could thus be used to sanctify the whole founding cohort by association, Franklin's personal place in the American and evangelical pantheons also gained strength by association, particularly as he was remembered in connection with two venerated Georges: Whitefield and Washington. Notwithstanding his joke that George Whitefield's prayers for him appeared to have gone unanswered, Benjamin Franklin's affiliation with that evangelical preacher seems to have silently lifted his reputation among evangelicals who knew that the two men had enjoyed each other's company. Without mentioning Franklin's dismissal of Whitefield's prayers for him, the *Advocate* repeatedly published anecdotes in which their friendship was in view. In the same period, as George Washington was increasingly celebrated, it could only help Franklin's posthumous reputation to be recalled in the same breath. By the 1830s, Franklin and Washington were regularly recalled in tandem in books and newspapers, including the *Advocate*, and, in 1832, Methodist minister Thomas S. Hinde volunteered to James Madison: "my mind is often drawn to the agents, through whom those temporal blessings we enjoy were obtained," and recently "I found myself on a visit" to the eastern seaboard, and "soliloquizing at Washington['s] and Franklin[']s tombs."[87]

Benjamin Franklin appears to have foreseen that, in the long run, George Washington would more than eclipse him in popular memory. In a codicil to his last will and testament, Franklin made peace with Washington's ascendancy, while deftly maneuvering to share in his fame, giving "my friend, and the friend of mankind[,] *General Washington*," his "fine crab-tree walking-stick, with a gold head curiously wrought in the form of the cap of liberty," noting: "If it were a Sceptre, he has merited it, and would become it."[88] Yet, the grasping, hands-on practices by which Americans—including evangelical Americans—would remember George Washington, and, by the 1830s, the last surviving privates from his army, owed more to patterns by which George Whitefield was remembered than to Franklin-related precedents. By the time that Willbur Fisk and Charles Downey were deciding what to make of Achmet's Washington relics in Middletown in the 1830s, their coreligionists, notwithstanding Protestant objections to the Catholic cult of saints, had learned to seek and to venerate relics of a dead hero. This they had done first at George Whitefield's tomb at Newburyport and only later at George Washington's crypt at Mount Vernon.

From Whitefield to Washington

Following his death in 1770, the Reverend George Whitefield, a founder of transatlantic Methodism, a hero to evangelicals in both Britain and America, and Franklin's friend, was entombed at the Old South Presbyterian Church in Newburyport, Massachusetts. In the ensuing century and a half, until the 1930s, when his crypt's exterior was remodeled to bar access to his corpse, scores of evangelicals, especially Methodists, undertook pilgrimages to Newburyport, not merely to see where Whitefield was buried, but to view, handle, and even steal away with some of his bodily fragments.[89] In 1832, for example, the *Christian Advocate* reprinted a first-person epistolary testimony of an evangelical devotee who visited "the tomb of Whitefield in order to obtain a sight of the venerated remains": "Said I," to the sexton, "can I see the remains of Whitefield?" "A rough, and rather eccentric old man ... responded: 'Yes, but it will cost you something.'" For a "fee" of "twenty-five cents," the sexton, candle in hand, led the pilgrim "through a scuttle in the porch back of the pulpit," to a sanctum beneath, where "the bones of Whitefield are in good preservation, the scull [*sic*] in particular," evidencing "a form of face and forehead quite similar to the busts and prints we have of him." However strongly "I may have been tempted," to take other relics, admitted the correspondent, "I carried nothing away with me," except for "a large quantity of cobwebs and dirt." Evidently, prior pilgrims had not been so restrained. "One of the bones of the arm is missing, supposed to have been taken by some visitor."[90] By then, people had, in fact, been taking relics from the evangelist's tomb for decades, and, notwithstanding the pastor's British birth, transatlantic ministry, and prewar death as a good subject of King George III, many venerated Whitefield as a symbol of American identity.[91]

In September of 1775, en route to Canada for a planned assault on the British stronghold at Quebec, Continental Army officers under Benedict Arnold had stopped at the church where in 1770 Whitefield preached his last sermon and was interred beneath the pulpit. From that pulpit, Arnold's chaplain, Samuel Spring, preached to the Patriot troops. He took as his text "If thy spirit go not with us, carry us not up hence," and marveled ever after that he had "preached over the grave of Whitefield." Afterward, "Someone" in the group "requested a visit to Whitefield's tomb." The "officers induced the sexton to take off the lid of the coffin," and Arnold and his entourage viewed "with awe and reverence" the corpse, which, after half of a decade in the tomb, had "nearly all returned to dust." Yet, "some portions of his grave-clothes remained." Reverend Whitefield's "collar and wristbands" were "in the best preservation." Those the officers removed, "carefully cut in little pieces, . . . divided . . . them" among themselves, and pressed on to their ill-fated invasion of Canada.[92]

Relic-gathering forays into Whitefield's crypt were only beginning. In 1823, Nathan Bangs published a biography and memoir of Methodist itinerant preacher Jesse Lee that related how, in June of 1790, Lee and some of his evangelical friends, by opening Whitefield's coffin, "were enabled to witness the fearful change which the king of terrors makes upon the most perfect forms." After twenty years in the tomb, Whitefield's "ears, hair, and a part of his nose had fallen off." Portions "of his gown," however, "remained," but "were quite hard to tear." The preacher "contented himself" with taking a "small relic of the gown," and "prayed that he might be endued with the same zeal which once inspired the breast of its wearer."[93] Later, Wesleyan University graduate Abel Stevens, a Methodist minister, future biographer of Nathan Bangs, and eventual editor of the *Christian Advocate,* visited the crypt. Stevens, in an 1843 autobiographical compendium in which he described his pilgrimage, portrayed himself in military terms, as a veteran of Methodist itinerant preaching whose "war-horse sleeps under the sod of a distant prairie," and whose "infirmities have compelled him to retire from the field," but who retains as prized material relics of his service, the old "saddle-bags" hanging "in his study before him," far "fuller of reminiscences than ever they were of anything else." In a reminiscence of his pilgrimage to Newburyport that Stevens published, then preserved in manuscript form in his mnemonically laden saddlebags, Stevens recalled that on his visit to Whitefield's Newburyport crypt the sextant opened "a small trap-door" in the vestry behind Whitefield's old pulpit "and we descended into a dark apartment, much like a common cellar," and through a door "into the vault, which extends under the pulpit," then by lantern-light beheld the "slight depth of black mold" that "covered the bottom of Whitefield's coffin," and upon which "lay the bare bones." The preacher remembered: "I took his skull into my hands," and "I held it with silence, thinking of the history of the 'seraphic man,'" and marveling at "What thoughts of grandeur and power had emanated from that abode of mind and stirred with emotions the souls of hundreds of thousands."[94]

Long ago, Richard Hofstadter warned fellow historians against try-ing to "draw, so to speak, a straight line from George Whitefield to George Washington," there having been "several paths to the revolu-tion."[95] Without tracing any such bright line, Mark Noll and Teresa Barnett have both seen significance in the fact that the generation of Americans who came of age prior to the American Revolution and lived through the founding era of the United States collectively revered no two mortals more than George Whitefield and George Wash-ington.[96] As British author Robert Philip noticed in 1837, American Christians in the young nation "would feel at a loss" if asked to choose between physically shaking hands with "two of their patriarchs—one of whom had shaken hands with George Washington, and the other with George Whitefield," and they "would venerate most a veteran who had known both" Georges.[97] Their parallel popularity was reflected too in the work of African American poet Phillis Wheatley, who gained inter-national notoriety in 1770 for her eulogistic poems lamenting White-field's passing, and urging readers to repair to Newburyport to "drop a tear upon his happy urn."[98] Five years later, she also wrote and sent laudatory verses to General Washington that caught the general's eye as he sorted his correspondence, leaving him grateful and impressed.[99]

The converging cults of Whitefield and Washington, of evangeli-cal and of patriotic remembrance, are also reflected in birth records, such as those of Massachusetts in the first half of the nineteenth cen-tury, recording entry into the world of George Washington Messinger, son of George Whitefield Messinger, in Wrentham in 1799; of George Whitefield Samson, son of George Washington Samson, in Plympton in 1808; of Washington Whitefield Temple in Reading, in 1819; and of George Washington Whitefield Hodgdon, in Newton in 1851.[100] In 1840, the *New York Evangelist* tellingly played off affinity for the two iconic Georges, relaying an anecdote from a reader in western New York: "Taking my pencil to note the name of a new acquaintance, 'How do you write your name?' said I. 'George W_____,' he replied." The reporter, "more in a tone of affirmation than of inquiry," responded, "George Washington," but "'O no!' he exclaimed; 'better than that—George Whitefield.'" That "little incident suggested to me" the apparently unanswerable "inquiry, which was the most useful man, George Whitefield, or George Washington?"[101]

Washington's Apotheosis

For any group seeking to positively connect itself with patriotic memory, George Washington was easily the most valuable individual with whom to posthumously affiliate. Yet, as with Franklin, annexing Washington to the evangelicals' cause would not necessarily be straightforward. There was no definitive proof that Washington was skeptical of Jesus's divinity, as Franklin had been. Yet, in thousands of surviving autograph writings, George Washington was strikingly quiescent about Jesus Christ. Respectful toward the Christian faith, he was not characteristically evangelical for it.[102] Yet, well before his death in 1799, he was on track to enjoy apotheosis in the affections of evangelicals, and his countrymen at large. Indeed, one of the first popular images exalting Washington was distributed by a Methodist immigrant from England, John Hewson. Hewson, who almost half a century later meticulously parceled out other images of Washington to his children in his will, made and marketed kerchiefs in 1776 bearing the likeness of General Washington on horseback, sword drawn, encircled by the words: "George Washington, Esq. Foundator and Protector of America's Liberty and Independency."

Owing to Hewson's idiosyncratic use of "Foundator" and "Independency" we can trace the resonance of the entrepreneurial Methodist's commercially manufactured Washington souvenir in a mutilated 1771 imprint of The New England Primer in the collection of the Free Library of Philadelphia. That textbook's frontmatter originally featured a pristine engraving of George III, "By the Grace of God, King of Great Britain, France and Ireland, Defender of the Faith, & C." Subsequently, someone—perhaps a passionate Patriot student assigned the textbook in the throes of the American Revolution—overwrote the page. Crossing out the king's name and title, the vandal encircled his face with the thrice-inked-in name "George Washington"; changed the caption to "George W"; and scrawled in the margin beneath the very slogan emblazoned on Hewson's mass-marketed souvenir handkerchiefs: "George Washington, Esq. Foundator and Protector of American Liberty and Independency."[103]

In the years that followed—embracing the balance of the Revolution, the Constitutional Convention, Washington's presidency and final retirement—George Washington's star generally continued to rise in popular culture, threatened only by the sharp partisan political

Frontispiece, 1771 imprint of *The New England Primer*. (Free Library of Philadelphia)

battles of the 1790s. Near the peak of those controversies, an unsigned letter in June of 1798 from "An Anonymous Scoundrel," as Washington dubbed the writer, taunted President Washington: "had you sir, retired at the close of the first congress," and not been involved in fights between emerging political parties you might have been remembered "by thousands, by millions," as "the example of a man approaching to a God!!!"[104] The projections of the "Scoundrel" missed the mark. In December of 1799, the shocking news of George Washington's death at his Mount Vernon estate accelerated a contested, yet seemingly inexorable, postmortem near-deification of George Washington in American memory, spearheaded by three sometimes intertwined groups, each of which sought to use the memory of Washington to support their own ideals: Federalists fighting unsuccessfully to prevent the "Revolution of 1800," as Thomas Jefferson termed his Democratic Republican party's ascendancy; Freemasons, who would respond to growing distrust of their fraternity by noting that Washington had been a Freemason; and clergy, feeling themselves, their offices, and by implication the Christian faith, disrespected as their individual authority was diluted by the proliferation of competing religious sects spawned in evangelical religious revivals that had begun in the early 1790s.[105]

Many of the eulogizing sermons that clergy preached amid gales of mourning for Washington that blew over the nation during the winter of 1799–1800 transported congregants rhetorically to Washington's burial site at Mount Vernon, and, in the years that followed, more than a few preachers personally visited his crypt.[106] In 1841, a correspondent in the *Christian Advocate,* recalled: "Never shall I forget, while memory lasts, the rush of feeling and of thought that pervaded my mind as I stood beside the tomb" of Washington, on a "sacred spot" that to "me . . . seemed like consecrated ground," until awakened "from my revery [sic], I plucked [as] a memento" a "twig from the cedar" tree hanging over the crypt, then "repaired to view" artifacts of the hero preserved in his mansion.[107] By then, evangelical preachers had been stopping off at Washington's tomb for decades, and, notwithstanding their well-known theological aversion to "popish" relics, some took away material remembrancers. On 2 January 1802, Congregationalist preacher and Massachusetts Historical Society member Manasseh Cutler wrote that he had just left "the venerable tomb which contains the remains of the great Washington. . . . I will not attempt to describe our feelings, or the solemn gloom as we approached the revered mound of earth," and the "precious monument which was the first object of our attention," and "all of us took boughs from the trees" surrounding the tomb as "precious relics of our own and our country's best friend."[108]

A decade later, Episcopal clergyman Theodore Dehon, in an October 1812 letter, marveled at how "vain appeared . . . all human distinction" as "I stood by [Washington's] coffin and saw him wasting into common earth, with no better exemption from this humbling doom of our race" than "obscure individuals," yet Dehon was heartened, too, contemplating "the worth of our holy religion in correcting the evils" of death, so that we may "believe of the great and good"—a company Dehon plainly assumed included Washington—that "the day of their death" as it is followed by their entrance into heaven "is better than the day of their birth." On the same pilgrimage, the preacher also visited Thomas Jefferson at Monticello and James Madison at Montpelier, and obliquely—yet, clearly—recorded his disappointment at their lack of interest in gospel matters.[109]

During an 1819 interlude at Mount Vernon, Congregationalist minister Samuel Worcester similarly found himself "lingering at" Washington's tomb, thinking about the "goodness of God in concealing the tomb of Moses" to keep it from becoming "a scene of idolatry," and musing that one could "not think it strange" that "if a nation ignorant of Him who made the earth and the heavens, should have a Washington, they should exalt him after death into a deity."[110] Another Congregationalist minister, Marcellus Post, regarded Washington's tomb as "the moral keystone in the arch of union and of empire" and vowed in an 1884 address: "Never shall I forget the lesson . . . when in the days of my youth. . . . I looked for the first time on the tomb of Washington" and there read "simply the text, 'I am the Resurrection and the Life: he that believeth in me, though he were dead, yet shall he live: and he that liveth and believeth in me shall never die.'"[111] One wonders if Post knew that the plaque bearing those evangelical words of Jesus was a late edition to the ensemble of Washington's tomb, appearing only on the "New Tomb," wherein Washington was reinterred in 1831, after evangelical revivalism appears to have touched the icon's heirs and possibly motivated them to portray their famous forebearer as an evangelical.

For his part, yet another Congregationalist clergyman, Oliver Alden Taylor, recalled his stop at Washington's grave as "one of the most interesting moments of my life,"[112] and on July Fourth in 1841, Presbyterian pastor Nathan S. S. Beman rapturously related "with what . . . emotions I have trodden the consecrated soil of Bunker Hill," and "mused in silence at the humble tomb of Washington," where "I . . . mingled in the conflicts of the historical past," and teleologically "reposed in the calmness of the prophetic future." Using the stock language of local memory theory, Beman gave thanks that: "There are many such hallowed spots on the American soil, sacred to the same associations" at which "the Christian freeman may stand . . . and pay his homage to the patriot's memory, and his adoration to the patriot's God."[113] Finally, several years later, in 1844, Methodist preacher Joshua Wells wrote to U.S. Army General Winfield Scott, an Episcopalian, gifting Scott with a relic "cane cut" from a tree near the tomb "on the Mount Vernon (General Washington's) estate." Wells could hardly have failed to be gratified by the general's response, which was to lavish praise on Methodism generally: "In my opinion, the Methodist Church has done more for the present and future good of the human race," Scott wrote in reply, "than any sect now on earth," and "vast numbers of the human family who would [otherwise] have been eternally ruined, are thus restored and fitted for the joys of another world."[114]

In the same era, Washington was made to become Word, in two popular textbooks appealing to Bible readers that re-rendered the history of the Revolution in "scriptural style." Verses 12–14 of the fifth chapter of Richard Snowden's historical primer, printed three years prior to Washington's death and republished in 1823, described the choice of who would lead the Patriotic forces in the Revolution thus: "the great Sanhedrin of the people, consulted together where they should find a man that would . . . order the battle for them," and "they chose *George*, whos[e] surname was *Washington*," a man "from the south country" with a "goodly inheritance on Mount Vernon, and flocks and herds in abundance."[115] Likewise, an 1819 *Historical Reader* by G. J. Hunt offered this explanation for why the seat of the U.S. federal government bears the appellation "Washington": "the name of the city" where "the Great Sanhedrin of the people," meaning Congress, gather together was "called after the name of the chief captain of the land of Columbia," George Washington, "whose fame extendeth to the uttermost parts of the earth."[116]

Word was also made flesh in the first few decades of the nineteenth century, as, with surprising frequency, discussants of biblical theology solidified their own, otherwise abstract, doctrinal polemics by remembering George Washington in the flesh as a material illustration. Thus, Nathan Bangs in an 1815 treatise against hyper-Calvinist theology argued that God's foreknowledge of events cannot be conflated with His foreordination of them, just as "General Washington, previous to his death, foretold that factions would arise in the United States, which would disturb the tranquility of the union—but it does not follow from thence, that either he himself, or his predictions, were the cause of the rise of such factions."[117] Twenty-two years later, contending for transmission of ministerial authority from Christ through successive generations of gospel preachers, including ministers of the Methodist Episcopal Church such as Bangs himself, the pastor refuted the claim that "because succeeding ministers in the church . . . could not, in the nature of things, testify from ocular demonstration to the resurrection of Christ" and lacked His "extraordinary gifts," Christ had no authoritative successors to his ministry; after all: "On the same principle it might be affirmed. . . . that General Washington could have no successor as president of these United States, merely because no one after him was inducted into office as the deliverer of his country from foreign oppression."[118]

In several instances, in the same era, evangelicals' church buildings and their environs were drawn into the contest for memories of Washington and the Founding. For example, in Alexandria, Virginia, in 1830, at a time when Freemasonry was controversial with many Americans—but less so among Methodist clergy, many of whom were themselves members of that fraternity—Freemasons, tasked with dedicating a new Methodist church's cornerstone, after ceremonially enclosing a copy of the Declaration of Independence and other artifacts into it, celebrated the stone's consecration by marching, with no sense of impropriety, "*in form*," from the Methodist church "to the tomb of Washington."[119] That same year, a writer for the *Christian Advocate* vicariously took readers on a winter coach ride to "WASHINGTON'S CHURCH," still extant at Pohick in Virginia, a "plain," yet "venerable," "brick edifice," filled with "moral grandeur" by the "associations attaching themselves to this sacred spot," particularly "that great spirit of our country," the "immortal Washington," a "Christian hero who," in that very church, the author confidently assured readers of the *Advocate*, found "religious relaxation . . . from the tumult of war" and "the cares of state," and now "reposes where the wicked cease from troubling, and the weary . . . rest."[120]

One year later in 1831, Presbyterians in Fredericksburg, Virginia, not so far from away from Pohick, wrote to the last surviving signer of the Declaration of Independence, Roman Catholic Charles Carroll of Carrollton, to ask for his moral and financial backing of their plan to honor not Mary the mother of Jesus, but Mary Ball Washington, the mother of George Washington. The Protestant petitioners envisioned a monument worthy of George Washington's mother, within which they would reinter her very bones as relics, and, as housing for the shrine, a new Presbyterian church building "worthy of the monument."[121] In 1834, the *Advocate* carried a story about a Methodist church building in Barkhamsted, Connecticut, at "Horse's Hill" as that promontory was then called until, on the Sunday of the new meetinghouse's dedicatory service, Pastor Daniel Coe stated to "the congregation that he had a desire to change the name of that place, and upon considerable reflection" had "fixed upon a name, in which he thought they would all readily concur—it was that of Washington hill, and if the inhabitants were pleased to adopt it they must signify their pleasure by a rising vote, whereupon the whole assembly arose, and" the site of the church "was accordingly pronounced WASHINGTON HILL." The article concluded with the observation that many other loci in America had unfortunate names that might be improved upon by citizens willing to follow "the example of the good people of Washington Hill."[122]

Over a dozen years later, though the *Advocate* took no notice of the story, another recently dedicated Methodist church—this one in Watertown, Massachusetts—was made to materially point back to the age of Washington; a gift from the local Unitarian church to their Methodist neighbors, a "vane surmounting" the new Methodist church's exterior, was "an historical relic," the "identical" weathervane "which graced the spire" of Carpenter's Hall in Philadelphia, where "the first Continental Congress," that counted George Washington among its members, was held in 1774.[123] The *Advocate* took no notice of that story. Had it done so, it might have reprised its 1828 reprinting of Benjamin Franklin's dictum that churches ought to prioritize print culture—building libraries—over ornamentation—outfitting spires. But in 1848, the *Christian Advocate* probably would not have done so.[124] By the 1840s, Unitarians and Methodists alike, could—as it seems that in Watertown, Massachusetts, they did—take it for granted that however much churches differed theologically over Jesus of Nazareth, patriotic relics that evoked George Washington and his fellow Founders of the United States would be received with unalloyed joy by any American congregation.

Discontents

By 1840, when Methodist student Charles Downey was deciding whether to accept Hamet Achmet's offer of six strands of George Washington's hairs in exchange for a piece of delivered furniture, American evangelicals, including other Methodists, had a honed habit of lauding and posthumously identifying with Washington. With their support and concurrence, he had become, for many in America, "the figure . . . we cannot dissociate from apotheosis,"[125] as one newspaper put it in 1838. In the same era, there were, however, some discontents, a few critics—Catholics, secular freethinkers, dissenting voices within evangelicalism itself, and even one of the last living representatives of America's founding elite, James Madison—maintaining that evangelicals' worship of, and postmortem affiliation with George Washington and other famous Founders was inaccurate, inconsistent, or overwrought. In September of 1835, Cincinnati's *Catholic Telegraph* pointed directly at the irony of Protestants purportedly against reliquary being attracted to locks of George Washington's hair: "Patriotism . . . , with its sacred instincts" to venerate relics is popularly accepted, so why "should not religion too have its relics?" Why "should" the Church "not value memorials capable[,] like the lock of the illustrious Washington's hair[,] of keeping alive and glowing feelings," especially such feelings of connection to the body of Christ as "should ever animate the Christian?" How can it be that "[w]hen the 'conquering hero' was an Apostle, a leader of the Spiritual host," it is "idolatry to preserve a lock of his hair," yet not "to receive with respect and guard with holy reverence the humblest relic of him who, in an inferior order, was 'first in the hearts of his countrymen?'"[126]

In 1830, freethinker Fanny Wright, dubbed "The Red Harlot of Infidelity" by her opponents, challenged patriotic American evangelical memory, arguing that the United States' leading Founders—including George Washington—had held "infidel" views anticipating her own.[127] To answer voices in Wright's camp, Episcopal minister E. C. M'Guire, having married into Washington's extended family, collaborated in 1836 with the icon's heirs to author *The Religious Opinions and Character of Washington*, a book-length defense of its subject as a vindicator "of evangelical doctrine," allowance being made for a "full development of the pregnant meaning" of George Washington's "statements."[128] Transparently tendentious, M'Guire's work, the *New York Review* reported, exposed him "to some laughter."[129] In 1831, as Fanny Wright's associate Robert Owen delighted in pointing out, James R. Willson, a Presbyterian pastor and legislative chaplain in Albany, New York, devoted a whole sermon to repudiating what he took to be fellow evangelicals' wishful thinking about the Founders.[130] In response, legislators in Albany voted 95 to 2 to condemn Willson for having "unnecessarily endeavored to detract from the fame of . . . the benefactors of our country," and rescinded his appointment as a chaplain.[131] Outside of the capitol, an angry mob burned the preacher in effigy, materially demonstrating how far residents of New York's Burned-over District, which had seen wave after wave of evangelical revivals, would go to defend the pietistic "memory" of the United States Founders that Reverend Willson dared to criticize.[132]

Eighteen years earlier, Willson had written a superficially friendly yet sternly proselytizing letter to James Madison—who had, over the years, received many missives from evangelicals trying, by turns, to either verify his approval of their doctrines or to convert him.[133] Willson warned Madison: "unless there is more respect paid to the '*king of kings & Lord of lords & prince of the kings of the earth*,' & to his bible, in our constitutions & by the dignitaries of this land: God almighty will soon do a thing which shall fill all ungodly hearts with dismay." James Madison did not respond, except to docket the letter in his files under the label "Revd & insane."[134] In 1833, Madison heard from another prominent evangelical: publisher, orator, and South Carolina politician Thomas Smith Grimké. Over several months in 1833, Grimké penned a series of letters to Montpelier, enclosing copies of his recent speeches, and begging Madison: "spare me, if you [have] any to spare, some autographs of Distinguished men," including, if possible, "those of the Members . . . of the Congress of 1776, and of the Convention of 1787."[135] Madison wrote back in 1834 with a "scanty supply of [the] autographs requested from me," lamenting "that my files have been so often resorted to" by autograph seekers "within a few years past, that they have become quite barren, especially in the case of names most distinguished."[136]

Madison also disappointed Grimké's thinly concealed evangelical hopes. Whenever the latter tried, even indirectly, to draw him out in support of distinctly evangelical theology, activism, or usable memory of the nation's Founding, the sage of Montpelier either ignored Grimké or vaguely adverted that he was "not prepared to accede to some of the opinions contained" in Grimké's writings.[137] In August of 1833, after Thomas Grimké sent two of his evangelical polemics to him, Madison responded: "My personal knowledge has discovered a few errors of fact in some of the political passages [of your work,] which future lights may correct."[138] Grimké anxiously asked Madison to show him his mistakes.[139] Madison pointed to the evangelicals' stock story, that Grimké had related, of Franklin calling for prayer at the 1787 Constitutional Convention, with its false claim that the convention had acceded to Franklin's request. That version of the story, favored by evangelicals, was, Madison had explained to Jared Sparks two years earlier, simply not true "in the extent supposed." Even as he corrected Grimké, Madison generously suggested that the preachy polemicist may have been led into believing the hagiographic version of the tale by an "erroneous" newspaper report "some years ago."[140]

Grimké responded by thanking Madison for the autograph relics that he had sent to him, and expressing shock that the Constitutional Convention had not acted piously, as he had assumed.[141] Thus, in a short cycle of letters, Madison encountered, and Grimké exemplified, leading features of early American evangelicals' participation in patriotic memory culture: seeking relics of the Founders; resorting to polemical preachment; and using cheap, mass-distribution printed pamphlets or newspapers to spread a pietistic version of American history to a mass audience. Unlike traditional Christian theology, with its emphasis on the universal, such nostalgic American evangelical hagiography would be provincially pro-American. Once promulgated it would, in evangelical style, be popularly conveyed across centuries of

U.S. cultural history, and frequently deployed to reinforce American evangelicals' faith in U.S. exceptionalism, and in what, at various times of American evangelical history, would pass for cultural conservatism.

Pohick's Ruins

On a rainy day, in the summer of 1837, the Reverend William Meade, assistant bishop of the Episcopal Diocese of Virginia, visited Pohick Church, "in the vicinity of Mt. Vernon, the seat of George Washington." No one was there, but the doors to the church were "wide open," and they were "inviting me to enter,—as they . . . invite day and night throughout the year, not only the passing traveler, but every beast of the field and fowl of the air." Climbing into the "lofty pulpit," of "the sacred chancel," Meade wondered: "Is this the House of God . . . built by the Washingtons, . . . the Lewises, the Fairfaxes . . . in which they used to worship . . . according to the venerable forms of the Episcopal Church?" Some of their names were "still to be seen on the doors of [their] deserted pews." Were these material vestiges of their faith, the bishop wondered, "destined to moulder piecemeal away, or, when some signal is given, to become the prey of" relic-seeking "spoilers[,] . . . carried hither and thither and applied to every purpose under heaven?" To prevent the continued deterioration and expropriation of George Washington's old church, Reverend Meade hoped that "reverence for" Washington, "the greatest of patriots, if not [for] religion[,] might be effectually appealed to."[142]

Taking up the old guard's cause, Pohick's new rector, W. P. C. Johnson, began collecting subscriptions in support of his church building's restoration. Contributors soon included such iconic figures as John Quincy Adams and Francis Scott Key. Nonetheless, in December of 1848, when the magazine editor Benjamin Lossing visited "the venerated Pohick . . . Church," he marked the continuing declension that Bishop Meade presciently feared. Where "Washington had worshipped" in high-church services, now "a Methodist meeting," noted Lossing, "was to be held." Arriving before the worshippers, Lossing, like Meade before him, found the church building in a vulnerable state, empty, with its doors "wide open, inviting ingress." Over the next hour, a "slow-gathering" group of Methodist worshippers entered. When "assembled, men and women, white and black, the whole congregation," including Lossing, "amounted to only twenty-one persons." Lossing, sitting in the same "pew, near the pulpit, where Washington and his family were seated Sabbath after Sabbath for many years," lamented the shameful "dilapidation" of once-prim Pohick, "around which clustered so many" patriotic "associations." Birds had come into the open building and desecrated its altar. No less shocking was the social status of the worshippers. In stark "contrast with former days, when some of the noblest of the Virginia aristocracy" attended Pohick in high-church style, now, no "choir, with the majestic organ, chanted the *Te Deum*, or the *Gloria in Excelsis.*" The "Decalogue was not read, nor did solemn audible responses, as in other days go up from the lips of the people." Instead an informal ethos prevailed. A "glorious hymn beginning 'Come holy Spirit, heavenly dove!' was sung" by the occupying Methodists "with fervor; and standing behind the ancient communion-table, a young preacher in homely garb," spoke affectively with striking effectiveness. Proclaiming "the pure Gospel of love," he "warmed the hearts of all present."[143]

What had happened? How had effusive, unwashed, mostly lower-class American evangelicals all but taken over the late George Washington's staid parish church? More largely how, by the 1840s, had evangelicals, as such, managed to retrospectively capture and yoke themselves to so much of American patriotic memory? Mead and Lossing were right if they perceived clues in the taking of relics from Pohick Church, for patriotic American evangelicals had benefited from an American cultural moment in which prevalent memory theory demanded relics; in which evangelicals were disproportionately represented among the Revolution's living relics, its surviving veterans; and in which a self-authorized, decentralized, almost-freewheeling view of authority within Protestantism itself, and especially within evangelical revivalism, left individuals free to choose in real time, subject only to their own conscience and theological understandings, how to regard, or respond to, relics, including relics associated with America's leading Founders. By 1840, even on the campus of Wesleyan University, one Charles Downey did not need the approval, tacit or otherwise, of a President Fisk or Bangs to certify, or to buy, a lock of George Washington's hair.

5

THE SCHOOLMISTRESS

In 1890, an earnest assemblage of women in Troy, New York, began a successful campaign for a statue of Emma Willard. Willard had been a local teacher, principal, and author. She had gained transatlantic fame as the leading American advocate for formally educating women. Documenting the legacy of excellence that they believed justified a public monument to her, the women of Troy solicited testimonials about Willard's teaching. Gleanings from the outpouring that ensued they published as an 800-page commemorative volume, *Emma Willard and Her Pupils.*[1] Among the anecdotes preserved was one contributed by the children of Cornelia Keeler, who had been a student of Willard's during the 1830s. Since deceased, Mrs. Keeler lived on in her children's memories. They particularly recalled listening with admiration as their mother repeated "verbatim paragraph after paragraph of logic which she had not seen since her school-days, and as readily" recited "genealogical tables as though learned but yesterday. When questioned by us as to how it was possible to remember so perfectly what was learned so long ago, she replied, 'I learned to study at Mrs. Willard's.' "[2]

Keeler's children's recollections of their mother's feats of memory would have pleased Emma Willard. In the 1820s and 1830s, Willard took pride in not only what she taught girls who came to her Troy Female Seminary, but also how she ensured that they would long remember what they learned there. Willard insisted that she had independently, if coincident with other pedagogues of the day, discerned the "true mnemonic" to be used in education, the most efficacious strategy for fostering lasting memories of academic lessons.[3] Significantly, Willard's beliefs about how to permanently instill her lessons reflected conventional wisdom about memory among educators in the 1820s and 1830s, inasmuch as they involved eager acceptance of then-popular physicalist recasting of the received "local memory" tradition, and her students, by all evidence, appreciated her emphasis on the tangible. For example, one of Willard's many effusively grateful pupils, Elizabeth Atwater, went on to garner her own relics illustrative of patriotic history of the sort that Willard especially loved to teach. A relative of the Washingtons, Atwater acquired locks of George and Martha Washington's hair and other historical relics unrelated to the Washingtons. Her lovingly constructed scrapbook containing the tresses and other artifacts is held today in the Chicago Academy of Sciences. The academy's entire Atwater collection instantiated early nineteenth-century physicalist memory theory, which Willard had argued that females must be formally taught to equip them to convey America's foundational patriotic memories to the nation's children.[4] Perhaps, then, it was telling, and certainly it was apropos, that Elizabeth Cady Stanton, who at Seneca Falls, New York, in 1848 would famously draw upon collective American memory of the Declaration of Independence to give voice to the emerging "Woman Movement," had been among Emma Willard's devoted students.[5]

To uncover how Willard, with other American educators in the new nation, adapted beliefs about pedagogy to changing memory theory and strategically employed physicalizing popular beliefs about how memory worked in order to argue for a prominent role for women in communicating national memories, one needs only to look with care at a large, representative sample of early American schoolbooks. Admittedly, it is no simple matter to discern to what extent the views expressed in, and the pedagogies endorsed by these textbooks reflected and shaped what went on in classrooms. Yet, textbooks, which "became more numerous during the early national era, . . . were seen by parents, teachers, and students alike as providing whatever structure and order, or in contemporary terms, 'system' there would be in the various subjects of the curriculum."[6] At a minimum, extant textbooks reveal what those educators elite enough to be published deemed important. Emma Willard's influential theories and practices as a textbook writer and classroom educator, as well as the reception of her

The 1895 unveiling of the Emma Willard statue. (Rensselaer County Historical Society, Troy, NY)

views, are well documented, offering clear insights into how changing memory theory and culture influenced American educators' patriotic retrospectives.

The Physicalist Turn in American Pedagogy

Had she lived to see it, Emma Willard might have taken particular delight in the fact that her admirers in late nineteenth-century Troy chose to commemorate her legacy with a physical monument. During the 1820s and 1830s, public monuments were commonly justified in terms of increasingly popular physicalist understandings of memory that were front and center in Willard's pedagogy. In the same era, with coauthor William Channing Woodbridge, Willard published a geography text that pictured prominently a monument in Baltimore to George Washington, reflecting their view that good teaching relied "upon the principle of making the eye the medium of instruction."

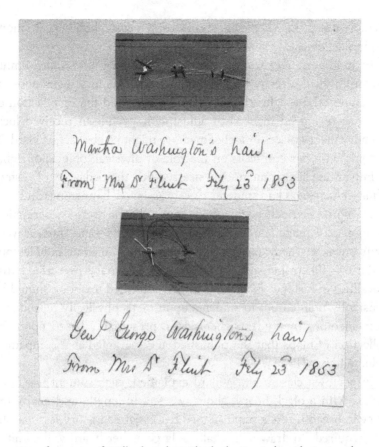

Page from one of Willard student Elizabeth Atwater's mid-nineteenth-century scrapbooks. (Chicago Academy of Sciences/Peggy Notebaert Nature Museum)

Their text's preface, written by Willard, explained that she and Wood-bridge would "admit little" pedagogically "which may not be traced to one of these two laws of intellect—first, that the objects of sight more readily become the subjects of conception and memory than those of the other senses; and secondly, that the best of all methods to . . . enable the memory . . . is to class particulars under general heads."[7] Thus, Willard and Woodbridge endorsed the view of memory gaining currency in the era, which continued the Classical emphasis upon conceiving of particular ideas to be remembered as organized in discrete rooms or loci, and then reified it biologically, treating enduring memories as primarily the effects of strong sensate, bodily perceptions of physical objects.

In another of her textbooks, her *History of the United States,* Emma Willard argued directly that traditional local memory techniques, or "mnemonics," though valuable "so far as they aid the recollection of facts" were indeed in need of adjustment.[8] While in received local memory theory places or loci of memory might be abstract, Willard, in keeping with her emphasis on the role of physical "objects of sight" in implanting lasting memories, stressed that the pedagogy of *History of the United States* had students closely associate happenings and personages in American history with concrete, real-world geographical locations. To make learning sensate for students—and thus, as Willard's physicalist view of memory would have it, memories of lessons enduring—the principal of Troy Female Seminary prescribed that "localities of history" mentioned in her published textbook should be constantly pointed out to students upon maps physically reproduced from memory by students themselves, presumably based upon the collection of maps that she published and marketed as a companion volume to her *History.*[9]

In her own classroom, Willard explained, each student was "furnished with a black board, about two feet in length, and nearly the same in breadth." As a pupil studied her assigned history lessons, she was required "to draw with chalk as large as her board will admit, a sketch of that part of the country which is the seat of the portion of history which the lesson contains; marking slightly the track of navigators and march of armies." For purposes of examination, the "pupil brings her black board to her classroom, and her recitation, in part, consists of the explanation, which, agreeably to the accounts derived from the book, she gives of her sketched map."[10] Such sensory-based, geographically centered historical instruction, Willard promised, would help "the present generation of our youth" to experience their nation's natural vistas as evocative of nationalistic memory. Pupils taught by her methods would "learn to connect the mental sublime of the story of our fathers with the natural grandeur of our scenery."[11] The territory of the nation would be their memory palace.

Willard's advocacy for sensory-driven "mnemonics" in education was part of a general bodily turn in contemporaneous pedagogy that began in the mid-eighteenth-century Enlightenment and continued well into the next century, as educators emphasized "concrete and observable" bodily "responses of the young . . . to the gradual derogation of . . . abstract" instruction. Part and parcel to these new understandings, physical exercise came to be seen more and more as a necessary partner of education.[12] Thus, an 1840 textbook on *Domestic Education* by H. Humphrey, president of Amherst College, argued that mothers should disregard advice from those who "*seem* to think that creeping is altogether too vulgar an affair to be tolerated in a good society," and allow children the "natural and inalienable" right to crawl about freely. "I dare say," averred Humphrey, "that Benjamin Franklin and George Washington were both great creepers in their infancy."[13] Physical strength, theorists stressed, was essential to remembrance.

Colorfully expressing what was becoming conventional wisdom on the subject, an article on "Development of the Mind" reprinted in one popular periodical in 1835 asserted that a person "gorging himself at dinner, must allow so much of the nervous energy to expend itself upon the digestive functions during the next three or four hours, that thought, which demands the same power to be at command in the brain is quite destitute of life. . . . Every uneasiness of the body . . . subtracts its part from the force that might serve the . . . memory."[14] With memory thus being widely understood as essentially physical, it is little wonder that American pedagogues in the period came to believe that, as William H. Brooks stated in an 1832 address at a meeting in Boston, Massachusetts, of the American Institute of Instruction, "the teacher," to be effective at exciting lasting memories in students, cannot possibly learn "too early" the "importance of the [physical] senses . . . and the importance of educating them to activity and accuracy." At the same meeting, speaking "On the Utility of Visible Illustrations," Walter Johnson pointed to Charles Willson Peale's Philadelphia museum as exemplifying the new object-oriented pedagogy's effectiveness and popularity. Thanks to growing acceptance in pedagogical theory that the "*eye of the auditor . . . is the chief coadjutor of the labor of instruction*," enthused Johnson, "truth now . . . frequently presents herself to the student under the attractive guise of visible" illustration.[15]

The new pedagogy was literally apparent in the textbooks of the 1820s and 1830s. Now as a matter of principle, albeit abetted by new technologies of printing, they drew more and more upon illustrations to convey lessons. Proponents claimed that the "Picture System" was more effective than prior pedagogies at working to "store the memory" of each pupil with crucial lessons.[16] Critics countered that pictures were spoiling children intellectually. Young scholars were becoming as dependent upon the external stimulus of pictures as drunkards were upon booze.[17] Such dueling appraisals notwithstanding, the "Picture System," observers agreed, was emblematic of a new era in which childhood education had become far more sensate than before.[18] The dawn of that era, one discussant suggested, had come in the 1820s with the publication of Willard and Woodbridge's popular geography, "one of the most highly-pictured school-books" in the United States, and a work that, in its preface by Willard, expressly enunciated fundamental philosophical and pedagogical reasons to teach with pictures.[19]

Whatever the precise influence of Willard and Woodbridge upon teachers, the attractiveness of physicalist pedagogies was generally enhanced by the growing popularity among American educators of Pestalozzianism and phrenology. Pestalozzianism, which drew upon views of Swiss educational theorist and educator Johann Heinrich Pestalozzi (1746–1827), was by 1825 "a subject of considerable interest" in the United States. Its leading patron among American teachers, William Maclure, stressed that the Pestalozzian system emphasized "use of all the senses," as did phrenology.[20] Both philosophies influenced teaching at Emma Willard's Female Seminary.[21] There, they may have informed, and presumably complemented, the physicalist epistemology that underlay Willard's conception of the "true mnemonic of history."[22]

In the 1820s and 1830s, as Emma Willard used her seminary and textbook writing to convey to the rising generation of American youth collective memories of the nation's founding epochs, she was almost certainly inspired not only by abstract arguments for popular physicalist pedagogical theory, but also by her personal, firsthand experiences of the efficacy of relics as foci of patriotic remembrance. Setting aside its usual aloof third-person narrative voice, Willard's *History of the United States* claimed that when Lafayette visited the United States during his 1824–25 memory tour he proved to be an evocative memory prop: to Americans who saw him, "there was an associated remembrance of those with whom he had lived; and there seemed to come back to us not only Lafayette, but Washington and Greene, and the heroes of the days of American glory" as "the feeling of communing with the illustrious dead . . . filled *our* hearts and excited *us* to the highest pitch of enthusiasm."[23] Willard's sudden use of the first-person plural voice reflected how much she treasured her private memories of meeting Lafayette in the flesh.

Passing through Troy, New York, in 1824 and 1825, Lafayette had favored her seminary with a visit. At his first appearing, the entryway to the institution was adorned with a banner: "We owe our schools to Freedom; Freedom to Lafayette." Willard met the general at the school's north gate, her teachers following in turn, and, behind them, her pupils, resplendent in white frocks with blue sashes, singing an ode that Willard had composed in Lafayette's honor: "And art thou, then, dear Hero come? And do our eyes behold the man . . . ?" Appropriately, given the seminary's pedagogical emphasis upon object-based learning, each student wore a satin badge bearing a print of Lafayette's visage, a concrete souvenir of their face-to-face encounter with him. In the years following, many of the girls faithfully preserved their badges, passing them on to their children as heirlooms.[24]

In the course of the general's visits to the Troy Seminary, Lafayette and Willard, as one of Willard's pupils, Annie McDowell, later recalled, "charmed . . . each other."[25] Subsequently, when Willard received letters from Lafayette, she treated them as treasured artifacts. She read them to her school's assembly. Consistent with her physicalist pedagogy, she required the listening "young ladies" of the seminary to "transcribe" them for their edification. One of Willard's students, Arabella M. Pearson, lamented decades afterward that though she had then failed to "appreciate this privilege," she now deeply regretted not having retained her copies.[26]

In late 1830, Willard, seeking a respite from her duties as principal of the seminary, left the United States for a several-months holiday in France and Britain. Not surprisingly, the highlights of Willard's trip were the times she spent with Lafayette. Revealingly, her correspondence of that period is freighted with the terminology of contemporaneous physicalist memory theory, and objectifies Lafayette's body, indicating what she thought his physiognomy evidenced about his character, and highlighting—in tones romantic, but not particularly erotic—occasions when the old relic of the American Revolution and the American school principal physically touched.

Examples of how Willard chronicled her Old World exploration in language associated with physicalist ideas about memory include descriptions in her journal of how particular geographic loci and "various objects, which everywhere present themselves to my view"—especially "fine monuments"—were awakening in her thinking vivid "historical associations," giving rise to ardent feelings the likes of which she had never before felt, "except it might have been in visiting the tomb of Washington" at Mount Vernon.[27] Her diary also betrayed her personal applications of, interest in, and friendliness toward transatlantic theories and practices of physiognomy and phrenology then being used in the United States to support the self-conscious turn to bodily artifacts and props in collective American memory. Willard judged France's queen to be someone of "agreeable physiognomy." Meeting another French royal, she declared: "I liked the general cast of his physiognomy better than that of any other of the family, except the Queen's." Introduced to a Scottish philosopher, she "marked his physiognomy" too. Following a face-to-face discussion with George Combe, the leading transatlantic evangelist of phrenology, she wrote: "In regard to his opinions some struck me as true the moment he announced them," but "with respect to others I was not prepared to judge." Whatever uncertainty she had about details of Combe's phrenological system, she hinted at her confidence in the usefulness of analyzing heads as physiognomic clues of character when she enthusiastically recorded her visit to the studio of the French sculptor who had "made that fine model of the head of Lafayette, from which the plaster casts multiply, for his millions of children in America." That likeness, Willard gushed, was "the true expression" of Lafayette's "paternal features." Busts of other famous persons in the artist's studio allowed her other physiognomic insights. She swelled with nationalistic pride when told that a "remarkable head" that had caught her eye was indeed the bust "of a man of great talents," American author James Fenimore Cooper.[28]

In her travelogue, Willard's most inspired argument from a person's physiognomy to claims about their character involved her beloved Lafayette. While listening to French scientist Georges Baron Cuvier lecture, she analyzed the speaker in physiognomic terms, using Lafayette as a basis for comparison: "I compared the physiognomy of Cuvier with that of Lafayette," and found "in each, the peculiar differences of their character. They have both noble countenances; but mental strength is Cuvier's leading characteristic,—benevolence that of La Fayette." While "Cuvier's visage invites students to approach with profound respect, and ask for knowledge, La Fayette's beckons the unfortunate to come with confiding love, and receive sympathy and protection."[29] Such episodes in Willard's accounts of her time in France treated Lafayette's body as a revealing, memory-evoking relic of a heroic age, a historical artifact that Willard, however chastely, was eager to personally observe and touch. Thus, she excitedly recorded an occasion on her European trip when she "saw again the benignant face of Lafayette, and felt the kind paternal grasp of his hand," another when he "moved" his eyes "slowly around till they rested . . . on myself," yet another when "I looked at him and met his eye" which shone with "precisely the same expression as I marked when we sung to him in Troy," and an unforgettable incident when she helped him to escape the crush of an admiring French crowd at the theatre: "In the enthusiasm of the moment, I . . . handed him over the seats . . . unconscious . . . that I was making myself a part of the spectacle."[30]

Emma Willard was not the only American textbook author whose interest in using concrete objects and visible illustrations appears to have been fired *both* by physicalist pedagogical theory *and* by vivid personal experiences with artifacts and loci evocative of the American Revolution. A passionate devotee of physicalist memory theory, John Fanning Watson used Revolutionary War relics and personal visits to historical sites to buttress his own consciousness of the past. Implementing physicalist principles of memory education, Watson produced children's textbooks that used eye-catching engravings, à la the Picture System, to "multiply" in young readers' minds "local associations of ideas which bind . . . to the paternal soil," and he encouraged students to begin to use local extant buildings from the Revolution as memory palaces, portals into their nation's storied collective memory.[31]

Similar, but more influential, was the work of Samuel G. Goodrich. Goodrich, one of the best-selling textbook writers of the 1820s and 1830s, eventually sold millions of copies of his curricula. His fictional alter ego "Peter Parley," the genial narrator of his most famous works, was all but synonymous with the Picture System of education. In his textbooks and his autobiography alike, Goodrich explained his allegiance to object-based education. Illustrations in textbooks, he argued, were uniquely effective for "fixing . . . ideas permanently in the memory of the pupil," and "the truth art of teaching children" respects the principle that "their first ideas are . . . formed of images of things palpable to the senses," especially to the "eye—the master organ of the body as well as the soul." Thus Goodrich, who prided himself on his Christian orthodoxy even when he was accused of having a reductively "materialistic" conception of learning, insisted that "old theories . . . that education should . . . seek to spiritualize the mind, and lift it above sensible ideas" should give way to pedagogies that prioritized physical processes of learning, facilitating academic memorization and understanding by showing "things capable of representation," especially by means of engravings in textbooks.[32]

As Goodrich punctuated his textbooks with engravings, as "sensible" evocations of historical happenings that he wished to sustain in Americans' collective memory, he was, like Emma Willard, influenced not only by physicalist theories of pedagogy, but also by firsthand experiences of the efficacy of patriotic memory props. Tellingly, Samuel Goodrich recounted his own acquisition of childhood memories in mechanistic, physicalist terms. In the 1850s, he recalled how, as a boy hunting in Connecticut, every "bird that flew, every corpse and thicket, every hill and dale—every thing that my senses realized, my memory daguerreotyped."[33] He long remembered the moment when, in his youth, he sighted the *Connecticut Courant*'s report of President Washington's 1799 death: "The paper was bordered with black, which left its indelible ink in my memory."[34] His boyhood hometown, Ridgefield, Connecticut, he remembered ever after as a site suggestive of historic Patriot heroics. He could hardly do otherwise, having, in childhood, listened by the hour on Saturday afternoons as a local war hero, "Lieutenant Smith, . . . sword in hand" narrated to the town's wide-eyed boys personal memories of Revolutionary War fighting at Ridgefield, frequently "punctuating his discourse with a present cannonball, sunk six inches deep into a corner-post of the very house in which we sat." Lieutenant Smith's object-based pedagogy, Goodrich harrumphed, was much more effective than that of a traditional schoolmaster who, by not appealing to their senses, failed to teach students memorably.[35]

As living relics, not only Smith, but every "old man" and "every old woman" in Ridgefield, "had stories to tell, rich with personal observation. Some had seen Washington," and "one was at the capture of Ticonderoga under Ethan Allen"; another "had witnessed the execution of André" and still another "had been present at the capture of Burgoyne." The very landscape of Ridgefield was filled with physical remains from the war.[36] As a four-year-old boy, skipping barefoot down a lane in Ridgefield, Goodrich traversed a "patch of earth, blackened by cinders, where my feet were hurt by pieces of melted glass and metal." Young Goodrich "inquired what this meant." He was told that "there a house was burned down by . . . British troops" who had come upon it during the Revolution. It "may seem trifling," the textbook writer admitted years later, to make so much of a minor physical injury sustained during his boyhood cavorting. Yet, that injury, in its impressive, painful physicality, ensured that "Every time I passed the place, I ruminated on" the "story of the house burned down by a foreign army." Soon Goodrich was "the master of the whole story and of other similar events" of the Revolution "which had occurred all over the country." So, in a direct, physical way, Goodrich was "initiated into the spirit of that day," being made to memorably feel in his own body an agonizing aftereffect of the perfidy of "foreign" forces during the Revolution.[37]

"Peter Parley," the fictive storyteller in Goodrich's texts, was too kind to use shards of broken glass to painfully impress upon students the importance of the Revolution. Yet, Goodrich's best-selling "Peter Parley" textbook series did proclaim and practice a sensory-driven, physicalist pedagogy. His *First Book of History* taught that "the memory of the pupil" must be appealed to with sense objects.[38] It thus conveyed lessons that Goodrich deemed worthy of remembrance through evocative pictures.[39] Goodrich's history also highlighted manifestations of physicalist patriotic American memory culture outside of the classroom, as when Parley exclaimed: "I must not forget to tell you of La-Fayette's visit to this country" in the 1820s. "I suppose many of my little readers saw him."[40] Thus textbooks of the period highlighted, and often suggestively juxtaposed, *both* tenets of contemporaneous physicalist memory theory *and* extracurricular real-world happenings in patriotic American memory culture that accorded with a physicalist pedagogy.[41]

Teaching American Memory Culture

Significantly, early American textbooks advertised their physicalist perspectives on memory not only in their prefaces aimed at teachers.[42] In the bodies of the texts as well, in sections meant for students to study, physicalist memory theory was directly taught. An 1828 reader featured a passage asserting that bodily and mental development are necessarily coeval: "As the body passes through infancy and childhood, so does the mind. Feeble at first, it 'grows with the growth and strengthens with the strength' of the corporeal system." The same book printed another selection that made the complementary assertions that "it has been found that all mental susceptibilities are strengthened by exercise[,] much the same as our bodily powers; and the faculty of memory certainly not less than others," with "conceptions of *sight*" being very vivid and more easily recalled to remembrance than others. In an apparent allusion to the local memory tradition, the excerpt continued: "our remembrances are assisted by the law of contiguity in place, which is known to be one of the most efficient aids" of memory.[43]

An 1830 government textbook by William Sullivan indicated that it was when "the senses have conveyed to the mind a knowledge of things without us, that we have the power of retaining that knowledge, and can recall the impressions made, and think of them."[44] An 1831 reader for young women included a passage on the human "faculty of associating remembrance of characters and events, which have most interested our passions, with the [physical] spot whereon the former have lived and the latter have occurred." It explained that "the potency of local associations is not limited to the sphere of our personal experience," but also made "sacred or fabulous history" more memorable, creating in the mind of the person who remembered something historical "a train of perception which either rush unbidden on his mind, or are courted by voluntary efforts." Most efficacious of "all the object of mental association" in evoking historical memory, the essay explained, were such relics as "ancient extant buildings and ruins."[45] Similarly, an 1832 reader put together by J. L. Blake stressed that "human nature" demanded "objects, whether animate or inanimate" to abet recollections of "persons whose memory we love and admire."[46]

Textbooks not only taught physicalist memory theory abstractly, but also acquainted students with performances of patriotic American memory that smacked of self-conscious physicalism. Passages that did so were often in the first person, in effect allowing reciting students to experience vicariously the recollections being conveyed. Thus, an anonymous piece in Moses Severance's 1835 reader, *The American Manual*, on "The Grave of Jefferson" described how "I ascended the winding road which leads from Charlottesville to Monticello, up the miniature mountain" to the "spot"—a word charged with significance in local memory theory—at which is the "grave of Jefferson," where "the visitor sees . . . a low unmortared stone wall, which he enters by a neat wooden gate" to find the humble "resting place of the patriot and philosopher."[47] James Hall's 1834 *Western Reader* had its intended audience—western youth residing in regions far from where the Revolution had occurred—effectively share the experience of someone living at the time of George Washington's death in a place charged with memories of the Revolution: "And when the news arrived (I was then a little lad at school,) that the great Washington was dead we all wept" in a "scene of spontaneous sorrow" the "impression" of which will never "be effaced while memory endures." Using language strikingly congruent with sensate, locality-oriented memory theory, the reminiscence continued with a caveat about how memory of George Washington had been transmitted to the young scholars: to be sure, "None of us—I mean the children at school—had ever seen him—but our fathers and mothers had seen him, and they told us about him—and we were in the vicinity of many of his disasters and of many of his brightest achievements."[48]

Similarly, an 1833 *Rhetorical Reader* by Ebenezer Porter had students practice public speaking skills by recounting in the first-person plural voice a visit to Washington's house and tomb at Mount Vernon: "We drove to the entrance of the old gateway, and alighted in the midst of what appeared to be a little village, so numerous and scattered were the buildings. About those which we came upon, there was an air of dilapidation and neglect that was rather unpromising." Yet, one of them, Washington's former mansion, proved to be an evocative memory palace filled with "rooms made interesting by the hallowed associations that came fast upon us as we traversed them" gawking at the relics with which they were furnished. Most inspiring as a locus of memory was the general's tomb: "It was a happy moment to visit the spot. . . . Who can analyze his feelings as he stands before that sepulcher! Who can tell the story of his associations. . . . Strange power of human mind! What intimation does this rapid communion with the past, and with the spirits of the past, give at once of their immortality and our own! . . . It was with reluctance I turned away, after gathering a relic or two."[49]

Reflecting the jointly physicalist and physiognomic turn in patriotic American memory culture, textbooks evidenced clear interest in bodies of the Revolutionary generation as reminders of, and clues about, the nation's founding epochs and leaders. An 1836 reader compiled by John Hall urged students to "Mourn Washington's death, when ye think of his birth," and bemoaned that "the dust of his body is all that is left" to "hallow his funeral pile."[50] An 1840 textbook life of Washington described him as someone with "whose countenance it was impossible to connect any other qualities than those of wisdom, benevolence, and magnanimity," and just before ending with an engraving of Washington's tomb, quoted an apologia for interest in Washington's body: "'It is natural . . . to view with keen attention the countenance of an illustrious man with a secret hope of discovering in his features some peculiar'" physiognomic traces "'of excellence,'" and such "'expectations are realized in . . . viewing the person of Washington.'"[51] An 1805 collection of exemplary lives, after going into great detail about Washington's death and burial, lingered over his "shrouded corpse—the countenance still composed and serene . . . so that it seemed to express the dignity of that spirit which so lately actuated the lifeless form."[52] An 1810 reader offered a reverent description of Washington's physiognomy: "General Washington was in his person about six feet in height, his eyes were gray, but full of animation; his visage was serene." His "limbs were well proportioned and muscular, and his deportment carried an air of solemnity in it, that was altogether awful to folly."[53]

Emblematic of how, increasingly, not only Washington's body, but also those of Revolutionary War veterans generally were being revered as relics of the Revolution, that same 1810 anthology included a selection lamenting that: "in the last six years" of the Revolution "upwards of eleven thousand persons died on board the [British] prison ship New Jersey . . . stationed in the East River near New York. On many of these, the rights of sepulcher were never, or were but very imperfectly, conferred," and for years "after the war was ended, their bones lay whitening in the sun, on the shores of Long Island."[54] Similarly directing bodily attention to rank-and-file veterans as icons of patriotic memory, A. M. Blake's 1830 *Historical Reader* featured a poem celebrating old men in America who, having fought in the Revolution in their youth, could now "strip their sleeves" to "show their [battle] scars."[55]

Prominent in the Parthenon of Revolutionary veterans pointed out to children as relics of nationalistic memory was Lafayette. When "Peter Parley," in Goodrich's *First Book of History*, exclaimed of the Frenchman "I suppose many of my little readers saw him," he was only being realistic.[56] During Lafayette's 1824–25 tour of the United States, children were often given pride of place in welcoming him. In 1824, reporting Lafayette's triumphal visit to Philadelphia, Sybilla Simmons observed that "on tuesday morning he received all the schools in the state house yard." It "was absolutely crammed full," and "all the streets round." Some "of the schools spoke[e] addresses and sang songs of welcome." Everywhere Lafayette went, she observed, "everybody wanted to shake hands with him."[57]

In 1824, visiting Bunker Hill, Lafayette expressed a "wish to sub-scribe" in support of the monument that was to be erected on the site. Utilizing the hero's cachet with the rising generation, the Monument Association placed Lafayette "at the head of the list" of pledged donors, but asked the hero "not to place any sum against his name." Eventually, the association promised, a sum *would* "be placed against the name of Lafayette" equal to "the whole amount of all the sums, which the little children throughout the state . . . subscribe, or give to the erection of the Monument." Thus the "little ones" will show "gratitude to this . . . noble benefactor" and their efforts at physically commemorating the battle of Bunker Hill would identify them with Lafayette.[58]

Whether they ever personally glimpsed Lafayette during his tour, or subscribed to the Bunker Hill Monument in his name, schoolchildren could easily meet him vicariously in school textbooks, which, after 1824, commonly drew attention to his storied visit, often while impli-cating the general in physicalist practices of patriotic American mem-ory. Thus, Emma Willard's *History of the United States* stressed that Lafayette "arrived in season to participate in the ceremony of laying the corner stone of a monument which was to commemorate the battle of Bunker's Hill," and noted that, during a visit to Washington's tomb at Mount Vernon, Lafayette was presented by "Mr. Custis, the adopted child of Washington" with "a ring containing a portion of the locks from that venerated head, which for so many toilsome days, and un-pillowed nights, had devoted all its energies to that cause for which La Fayette had toiled and bled with kindred devotion."[59] It was, to say the least, not without reason that President John Quincy Adams, as cited in an 1833 textbook, promised Lafayette: "our [American] children in life and after death shall claim you for our own."[60]

Physicalism and Women as Teachers

In the opinion of Emma Willard, and of other influential pedagogues of the era, if the rising generation did lay claim to the United States' natal memories it would be largely owing to the exertions of women. The preeminently physical nature of memory itself, coupled with the logistics of most Americans' early childhoods, Willard argued, entailed as much. In 1819 Willard petitioned New York's legislature in physicalist idioms: "the ductile mind of the child is" chiefly "intrusted to the mother; and she ought to have . . . a knowledge of this noble material, on which it is her business to operate, that she may best understand how to mould it to its most excellent form." Women should be prepared to reason pedagogically not only as mothers, but also as teachers in "common schools." The feminization of the American teaching profession that was at the time manifestly under way could, argued Willard, be a special benefit to the United States' rising generation. Women, she argued, had been given by "nature. . . . in a greater degree than men, the gentle arts of insinuation to soften [children's] minds and fit them to receive impressions."[61] In 1836, reasoning similarly from the criticality of "first impressions" in forming the memories of children, Willard insisted that, because of their physical proximity to young children, American women ought to be taught well academically and should especially learn "the science of the mind," knowledge of which would prepare and motivate them to effectively convey "correct impressions" to their young charges, whose minds would thus be "indelibly stamped" with foundational knowledge well before they come "under the care of learned male instructors."[62] Willard thus argued from a physicalist assay of memory and education to an apologia for women as mothers and educators, and, hence, to a rationale for liberally educating women.

In the 1830s, the patron saint of Americans espousing such reasoning was "Mary, the Mother of Washington."[63] Only a few years before, George Washington's mother had been little known to most Americans.[64] Then, beginning in the late 1820s, popular essays drawing primarily upon writings of Mary Washington's great-grandson, George

Washington Parke Custis, began to posthumously introduce her to the American public.[65] Among the articles was one published in 1831 in a leading women's magazine. It reported that when George Washington visited his chronically ailing mother for what the general presciently knew would be the last time, he wept as "memory, retracing scenes long past, carried him back to the paternal mansion, and the days of his youth, and there, the center of attraction was his mother; whose care . . . prepared him to reach the topmost height of laudable ambition."[66]

The language, emphasizing George Washington's memory of a locale (his boyhood home) and of an embodied object (his mother, its "center of attraction"), was the very sort then affiliated with physicalist memory theory. It may well have been meant to suggest anachronistically that Mary Washington had presciently influenced young George to remember important things, including his mother, in ways prescribed by physicalist adaptations of Classical local memory theory that were more current in 1831 than in Mary Washington's lifetime.

In any case, it soon became a commonplace that Mary Ball Washington had used her physical proximity to her son, as his maternal caregiver, to impress upon him foundational lessons that underwrote his history-making exploits. In Lydia H. Sigourney's judgment, cited in an 1831 school reader, Mary Washington evidenced the "immense force of first impressions," which was "on the side of the mother. An engine of uncomputed power is committed to her hand. If she fix her lever judiciously, though she may not, like Archimedes, aspire to move the earth, she may hope to raise one of the inhabitants of earth to heaven."[67] In 1833, the *Christian Watchman* similarly used physicalist language to explain that the lesson of Mary Washington's life was that mothers shaped their children's' formative memories: "Impressions made in infancy, if not indelible, are effaced with difficulty and renewed with facility; and upon the mother therefore, must frequently, if not generally, depend the fate of the son."[68]

Complementing popular invocations of Mary Ball Washington as an exemplar of the effectiveness of a physicalist pedagogy for teaching if practiced by children's nearest physical companions—their mothers—were contemporaneous efforts to make the tomb of Mary Ball Washington a physical center of pilgrimage. In 1831 locals in Fredericksburg, Virginia, seeking to build a monument at the "locality" of her burial place, explained that it would give "'a local habitation'" to her memory.[69] Advocates of the monument argued too that, as a physical tribute, it would work to educate visitors on the principle that "sight is the liveliest of impressions," and by its locality could draw attention not merely to Mary Washington, but also to her pedagogy. Mary Washington, they reported, was buried at "a favorite spot" of hers, a "beautiful" unspoiled location to which she often repaired with her only daughter and grandchildren. "It was *here* that she impressed upon their infant minds the wonderful works of the great Creator of all things."[70]

Mary Ball Washington not only exemplified popular physicalist pedagogical rationales for recognizing mothers as key educators. As the allusion to her teaching her grandchildren to view Creation as a reminder of the Creator suggested, she was also enlisted to highlight another emphasis in American memory culture generally, and in contemporaneous American pedagogy particularly: spiritual values.[71] In the wake of waves of evangelical Christian revivals in America between 1790 and 1840, Americans were eager, however ahistorically, to remember the Founders as evangelical exemplars. Invoking Mary Ball Washington teaching her grandchildren to revere the Creator may have generically reflected that impulse, as it implied longstanding evangelical piety in Washington's family. It could also have reflected contemporaneous opinion that women were endowed by God with a greater ability than men to teach spiritual values to children. Concurrently, educators were showing "a tendency to prefer the moral to the intellectual or academic values of education," and women were displacing men as children's formal instructors. Few American women had themselves received enough of an education to teach a rigorously academic curriculum, but their deficiencies as teachers appeared less glaring in an era when an increasingly "large segment of opinion was inclined to discount the 'intellectual' training women were not as yet qualified to conduct."[72]

At all events, textbooks of the day offered ready assistance for all who wanted children to remember the Founders as a means of spiritual edification. Yet some curricular attempts to integrate faith and learning were less than adroit. John Hubbard's 1820 reader concluded an extended comparison of "Opposers of the General Government of the United States" to "Ancient Jews" who rebelled against God's leadership of them through Moses with an ambiguous caveat: "I beg I may not be understood to infer that our general convention was divinely inspired when it formed the new federal constitution." However, "I have so much faith in the general government of the world by Providence, that I can hardly conceive a transaction of such importance to millions, should be suffered to pass without being . . . guided . . . by that . . . beneficent Ruler, in whom all inferior beings live, move, and have their being."[73] An 1831 reader hinted by association and implication that the United States' two best-remembered Founders must have been Christians: "The people of . . . the United States of America (where we live,) are Christians. When Christians say anything happened on a particular year, as—Dr. Franklin was born in 1706, or George Washington died in 1799—they mean that one was born 1706 years after Christ was born, and the other died 1799 years after Christ was born."[74]

In the work and biography of Noah Webster one can see clearly how post–Revolutionary War revivalism in the Second Great Awakening encouraged a spiritualized "memory" of the Revolution in at least one prominent educator. Webster's popular *History of the United States*, published in 1832, sought to persuade "American youth" that "the genuine source of correct republican principles is the Bible, particularly the New Testament or the Christian religion." Webster taught that: "During the war of the revolution, the clergy were generally friendly to the cause of the country," so much so that the "present generation can hardly have a tolerable idea of the influence of the New-England clergy in sustaining the patriotic exertions of the people, under the appalling discouragements of war." However, the "writer remembers their good offices with gratitude," and drew from that memory the lesson that those "who destroy the influence and authority of the Christian religion sap the foundation of public order, of liberty, and of republican government."[75] Yet, such fervent religious sentiments, however much Webster was by then associating them with his memory of the "black regiment" of Patriot clergy during the Revolution, stemmed as much from his own postwar personal conversion to evangelical Christianity as from the residue of his own feelings at the time of the War for Independence. During the era of the Revolution, Webster, who served with the Patriot forces, had, as he later acknowledged in private correspondence, had "doubts respecting . . . doctrines of the Christian faith" and did not "make a profession of religion." However, nearly thirty years later, though Webster had been especially hostile to evangelicalism as too given to "enthusiasm," he was caught up in a "revival of religion" that "took place in New Haven," Connecticut, and he "was led by a spontaneous impulse to repentance, prayer, & entire submission & surrender . . . to my maker & redeemer." Thereafter, it was Webster's "earnest" desire to "cherish evangelical doctrines." His *History of the United States*, mixing history and preachment, was clearly influenced accordingly.[76]

One of the most common ways in which textbooks implied affinities between Christianity and patriotic memory was by treating the Bible and the United States' founding documents as equally worthy of reverence, and, presumably, as eminently complementary. Charles Prentiss's 1820 *History of the United States of America* declared that "the Constitution of the United States ought not only to be studied in our schools, but should find a place on every family shelf with the bible and the catechism."[77] Samuel Williams's 1824 *History of the American Revolution*, immediately after claiming that next to "the Bible, the history of the American Revolution is most deservedly entitled to the attention and reverence of the youth of our country," referenced "that sacred instrument, the Declaration of Independence."[78] Similarly, Emma Willard's *History of the United States* included the texts of the Declaration of Independence and of the U.S. Constitution in its appendices, and soberly announced that those documents "should be studied by the youth of our country as their political scriptures."[79]

The process of cultural change by which the Declaration of Independence came, particularly in the 1820s and 1830s, to be regarded as *American Scripture* was explored decades ago in an excellent book of that title by Pauline Maier.[80] Maier's study did not focus upon changing memory theory in the period, nor upon textbooks. A history doing so could, by contrast, suggestively relate early nineteenth-century textbooks' didactic religious and patriotic invocations of icons of American memory, such as the Declaration of Independence, to the changing pedagogy of memory in the period; the fact that educators were tending to "prefer the moral" and religious "to the intellectual or academic values of education," can be readily explained in terms of a contemporaneous commonplace about memory that Emma Willard reiterated in the preface that she wrote to *A System of Universal Geography*: memory and memorization were not for storing unlimited numbers of particular facts, but for keeping in mind judiciously chosen particulars that illustrated universal—or at least still-applicable—truths.[81] In other words, recollections should be useful. Applied to collective American memory, the pedagogues' utilitarian concept of memory meant *deliberately* teaching students to recall particulars from, or about, the past not as things-in-themselves so much as relics, or tokens—discrete (and, to be most effective, concrete) reminders, less of the "pastness" of the past and more of its timeless "lessons."

What by an empiricist standard of historical objectivity may appear to have been tendentious moralistic or religiously inspired invocations of national memory in the early nineteenth century were often quite justifiable by avowedly pragmatic beliefs about memory to which American educators in Emma Willard's day were beholden. By the light of their suppositions, the Declaration of Independence could properly appear to Willard and fellow educators less as a window for students into what was irrecoverably unique about the Founding era and more as a reminder of still-valid principles. The Declaration, by its historical associations, was, as a memory prop, effective at bringing to mind those principles. Serving as President James Monroe's secretary of state, John Quincy Adams exemplified, acknowledged, and contended for such a history-transcending role for the Declaration in American memory. Brandishing the authentic autograph in his hand, Adams declared to an 1821 Independence Day celebration: "fellow citizens," the "primary" historical "purpose of this Declaration, the proclamation to the world of the causes of our Revolution," is not that upon which "your memory delights to dwell." Historical "enumeration of intolerable wrongs concentrated in this Declaration" were in 1821 "no more [of] interest to us than . . . the apple on the head of the Child Tell." The "interest which quickens with the lapse of years, spreads as it grows old, and brightens as it recedes is in the [timeless] principles" that the Declaration "proclaims."[82] Educators of the era, by their own, contemporaneous view of memory, were disposed with Adams to accept the sort of incomplete memory of the Declaration that he saw was necessary for that document to speak with continuing immediacy to a new generation.

A student who more than heeded her instructress Emma Willard's charge to "the youth of our country" to let the Declaration of Independence guide their current-day "political" activities was Elizabeth Cady

Stanton.[83] As a small child, Stanton experienced the period, prior to the turn toward emphasis on the Declaration's "principles" that Adams marked in 1821, when what most resonated when the Declaration was read at patriotic observances were its historical allusions to particular purported British transgressions. We "need not wonder," Stanton later commented, "that our patriotism in those early days was measured by our dislike of Great Britain."[84] When she grew older, Stanton studied under her hero, Emma Willard, at the Troy Female Seminary, graduating from that "intellectual mecca" in 1832.[85] In 1848, Stanton, in an influential act that comported with Emma Willard's appeal to students to regard the Declaration as among "their political scriptures," suggested and abetted the composition of a "Declaration of Sentiments," patterned after the Declaration of Independence, which expanded its arguments to contend for women's rights.[86] Stanton's biographer, Elisabeth Griffith, has written that it was from Emma Willard that Stanton learned to reverence natural rights theory, the basis for the Declaration of Independence.[87] Thus, Stanton's history-making, but noticeably ahistorical, application of America's eighteenth-century Declaration of Independence from Britain to the plight of women in nineteenth-century U.S. culture may have been a fruit of the pragmatic view of memory current among the teachers of Willard's generation, which encouraged them to teach students of Stanton's generation to abstract time-transcendent principles from the past and its relics, including from the Declaration.

Certainly, Stanton's teacher Emma Willard was relentless in coupling self-consciously scientific physicalist memory theory with the logistical fact that women were increasingly physically responsible for the care and teaching of small children. She put a scientific gloss on an old argument for broadly based, civics-oriented education of females as the republic's future mother-teachers, schooling of the sort Willard offered through her Troy Seminary and upon which her pupil, Stanton, drew in 1848 at Seneca Falls. Willard recognized that changing memory theory had political applications and ramifications. Altered understandings between 1790 and 1840 about the nature of memory crucially influenced choices from among, and valences of, strategies by which Americans—not only elites; but also average evangelicals; common veterans; Blacks; and women such as Willard—could, and did, deploy patriotic memory to demand political rights and influence.

Transformations in what they believed about the faculty of memory itself influenced not merely how early Americans regarded extant locks of George Washington's hair, but what they were prepared to believe about each other's legitimacy as his, and the other Founders', political and cultural legatees.

EPILOGUE

The Continuing Career of Washington's Tresses

Francis Edmonds's 1844 work *The Image Pedlar* takes its viewer into a middle-class American home. At the scene's center a traveling salesman shows the resident family his wares—small statues of historical figures, including heroes of the American Revolution. To one side, a small boy is decked out in a makeshift Revolutionary War uniform. He examines a large bust of Washington as he listens wide-eyed to an elderly man. Perhaps that man is his grandfather. Perhaps Grandfather is recounting battlefield service under Washington. Across the room, a mother surveys the scene while holding her infant. The viewer suspects that by the time the baby is grown up enough to comprehend tales of the Revolution, the old veteran will be dead. It may then fall to the mother to tell the children about America's War for Independence. Doing so, perhaps she will use such props as the history-themed statuary being peddled in her home.[1]

If the painting suggests confidence in how intentionally Americans were passing on national memory, it is also easy to discern uncertainty. When America's founding generation was in the grave, would the rising generation adequately recollect their nation's natal epoch? A younger man in the scene, looking more than a bit like the artist Edmonds himself, appears ambivalent. So does a young woman washing dishes. An elderly woman, presumably the old veteran's spouse, seems almost hostile.

One ambitious politician in the era who expressed angst about the generational transition under way was Abraham Lincoln. In 1838, to the Young Men's Lyceum in Springfield, Illinois, Lincoln extolled the

Francis Edmonds, *The Image Pedlar*, 1844. (New-York Historical Society)

"legacy bequeathed to us, by a *once* hardy, brave, and patriotic . . . race of ancestors." However, he warned, memory of exemplary acts during the Revolution "*must fade, is fading, has faded,* with . . . circumstances that produced it." If the twenty-eight-year-old had then ended his remarks, he might be interpreted simply as having echoed Puritan jeremiads that notoriously fretted about whether the young would carry on their parents' divinely appointed errand. Lincoln continued, however, using language that exemplified physical, concrete, bodily preoccupations common in discussions of memory in the 1830s. He observed that at the end of America's War for Independence, "a *living history*" of that conflict in the concrete "form of a husband, a father, a son, or a brother . . . was to be found in every family—a history bearing the indubitable testimonies of its own authenticity, in the limbs mangled, in the scars of wounds received in the midst of the very scenes related." It was "a history that could be read and understood alike by all, the wise and ignorant, the learned and the unlearned." Now, "*those* histories are gone," the war veterans who embodied them having been felled by the "artillery of time." Where once the veterans stood like a solid cohort of giant oaks, there remained by 1838 "only here and there, a lonely trunk despoiled of it verdure, shorn of its foliage; unshading, and unshaded . . . to combat with its mutilated limbs, a few more . . . storms, then to sink and be no more."[2] The vivid organic metaphors would have evoked for some listeners "The Last Leaf," Oliver Wendell Holmes's 1832 poetic notice of a passing Revolutionary War soldier:[3]

I saw him once before,
As he passed by the door,
And again
The pavement stones resound,
As he totters o'er the ground
With his cane.

They say that in his prime,
Ere the pruning-knife of Time
Cut him down,
Not a better man was found
By the Crier on his round
Through the town.

But now he walks the streets,
And he looks at all he meets
Sad and wan,
And he shakes his feeble head,
That it seems as if he said,
"They are gone!"

The mossy marbles rest
On the lips that he has prest
In their bloom,
And the names he loved to hear
Have been carved for many a year
On the tomb.

My grandmamma has said—
Poor old lady, she is dead
Long ago—
That he had a Roman nose,

And his cheek was like a rose
In the snow;

But now his nose is thin,
And it rests upon his chin
Like a staff,
And a crook is in his back,
And a melancholy crack
In his laugh.

I know it is a sin
For me to sit and grin
At him here;
But the old three-cornered hat,
And the breeches, and all that,
Are so queer!

And if I should live to be
The last leaf upon the tree
In the spring,
Let them smile, as I do now,
At the old forsaken bough
Where I cling.

A quarter century later, less than a dozen Revolutionary War veteran pensioners were known to be clinging to the bough. Their descendants were killing each other in the American Civil War. Persuaded that national memory might be materially revived by viewing *Last Men of the Revolution* and loci associated with them, the Rev. E. B. Hillard published survivors' photos, biographies, and renderings of their homes in his book by that title. One whom Hillard sought to interview and daguerreotype, Daniel Waldo, died too soon. Apparently anticipating that readers might forlornly ask, "Where's Waldo?" the reverend reported consolingly that "a lock of his hair" was extant, a material relic of the old soldier.[4]

A few months before Hilliard's manuscript went to press, President Abraham Lincoln traveled to the Gettysburg, Pennsylvania, Civil War battlefield to "dedicate a portion as a final resting place" for thousands of soldiers who there had lately perished. Lincoln declared that the war was testing whether the United States, "dedicated" at its inception in the Revolution "to the proposition that all men are created equal," could "long endure."[5] In Lincoln's Gettysburg Address, allusions to the opening words of the 1776 Declaration of Independence were effectively revisionist. The Declaration had been vague and idealistic. The Address was specific and concrete. The Declaration had cited universal principles, true anywhere, anytime "in the course of human events." The Address reasoned to the ethical imperatives of equality and abolition of slavery from concrete happenings that had occurred "here"—a word Lincoln revealingly used eight times during his brief remarks—at Gettysburg itself, "four score and seven years" after the Declaration's promulgation. Thus, with pointed particularity, in language consistent with physicalized local memory that underpinned a large swath of patriotic commemoration in the America of his youth, Lincoln transmogrified Gettysburg into a memory palace.[6]

As patriotic lodestones, Lincoln supplemented the old memory of the Revolution with the fresh memory of Union sacrifices in the Civil War. For the next half century and beyond, Americans oriented themselves culturally with reference to recollections of their Civil War. Many worked to embalm that struggle in American memory by the sort of physicalist means that were self-consciously relied upon in Lincoln's, and the nation's, youth to preserve memories of the American Revolution. Yet, though the ascendancy of physicalist memory theory in the era of the early republic effectively abetted the democratization of America and its memories of the Revolution, the same appears from secondary sources to have been less so where memory of the Civil War was concerned. David Blight has traced how in the years following Lee's surrender at Appomattox the nation constructed consensus narratives about the 1861–65 war, jettisoning recollections of substantive racial conflicts to allow White Americans North and South to readily reconcile. Memory of the Civil War was supported with monuments and relics aplenty, of course. By the late nineteenth century, Union and Confederate veterans were coming together in "reunions" at formerly war-torn sites, including Gettysburg, where they peaceably exchanged war stories and locks of each other's hair. Yet, African Americans, including Black Union combat veterans, were deliberately excluded. Lincoln's fears, evident in his 1838 address in Springfield and again at Gettysburg in 1863, were justified: Americans, their putative devotion to "memory" notwithstanding, proved all too willing to ignore key lessons from their nation's past.[7]

Washington's Hair in After Years

People did, however, continue to retain, and brandish, a lot of George Washington's hair. Teasing out a few of his filaments' cameo appearances from the era of the Civil War to the present will here supply concluding clues, if not quite evidence, suggestively highlighting certain long strands and key breaks—important continuities and significant split ends—in American cultural history.

Consider the remembrance offered to a *St. Louis Post-Dispatch* reporter in 1913 by eighty-one-year-old former Union general James Grant Wilson of New York. The *Post* observed that Wilson, born in 1832, "embodies in his own career the history of the United States" since the era when the Founders yet lived. Wistfully, the old man recalled that when but seventeen years old, in about 1849, he spent a day at Mount Vernon with two Virginian lads. During his visit, George Washington Parke Custis quizzed the boys about the life of George Washington. Having by chance recently finished reading a biography of Washington, young Wilson answered most knowledgeably. "You should be ashamed," said "Mr. Custis to the two Virginians, 'to let young men come here from the North knowing more about Washington than you do.'" Turning toward Wilson, Custis retrieved "a small packet" that held "a little of George Washington's hair," and gave it to Wilson as a reward. Subsequently, James Wilson put that hair in a ring. He showed it to the widow of Alexander Hamilton. She donated fragments of her late husband's mane to be put with Washington's. Abraham Lincoln consented to the addition of his tresses when "Gen. Wilson visited him in the winter of 1864–'65." Going "to the White House hoping to get this memento of the President," Wilson brought along "a pair of scissors." He told Lincoln "how he had come by the hair of Washington and Hamilton and asked for a lock to add to these two." The president answered cheerfully, "'Why, take all you want,' and in a jiffy Gen. Wilson took out the scissors and snipped off a small bit."[8] The ensuing juxtaposition of his own tresses with Washington's might have had real meaning for President Lincoln. In 1848, as a United States senator lambasting President James K. Polk's aggressive invasion of Mexico, Lincoln insisted that a U.S. president ought ever to be mindful "that he sits where Washington sat."[9]

On 16 October 1871, in a ceremony to dedicate a new Boston post office, President Ulysses S. Grant held the lock of Washington's hair that had been given to the Masons' Grand Lodge of Massachusetts in 1800 by Martha Washington. The lodge's grand master, Charles S. Woodbury, then solemnly proclaimed that the Founder's hair "through vicissitudes of fortune hard to endure, and conflagrations, which have devoured Masonic Temples, has been spared." When James Grant Wilson befriended U. S. Grant, the indefatigable Wilson, with Grant's blessings, took a cutting of General Grant's coiffure and placed it in his keepsake ring along with Washington's, Hamilton's, and Lincoln's locks.[10]

Yet, it is the nature of a mute, merely material relic—especially a small, portable one, such as a few filaments of George Washington's hair—that it might physically be snatched up by anyone on any side of any controversy. In fact, Lincoln's best-known military opponent had his own affiliation with the Founder's follicles. Robert E. Lee, who married into George Washington's Custis relations, kept locks of George and Martha Washington's hair at his Arlington estate. With the coming of the Civil War, fearing that Union troops might overrun Arlington and steal the relics, Lee, as he later recollected, packed the hair into "a French and Rosewood dressing case with a leather cover" and sent it to Edward C. Turner's home for safekeeping. Subsequently, Union troops pillaged Turner's residence. An enterprising federal soldier swiped the follicles. He sold them to someone who, after the war, returned the strands to a grateful Robert E. Lee. Today, the very hair may be seen at Arlington.[11]

Reconstruction

In effect, Washington's hair had become everything and nothing. It was, and still is, an attention-getting token, but one materially subject to appropriation and expropriation by nearly anyone associated with any cause. Superficially prized, the extant follicles have been cultural flotsam, carried hither and yon with shifting currents of American social history. Thus, in 1876, as federal post–Civil War Reconstruction policies on race were unceremoniously abandoned, the hair was there. A display of George and Martha Washington's hair was an attraction at the Centennial Exhibition in Philadelphia. That grandiose gathering had as its theme the adamantly inorganic, self-consciously modernist assertion: "Machines Are Remaking Society." As the "Centennial" designation indicated, the affair was simultaneously a celebration of the 100th anniversary of American Independence. One display blended the mechanical and commemorative themes of the exhibition and hinted that death itself might be vanquished by mechanism. It was a nine-foot-tall replica of the first president's Mount Vernon tomb. From it, a George Washington automaton regularly rose from the dead to celebratory salutes from a klatch of mechanical toy soldiers.[12]

An orgy of chest-thumping patriotic self-congratulation, the Philadelphia exhibition incidentally, yet significantly, made it harder for Americans to see their cultural weaknesses, including racism rebounding in the wake of the Emancipation Proclamation, Union victory in the late Civil War, and a trinity of constitutional amendments—the Thirteenth through the Fifteenth—that had been aimed at locking in gains for racial equality.[13] In 1876, too, the winner of the U.S. presidential election was too close to call. Wrangling over who had won the White House persisted into 1877. Finally, Republican Rutherford B. Hayes was certified the victor over Democrat Samuel J. Tilden. Reportedly, a bargain was struck: Hayes's advocates pledged that President Hayes would order federal troops to stand down in the South. Then, southern "Redeemers" could effectively reconstitute systematic social and political repression of African Americans. "As matters look to me now," wrote the chairman of Kansas's Republican state committee on 22 February, Hayes will become the next president and "'I think the policy of the new administration will be to conciliate the white men of the South.'"[14] That same day, ebullient over Hayes's clearing path to the White House, one of his backers, John Hay, presented Rutherford Hayes with the lock of George Washington's hair that is today kept at the Rutherford B. Hayes Presidential Center in Fremont, Ohio.[15] One wonders if President-elect Hayes, upon receipt of the hair, thought, if only for a moment, of the African American Revolutionary War veteran Hamet Achmet and his famous hair relics of Washington. Near the height of Achmet's burgeoning reputation as a patriotic memoirist, in 1837 and 1838, Rutherford Birchard Hayes, who boasted that he loved to take long walks in that town as a young man, attended a school for boys in Middletown, Connecticut, that occupied a building less than 1,700 feet from the most likely site of the old Black veteran's conspicuous cottage.[16]

Jim Crow and the Gilded Age

In the wake of Reconstruction's betrayal under President Hayes, the dominant culture's racism became all the more evident in popular acts of social and political terrorism, most notoriously in executions by White mobs of African American citizens. On the same page as it described a "nearly pure, white and glossy" sample of George Washington's hair on view in a museum in Washington, DC, an 1884 edition of the *Weekly Wisconsin,* a Milwaukee newspaper, reported the lynching of "Henry Kilburn (white) and Ben. Strong (colored)" by "fifty masked men" who, accusing Strong of being implicated in a murder for which Kilburn had legally been charged, broke into a Jackson, Kentucky, jail, and, for good measure, hanged both men. On the same page too was a story about an African American in Texas "named Gibbs." Apparently, he was an itinerant farmhand. Gibbs was accused of murdering his employer's wife because "she would not allow him to sit at the supper table with the family." The "whole community turned out, and on Sunday afternoon overtook Gibbs, . . . chained him to a post and burned him to death." Lest readers think their countrymen's vigilantism unjustified, the report allowed: "Gibbs was an escaped convict and was considered a very bad negro."[17] Somewhat similarly, a 1906 edition of a Binghamton, New York, newspaper, on the same page as it enthused that a lock of Washington's hair was a "prized keepsake" in a memorial prayer chapel at Valley Forge, reported less happily that U.S. Senator Benjamin Tillman of South Carolina, already notorious as a race baiter, endorsed "assassination to maintain white supremacy," and proclaimed: "lynch law is all we have left."[18]

When Tillman spoke those words, America was in the midst of its Gilded Age, as Mark Twain—or Samuel Clemens, if you prefer—and Charles Dudley Warner famously called the era in their cowritten novel by that title.[19] Historians of American history—who use periodization as convenient chronological shorthand—have often defined the Gilded Age and Progressive Era as extending, more or less, from the collapse of Reconstruction in 1877 to the first years of the twentieth century. One of the reasons that Twain and Warner dubbed the age "Gilded," a superficial coating of gold over base metal, was that there was then a growing awareness among Americans of widespread, barely cloaked hypocrisy and corruption in politics. In their

1873 novel, as in real life, the unfinished Washington Monument—constructed by fits and by starts between 1848 and 1884—loomed garishly over Washington, DC, materially evidencing the failure of contemporaneous politicians to emulate Washington's honorable, effective leadership.[20] A politician for whom Twain felt particularly "sorry and embarrassed," as he recalled that man's descent into the "sewer—party politics," was the ambitious John Hay.[21] Ever angling for personal gain, Hay courted President-elect William McKinley almost precisely as he had pursued Rutherford B. Hayes. Hay gave McKinley a ring containing Washington's hair, engraved with the interwoven initials GW and WM. McKinley wore that ring during his 1897 inauguration. Shortly thereafter, President McKinley appointed John Hay to an ambassadorship.[22]

The 1893 Chicago World's Fair

Washington's hairs were present at the quintessential public spectacles of the Gilded Age, world's fairs. At the 1893 Chicago World's Columbian Exhibition, the Founder's follicles given to France's Lafayette by Americans during his celebrated memory tour of the United States in the 1820s were in the French pavilion's exhibit of mementos "precious in the eyes of patriotic peoples of both countries."[23] A visitor to the fair who missed Washington's reliquary there might yet see his tufts in the Virginia Building, a replica of Washington's Mount Vernon mansion.[24] An alcove in the rotunda of the Government Building afforded a third opportunity to view "bright auburn" clippings from Washington's dome.[25] One tourist who may well have seen the hair on Independence Day in one, two, or even all three convenient venues was Anna Williams. On 4 July 1893, the attractive young woman wrote excitedly from Chicago to relatives in Texas that she had "taken in the fair" to her "heart's content."[26] If Anna overlooked George Washington's follicles on the Fourth, she might still have been impressed with Washington's physiognomy that night. After dark on the Fourth, the fair featured a stunning fireworks display, including thousands of rockets and huge searchlights. The hard-to-overlook spectacle captivated hundreds of thousands of spectators. Its climax involved a massive pyrotechnic rendering of George Washington's face that "burned before" crowds who "beneath . . . lay outlined like the children of Israel encamped on the holy land." Anna Williams probably witnessed it. The next day, 5 July, she may also have noticed the front page of the *Chicago Tribune,* adorned with an artist's evocative sketch of the phosphorescent Washington.[27]

In any of these scenarios, Washington's visage would have been among the last that Williams lived to see, for lurking at the fair was a murderer. Later, he would be dubbed America's "first serial killer." Born Herman Mudgett, he took the name H. H. Holmes as an alias. Holmes was a medical-school graduate. The "Class Prophecy" that satirized his graduating cohort unfavorably compared his character to that of George Washington. Presciently it suggested that Holmes's solicitous manner with women and academic bona fides were only concealments for the newly minted doctor's fundamentally alienated, misogynistic character: "Unlike George Washington, no widow shall find favor in his eyes. After being charged with innumerable Don Juan escapades for which he is not responsible, he will retire to write a book on the 'Oppression of Man.' This book will make women very unpopular."[28] Holmes was inclined to dehumanize others, especially women, viewing them clinically rather than as integrated members of a metaphysical body politic in which he too was necessarily a conjoined member. He seems to have regarded people as infinitely separable, individual, reducibly material integers, mere machines that he might disassemble at will. Anna Williams became one of his victims.[29]

Holmes murdered Anna, as he would others, with, and within, a labyrinthine "castle"—disguised as a functioning pharmacy, "World's Fair Hotel," and suite of offices—that he had personally designed and ordered constructed for his nefarious purposes. As his "castle" was being built, Holmes exploited the bustling, inorganic, fragmented, atomized, individualistic, anonymous ethos of the modern city. Subcontractors he engaged to work piecemeal raised his house of horrors. They came, innocently fulfilled individual work assignments, then left. They did not truly understand Holmes, each other's contributions to his project, or the larger layout of the building. Only H. H. Holmes knew its comprehensive purpose and design. Beneath its gilded surface, Holmes's "castle" was a vast machine of interlocking, ingenious mechanical contrivances. Parts included valves for the release of poison gas, a dissection platform, and a custom, large-capacity, high-temperature, industrial-grade oven. Combined, they made possible the surreptitious,

efficient, self-consciously sophisticated, and medicalized dismember-
ment of human beings. Designed and assembled by well-educated, technologically savvy, scientifically literate moderns, Holmes's factory may
have been the first for murdering people. As the history of European
fascism of the twentieth century illustrates, it would not be the last.[30]

In retrospect, H. H. Holmes's well-oiled murder machine appears
as the very instantiation, in hyperbolic form, of the dystopian fears
that were sweeping over historian Henry Adams, the great-grandson
of President John Adams, during his own visit to the 1893 World's Columbian Exposition. Henry Adams had long been proud to be connected organically, by blood, to the Revolution and Founding. Yet, at
the Chicago fair he recognized with alarm that developing technology
was effectively parting whatever strands still joined his world to that
of his forebearers. An exhibit in Machinery Hall featured dynamos,
hulking exemplars of emerging electrical technologies. Henry "lingered long among the dynamos, for they were new, and they gave to
history a new phase."[31] As an Adams, he conceived of himself as the in-
trepid defender of "his eighteenth century, his Constitution of 1789, his
George Washington."[32] The surging electrified world of dynamos and
their like he recognized as threats to those ideals—indeed, to all ideals.
Adams interpreted popular mania for electromechanical technologies
as evidence of modernity's excessive concern with material, physical
means to the exclusion of valuing metaphysical principles necessary
for choosing right ends.[33]

As a historian, Henry Adams argued that George Washington, by
happy contrast, had labored to ensure that the United States' physical development would serve considered metaphysical ends. A former surveyor, Washington had intended that the nation's material
infrastructure—its roads, canals, and developed river system—would
be deliberately situated to serve American policies. He envisioned avenues of transport laid out as crisscrossing lines, effectively serving as
sinews, binding the body of the nation together across its topographic
sections. More precisely, the United States' built-up transportation
network would, by implications of its very geometry, draw the whole,
embodied nation's allegiance toward its new capital city, Washington,
DC. That locus, by its namesake's design, was to have been located
on "converging avenues" of the completed system, and so become the
country's logistical, as well as its political, heart. Within the capital,

President Washington hoped to see founded a great national university, the brain of the whole "corporeal system."

Yet, Adams's histories lamented, George Washington died before his plan for physical and educational integration was realized. The complex political organism that the Founder meant to create was too much "the product of Washington's single mind and . . . commanding personality" to survive his passing. The integrative scheme was all but buried with the Father of His Country in the loam of Mount Vernon.[34] Thereafter, in Henry Adams's telling, there followed a long, terrible national declension—a renting asunder of the United States' body from its spirit by modernism, materialism, commercialism, and "leveling" democratic individualism. Ironically employing terms of the very scientistic reductionism that he thought was encouraging neglect of America's metaphysical vitals, Adams wrote that the decline might be represented scientifically, numerically, and formulaically. "When General Washington died, the democratic system of averages began its work, and the old inequality sank to a common level. By 1828, a level of degradation had been reached, and it was the level of Jackson." The "fall in intelligence and intellectual energy of the democratic community, in twenty-five years . . . exactly corresponded to the interval which separated George Washington intellectually, from Andrew Jackson."[35]

In the aftermath of the Civil War that rent the country's collective body just as it tore the personal, individual bodies of hundreds of thousands of its citizens, Adams hoped that Ulysses S. Grant would be a second George Washington, not only first in war, but also first in peace—stitching the country together under his administration. When Grant, to Adams's thinking, entirely failed to be such a figure, the historian opined that the "progress of evolution from President Washington to President Grant, was alone evidence enough to upset Darwin."[36] The nation, Adams judged, for reasons that included a naïve embrace of reductive scientism, had artificially set truths of physics at cross purposes with truths of metaphysics, pitting "flesh" against "spirit." Standing in the shadow of the imposing dynamos on display in Chicago, Adams saw them as heralds of the spirit-crushing, encroaching power of scientific materialism and consumerism in the western world, which—by brute, material force—would soon become the dominant strand in American culture. In the raging war between "the flesh" and "the spirit," he lamented, flesh would prevail.[37]

Seven years later, in France—Lafayette's homeland, to which, presumably, that Frenchman's ring containing Washington's hair had been returned after the 1893 Chicago fair—Adams attended the 1900 Paris Exposition. Again, Henry Adams literally stood in the shadow of displayed dynamos for hours at a time. Again, he pondered significances of their awesome power—the power of the machine age. With fascination and fear, the great-grandson of President John Adams judged that western societies, impressed with their own technological prowess, were presumptuously rejecting traditional Christian confidence in received, intrinsic, theological, epistemic, and moral principles to which all humans ought to be beholden. Modern worshippers of machines, Adams apprehended, recognized only scientific description, not ethical prescription. Any people who materially acquired the requisite technology might muster present material force to any ends, without accountability, limits, or mercy.[38] Thus, the thirty-foot tall dynamos before which Henry Adams meditated in Paris in 1900 only reified longstanding concerns that he had expressed decades earlier. Human beings, drawn to science by a lust for power to—for example—"cruize [sic] in space," might, Henry Adams had privately averred in 1862, trap themselves in a net of their own making. The internal logic and power of cutting-edge machines would finally overwhelm their creators, until inventors would be the slaves of their own inventions, and "science will be the master of man."[39]

The 1904 St. Louis World's Fair

If the 1893 Chicago World's Columbian Exposition and 1900 Paris Exposition left Adams in a lather over modernity's uncritical embrace of mechanism, his visit with John Hay to the 1904 World's Fair in St. Louis offered nothing to wash away his fear. De rigueur, well-attested Washington lovelocks were carted to the banks of the Mississippi for display at the fair—this time by the state of Massachusetts.[40] Perhaps, during their time at the fair, Adams and Hay happened into the Massachusetts Building and glimpsed the Founder's hair. If so, neither likely found that display particularly novel. Hay had already twice trafficked Washington's locks to political patrons. Adams, though he confessedly held Washington in special esteem as "the pole star" of American politics, had been born into a social circle in which "A President" of the

United States "was a matter of course in every respectable family."[41] What did garner Henry Adams's attention in St. Louis was what he termed the "new American" who "showed his parentage proudly." Mistaking the sophistication of American society's technology as an index of Americans' freedom, the average citizen of 1904, Adams lamented, was unabashedly "the child of steam," and the "brother of the dynamo," and therefore, by inevitable implication, in bondage, the "servant of the powerhouse" as completely as any "European of the twelfth century" had ever been "the servant of the Church."[42]

As Adams brooded about unhappy, ironic outcomes that he thought a mania for technology was fast bringing to American society, a wider, not-unrelated international conversation was already under way at the fair. Communicated in words, deeds, exhibits, newspapers, and pageantry, it concerned the interrelatedness of advancing technology, modernity, western imperialism, and the increasing role of the United States in world affairs. At the fair's opening, its president David R. Francis enthused that it had "exhibits of every country and every people, classified . . . in a manner unequalled for clear and competitive comparison." The fair was a "congregating of the grades of civilization as represented by all races from the primitive to the cultured."[43] Choreographed to make judgments about peoples' relative rankings culturally and biologically, the 1904 St. Louis World's Fair had real affinities with the pseudoscientific, politically charged assays of human bodies in which patriotic, ethnocentric opinion-makers going back to nineteenth-century Philadelphia had dealt. Recall Charles Willson Peale's museum of natural and political history, wherein, in the 1820s, portraits of the U.S. Founders enjoyed pride of place above taxidermical displays of other living creatures. Recollect Peter A. Browne's mid-century address to the Academy of Natural Sciences, comparing samples of George Washington's hair to strands from the head of a "pure negro," to claim that legalized racial discrimination in American politics and society simply reflected the best science. Several decades and eight hundred miles on, in 1904 at the World's Fair on the banks of the Mississippi, the names of the protagonists and the precise terminology was different. The essential tactic—torturing science to give preconceived scientisitic answers to questions categorically cultural and political—was the same.

Anthropologists at the 1904 St. Louis World's Fair pledged to "carefully measure the different tribes of people at the Fair, and to draw from the results of the measurements scientific deductions as to the progress of the human race." A 23 May 1904 article in the *St. Louis Post Dispatch* disclosed that measurements of World's Fair "President Francis will be compared with those of an Igorrote chief and a Patagonian giant, while Secretary Stevens and Director Taylor will be compared with Visayans and hairy Ainus and the exact degree of progress that has been achieved by intellectual man will be scientifically determined."[44] Given the inevitable cultural biases of the scientists involved, much of the putatively scientific research done at the 1904 fair was interpreted as vindicating western, including American imperialism abroad and privileged intellectual and cultural authority at home for the scientists themselves. One did not have to read research reports or attend lectures to be pushed toward such lessons. Years after taking the Philippines from Spain in the Spanish-American War, the United States in 1904 was still engaged there, fighting a bloody counterinsurgency campaign. Against the backdrop of that conflict, the U.S. government sponsored a massive "Philippine Village" at the World's Fair. It featured fenced-in Philippine headhunters and other underdressed "primitives" from the region, effectively juxtaposing them with impeccably uniformed Filipino Boy Scouts. The scouts, having submitted themselves to American military training and discipline, were relatively freely deployed across the fairgrounds. The conclusion that visitors were meant to draw was obvious: American political and military rule in the Philippines was an objective, unalloyed, civilizing good for Filipinos.[45]

Yet, that spring, an interested critic of American imperial ambitions, Queen Liliuokalani, the former monarch of Hawaii, came to the fair. Illness kept her in her hotel for most of her stay. If, during her brief ambulatory time in St. Louis, she somehow made her way into the Massachusetts Building and there saw George Washington's hair, she probably found the display provoking and familiar. In 1893, Queen Liliuokalani had been ousted in a rebellion largely fomented by American business, diplomatic, and military leaders. They had sought Hawaii's annexation by the United States, which was effected in 1898. By the time of her 1904 trip to St. Louis, she was busily lobbying the United States to again recognize her as Hawaii's rightful ruler and restore her throne. Part and parcel to that public relations offensive, Liliuokalani penned an autobiography. In an evocative section, she enthusiastically recounted touring Washington's Mount Vernon estate during visits to the United States. For example, in May of 1887, as Hawaii's princess regent, Liliuokalani had accompanied her brother's wife, Queen Consort Kapiolani, to Washington's estate. Kapiolani was "so visibly affected that when she returned to" nearby Alexandria, Virginia, "some body [sic]," reported the *Alexandria Gazette*, presented her with what was "represented to be a lock of Gen. Washington's hair . . . obtained from a descendant of an Indian girl, a captive of Washington, raised at Mount Vernon, who, after marrying two white gentlemen, subsequently married a negro." The *Gazette* laughingly judged the "whole . . . story" of the hair's provenance to be nothing more than "the creature of a vivid imagination."[46] That humbug, if humbug it was, managed to reference racial taxonomy in American culture and to mockingly put the would-be queen in her place, scorning the Hawaiian's efforts to possess a piece of George Washington, suggesting that by her credulous acceptance of the gift of "Washington's hair" she had shown herself and her people to be racial diminutives, fit subjects for American rulership.

Superficially, by her receipt of the strands, Hawaii's queen consort had, however, joined the swelling ranks of nineteenth-century foreign notables to whom American citizens presented supposed locks of Washington's hair as calling cards of the United States' growing global influence. Not only Marquis de Lafayette and Simón Bolívar, but also Lord John Russell, Lajos Kossuth, Apollonio Jagielo Tochman, and Otto von Bismarck received parcels of Washington's tresses.[47] By 1904, the royal family of Hawaii knew firsthand that receipt of a gift of Washington's hair offered no reprieve from American imperialism, an imperialism that, at the St. Louis exposition that year, was far more conspicuous than the little hank of Washington's wool on view in the Massachusetts Building. This is not to suggest that more attention to hirsute Washington tokens could have changed American attitudes about imperialism. Washington, as those Gilded Age American political leaders who swam against the prevailing currents to oppose imperialism were delighted to recount, had indeed argued for a restrained U.S. foreign policy. Yet, that was an involved historical truth, not readily signified or evaluated by such tokenism as the cult of George Washington's hair afforded.[48]

The Hair after 1904

For the balance of the twentieth century, and well into the twenty-first, public attention to circulating putative fragmentum of Washington's tresses more or less continued to track the larger trajectory of change in American society. In 1909, a Michigan newspaper made light of serious debate about the rights of women in the American body politic with a dismissive quip: "If but a single lock of Washington's hair was left for posterity[,] it is time to look into the Widow Custis's views on woman's rights."[49] Nine years later, as American troops were mustered into World War I, the Historical Society of Pennsylvania held "varied entertainments for the enlisted men of the Army, Navy Marine Corps and Allies of the United States" at which a gold "locket containing hair of Washington" was on display.[50] Following professionalization of historical studies early in the century, there was in 1922 a brief, but surprisingly heated, dust-up in American newspapers about the validity of Harvard professor Alfred Bushnell Hart's public insistence that Washington's hair was red, an assertion challenged by laypersons who, in an exhibition of democratic empiricism, dipped into their own holdings of the Founder's follicles to give answer.[51]

With increasing litigation and legal formality in twentieth-century America, inherited locks of Washington's hair were mentioned in newspaper accounts of probate proceedings.[52] In 1925, as Americans argued over whether or not to recognize the League of Nation's Permanent Court of International Justice, a newspaper, the *Pharos-Tribune*, in Logansport, Indiana, observed that hair "cut from" Washington's "proud fighting head" was extant at Mount Vernon, and opined: "If its owner could come back[,] he would be" unhappily "surprised to find the American nation . . . actually discussing its submission to a world court established in Europe."[53] In the fateful spring of 1939, with a Second World War evidently imminent, the *New York Times* offered a hank of encouragement. At the World's Fair in New York, Venezuela's "Ambassador Escalante" announced that his country "was happy to demonstrate her friendship for the United States" and he "unveiled a medallion containing a likeness of George Washington and a lock of his hair, presented . . . in 1825 to Simon Bolivar," and "brought here from Venezuela . . . to be placed in" his country's pavilion, exhibited upon its newly constructed "Altar of the Good Neighbor."[54]

In the latter half of the twentieth century, with a growing perception that crime was out of control in the western world, there were reports of heists of Washington's hair from collections in London, Paris, Albany, and Philadelphia.[55] To celebrate the memory of Washington, who throughout his storied military and political career famously eschewed every temptation to become a dictator, a hank of George Washington's hair—a portion of Simón Bolívar's stash that had recently been gifted to the White House by the government of Venezuela—was on display in the Oval Office on 22 February 1971, Washington's Birthday, as President Richard M. Nixon's secret automatic taping system recorded him musing that it would be "much easier" to "run this war" in Vietnam "in a dictatorial way," to "kill all the reporters, and carry on the war."[56]

In the 1990s, for at least a year—the evidence is unclear about whether it was longer—the nuclear-powered supercarrier U.S.S. *George Washington* patrolled the world's sea lanes with a lock of Washington's hair in its permanent onboard museum compartment that Mount Vernon had loaned to the U.S. Navy for displays for the inspiration of that ship's crew on renewable one-year contracts.[57] On 11 September 2001, when al-Qaeda terrorists piloted hijacked airplanes filled with innocent civilians into New York's World Trade Center in a multipronged attack on American lives, icons, and identity, concussions from the collapse of the South Tower cracked the foundation of nearby Federal Hall, where on 30 April 1789, George Washington had taken the oath of office as the first president of the United States, and in the basement of which, on that fateful day in 2001, two separate locks of President Washington's hair—one purportedly cut on the day of his first inauguration—were being held in storage by the National Park Service.[58] Fast-moving clouds of dust and debris swiftly engulfed other nearby buildings in all directions, including Fraunces Tavern, barely one half mile from Ground Zero, where, at the end of the Revolution, General Washington had bid farewell to his troops, and in which his hair was on public display that day in 2001, as it had been for many years, including in 1975 when it survived undamaged a deadly terror bombing at the tavern perpetrated by a group agitating for Puerto Rican independence from the United States.[59]

In the second decade of the twenty-first century, which saw intense debate in American culture—what some dubbed a "culture war"—over the proper and historic place of religion in the public sphere, David Barton, a self-styled, largely self-educated conservative partisan and polemicist, whom *Time* magazine in 2005 ranked third on its list of "The 25 Most Influential Evangelicals in America," purchased two locks of Washington's hair that he brandishes to visitors to the Aledo, Texas, headquarters of Wallbuilders, his private educational and lobbying organization, which exists to defend what Barton insists is "America's Godly Heritage" bequeathed to it by the Founding Fathers.[60]

With continuing public interest and confidence in the twentieth and twenty-first centuries in the evolving capabilities of science, locks of Washington's hair were variously tested to reveal his rare blood type, B; to confirm that he was a dietary "centrist"; and to verify the relics' authenticity.[61] For its part, in the 1990s, the Federal Bureau of Investigation undertook "analysis of head hairs purported to be from George Washington," attempting to determine their authenticity. Reporting to the Daughters of the American Revolution about samples it had furnished to the federal investigators, the bureau noted that there was too little DNA "to allow for conclusive DNA sequence analysis" that would, in turn, facilitate comparison with DNA samples taken from known, living Washington relatives. Thus, the laboratory leaned heavily upon microscopic comparisons of the Tavern's samples to other putative, documented samples of Washington's mane provided by such venerable institutions as Mount Vernon and Colonial Williamsburg. The final report explained that "microscopic characteristics . . . compared included cuticle, thickness and color, scale protrusion, pigment size and distribution, hair color, cortical fusi (air spaces), ovoid bodies, medulla appearance and other characteristics." The FBI's underwhelming conclusion: "not one of the samples could be excluded as possibly originating from George Washington."[62]

In 2007, reflecting the growing prominence and convergence of sports and marketing in American culture, the Topps Company, a leading manufacturer of baseball cards and bubblegum, expropriated George Washington's cultural cachet by inserting into each of three random, nondescript packs of its cards one "relic card," containing a strand of Washington's hair. Illustrating, perhaps, that Americans—as Benjamin Rush, a signer of the Declaration of Independence, once quipped—inhabit a "bedollared nation," given to enterprise at any opportunity, one lucky winner of a hairy Washington card soon listed his prize for sale on eBay, where, at any given moment, numerous parcels of "Washington's hair" of differing prices and provenances are generally for sale, and, in 2012, a three-year-old Chicken McNugget reputed to resemble George Washington's face was sold for $8,100 to benefit a charity.[63] In 2008, not to be outdone by Topps, the Upper Deck baseball-card company released its "Hair Cut" series, featuring a random deck of cards containing a lock of Washington's hair, with an extant sample of the general's autograph signature, as the company boasted that "microscopic analysis" was used to corroborate that the hair was Washington's.[64] One-half decade later, in 2013, the Upper Deck Washington card, still being borne along in the rapids of American commercial culture, surfaced on "Hair Force One," an episode of the highly rated reality-television series *Pawn Stars*.[65]

Five years later, in 2018, the discovery by a librarian at Union College in Schenectady, New York, of a likely lock of Washington's hair in a nineteenth-century volume set off a media frenzy, as the press—as has happened repeatedly in the nation's history—briefly rediscovered that Washington hair relics exist.[66] The next year, in 2019, when a group of visiting Black constituents noticed that a U.S. congressman had on view in his office a nineteenth-century book about Robert E. Lee opened to a particularly racist passage, a member of the congressman's staff defended the office display by noting that it included a lock of George Washington's hair.[67] That same year, an executive at Alphabet, the parent company of Google, a megacorporation that some had come to regard as the very reincarnation of Gilded Age monopolism, noted in a *Washington Post* interview that he was using his personal wealth to buy for private display in his home historical artifacts, including autograph documents in George Washington's own hand, and—of course—a bona fide lock of President Washington's hair.[68]

In 2007, the *New York Times* cited the judgment of "the world's pre-eminent historical hair collector (yes, there is such a thing), John Reznikoff," that "there are probably close to a thousand strands of Washington's hair in existence that can be reliably documented."[69] What is the cultural significance of so much bodily detritus handed down—sometimes credulously, sometimes incredulously—from the self-consciously physicalist patriotic memory culture that prevailed in the early American republic? Important cultural or historical lessons scientifically derived from physical study of the received hairs themselves may never be forthcoming. Yet, our generation continues to cling—sometimes with bemusement, but also with care, and interest—to the received relics. We seem impelled, as all intervening generations of Americans have been, to seek communion with the United States' dead parental generation. Like Lincoln at Gettysburg, we may yearn to see the Spirit of '76 reborn in our world in spirit and in flesh. Materially, technologically, scientifically, we are more capable than any prior generation of physically preserving inherited relics. To protect and display once-sacred artifacts from the Founding, we can build elaborate, bulletproof, argon- and helium-filled, climate-controlled casings to slow their natural, material decay, and surround them with motion detectors, security cameras, marine guards, or whatnot. Yet relics, especially the bodily relics of leaders now dead, do not mean in our secular, unenchanted, scientistic, and individualistic culture what they meant to early Americans who, even if they were already tacking swiftly in our cultural direction, were relatively nearer temporally and conceptually than are we to conceiving of society as a great body politic, a gathered cloud of witnesses, comprised, under Providence, not only of embodied, currently earthbound compatriots, but also, in a manner, of relics—of the received material instantiations of the "the living dead at work amongst us, from a past not left behind but entering into present life."[70]

"Touch It, Dude!"

Given Washington's reputation for probity, perhaps what the long, continuing career of Washington's hairy keepsakes reveals most undeniably is an abiding desire in generations of Americans for their ethics to be incarnated, for their nation's highest moral and metaphysical commitments to come to life, to be materially lived out head-to-toe in and by its most empowered leaders. In 2010, the *New York Times* featured an "Op-Art" cartoon, a composite of "Hair-Portraits"—depictions of the hair-as-worn—of each of the presidents of the United States from George Washington to Barack Obama, in order of their accession to the presidency. "Hair is a language," asserted accompanying text by art historian Penny Howell Jolly. "For the last 100 years, there have been very few stylistic developments of note" where the hair of presidents is concerned, but "the most significant change of late comes with our current commander in chief," President Barack Obama, "whose hair has brought welcome diversity to the presidential scalp."[71]

In 2009, a five-year-old African American child, Jacob Philadelphia of Columbia, Maryland, apparently drew a like conclusion in a moment during which the president of the United States of America was kindness incarnate toward him. Jacob's father, Carlton Philadelphia, had been due to leave his position on the staff of the National Security Council. He asked for a picture to be taken in the Oval Office of his family with the president. The request itself was unremarkable. Souvenir photos with the president have been made for departing White House staff and their relatives for many years, and across administrations. The group portrait with President Obama was soon arranged and taken. The Philadelphia family was about to be ushered out of the presidential sanctum. Then, five-year-old Jacob said meekly, "I want to know if my hair is just like yours." So quietly did he speak that the forty-fourth president of the United States, uncertain of what the child said, asked him to repeat his words. Jacob did. President Obama leaned over. "Why don't you touch it and see for yourself?" he offered.

Five-year-old Jacob Philadelphia and President Barack Obama in the Oval Office, 2009. (Pete Souza, the White House)

The boy seemed uncertain. "Touch it, dude!" the president urged. The five-year-old stretched out his hand. Solemnly he felt President Obama's hair, as a White House photographer scrambled to record the moment. "So, what do you think?" queried the commander-in-chief. "Yes, it does feel the same," said Jacob. Three years later, the *New York Times* reported that Jacob hopes to become president of the United States, "Or a test pilot." No one—certainly no one who knows what occurred in the nation in the years that followed—would simplistically suggest that a single American president allowing a single curious child to feel his hair could heal his nation's riven body politic. Yet, no one who knows the strange career of George Washington's tresses can be surprised if "Finding a Familiar Feel in a Pat of the Head of State," as the *Times* headline put it, augmented Jacob Philadelphia's confidence that one day he too might sit "where Washington sat."[72]

NOTES

INTRODUCTION

1. Elizabeth Wadsworth to Peleg Wadsworth, 19 January 1800, Coll. S-1247 MS-00–448, vol. 1, misc. box 5/5, Maine Historical Society, "Maine Memory Network," s.v. "George Washington's Hair," http://www .mainememory.net.
2. Peleg Wadsworth to Elizabeth Wadsworth, 14 April 1800, Coll. S-1247; cf., at the same location: Peleg Wadsworth to Martha Washington, 26 March 1800; Tobias Lear to Peleg Wadsworth, 5 April 1800.
3. Elizabeth Wadsworth to Peleg Wadsworth, 24 April 1800, Coll. S-1247. Peleg wrote cautioning Elizabeth not to "give it all away—hair by hair—Isabella must not have more than One." Peleg Wadsworth to Elizabeth Wadsworth, 3 May 1800, Coll. S-1247.
4. Elizabeth Wadsworth died in 1802, after willing the Washington relic to her sister Zilpah and suggesting that, in the future, if Maine gained statehood, it might be given to that state. Zilpah passed it on to her son, the poet Henry Wadsworth Longfellow. In 1899, his daughter gave it to the Maine Historical Society. See http://www.mainememory.net, accessed 3 December 2019. Today, at that internet site, "thousands" can at last see the relic, effectively fulfilling Elizabeth Wadsworth's wish.
5. Sarah J. Purcell, *Sealed with Blood: War, Sacrifice, and Memory in Revolutionary America* (Philadelphia: University of Pennsylvania Press, 2002), 150; cf. 206–7. Purcell, is not, to be sure, guilty of treating democratization as uncomplicated in its relationship with patriotic memory. She shows on p. 151, for example, that it was the need to inspire common citizens to be ever ready to become soldiers to defend the young nation in the early nineteenth century, a "period of growing international and domestic political tension," that was part of the rationale for holding up the common veterans of the Revolution as role models. Cf. comparable recognition of democratizing American memory in Len Travers, *Celebrating the Fourth: Independence Day and the Rites of Nationalism in the Early Republic* (Amherst: University of Massachusetts Press, 1997). Other "democratizations" noted by historians in the period involved such areas as religion and the franchise. See, e.g., Nathan O. Hatch, *The*

Democratization of American Christianity (New Haven: Yale University Press, 1989); and Robert H. Wiebe, *The Opening of American Society: From the Adoption of the Constitution to the Eve of Disunion* (New York: Alfred A. Knopf, 1984), esp. 143–67, where Wiebe argues that a "revolution of choices" in the young nation effected general democratization; a transportation revolution, Arminian evangelicalism, phrenology, and credit empowered people as arbiters of their own spatial, religious, cultural, economic, and, in effect, political destinies.

6. Gordon Wood has argued that a cluster of physicalist epistemological ideas contributed to the coming of the Revolution by suggesting an essential equality among human beings as alike-embodied sentient knowers. The present book reveals that by the 1820s and 1830s surging "sensationalism," to use Wood's label for physicalist epistemology, was underwriting increasingly popular physicalist assumptions about the nature of "memory" itself that, by their implications, supported a democratizing memory of the Revolution and Founding. Gordon S. Wood, *The Radicalism of the American Revolution* (New York: Vintage Books, 1993), 190, 236, and cf. 240; Gordon S. Wood, *The American Revolution: A History* (New York: Random House, 2002), 101–6. Wood points to Locke as an exemplar and source of such materialist, sensate epistemology. Cf. John Locke, *An Essay Concerning Human Understanding*, 24th ed. (London: Longman, 1824), 133, incl. marginal notes.

7. Cf. George R. Stewart, *Names on the Land: A Historical Account of Place-Naming in the United States*, rev. ed. (Boston: Houghton Mifflin, 1958).

8. Cf. "Life of Simonides," *New York Magazine, or Literary Repository* 1 (May 1796): 245–49; J. R. Murden, *The Art of Memory, Reduced to a Systematic Arrangement, Exemplified under the Two Leading Principles, Locality and Association* (New York: J. T. Murden, 1818), ix; Pliny Miles, *American Phreno-Mnemotechny, Theoretical and Practical; On the Basis of the Most Recent Discoveries and Improvements in Europe and America; Comprising a Phreno-Mnemotechnic Dictionary, and the Principles of the Art Applied to Different Historical and Scientific Subjects* (New York: William Taylor and Company, 1846), 82. See also the reference to "apartments . . . in which memory stores its merchandize [*sic*]" in "Dacinthus," "Essay on Imagination and Memory," *Massachusetts Magazine* (July 1792): 440. Generally, on Simonides, mnemonics, and the concept of loci, see Daniel L. Schachter, *Searching for Memory: The Brain, the Mind, and the Past* (New York: Basic Books, 1996), 46–47. On Cicero and other Classical influence upon early American thought in the context of the "American Enlightenment" see Carl J. Richard, *The Founders and the Classics:*

Greece, Rome, and the American Enlightenment (Cambridge, MA: Harvard University Press, 1994).

9. Cicero, excerpted in Douglas J. Herrmann and Roger Chaffin, eds., *Memory in Historical Perspective: The Literature before Ebbinghaus* (New York: Springer-Verlag, 1988), 78. Herrmann and Chaffin's fine publication conveniently anthologizes the most seminal passages in western literature prior to the late nineteenth century that bear on memory.

10. William H. Burnham, excerpted in Herrmann and Chaffin, eds., *Memory in Historical Perspective*, 233. By comparing excerpts at the following pages in Herrmann and Chaffin's chronologically organized anthology one can see, from the time of Simonides into the early nineteenth century, evidence of the pendulum of western thought about memory swinging, however irregularly, between views influenced by Plato's idealism and alternative theories informed by Aristotle's moderate realism: 21, 28, 38, 61, 73, 78, 80–81, 99, 106, 122–23, 126–27, 168, 177, 190, 192–93, 233. Frances A. Yates, *The Art of Memory* (Chicago: University of Chicago Press, 1966); Douwe Draaisma, *The Metaphors of Memory: A History of Ideas About the Mind*, trans. Paul Vincent (New York: Cambridge University Press, 2000); Kurt Danziger, *Marking the Mind: A History of Memory* (Cambridge: Cambridge University Press, 2008), esp. 42–47; cf. Dominik Perler, ed., *The Faculties: A History* (New York: Oxford University Press, 2015).

11. This book is the first full-scale historical study as such of how contemporaneous theories and practices of memory in early America correlated. Still helpful on the imperative of historicizing memory itself in histories of memory is Alon Confino's classic essay "Collective Memory and Cultural History: Problems of Method," *American Historical Review* 102 (December 1997): 1403. For an example of an important book on memory of a generation ago that offhandedly denied that such historicization might usefully be achieved for early nineteenth-century America is Michael Kammen, *Mystic Chords of Memory: The Transformation of Tradition in American Culture* (New York: Alfred A. Knopf, 1991), 95. Three published works that have begun the work of historicizing memory in American culture are: Susan M. Stabile, *Memory's Daughters: The Material Culture of Remembrance in Eighteenth-Century America* (Ithaca, NY: Cornell University Press, 2004); Seth C. Bruggeman, *Here George Washington Was Born: Memory, Material Culture and the Public History of a National Monument* (Athens: University of Georgia Press, 2008), especially 44; and Teresa Barnett, *Sacred Relics: Pieces of the Past in Nineteenth-Century America* (Chicago: University of Chicago Press,

2013), especially where the last work discusses "association items," as on p. 18. The present book details vectors of American memory culture only from 1790 through 1840. No thorough accounting is yet available of ideas and performances of memory in America before 1840, much less of the relationship between them. Yet, reading between the lines in existing histories that do have at least indirect relevance tentatively suggests that transatlantic memory culture in the century or so before 1790 was not nearly so self-consciously physicalist as it became in the half century that followed. Consider, the shocked, negative reaction that, Douwe Draaisma has noted, occurred in Britain's Royal Society in 1682 when Sir Robert Hooke argued for a reductively physicalist theory of memory. The view was easily dismissed as a foolish "provocation" by "Hooke's contemporaries." The latter, Draaisma notes, "denied the physicality of memory by placing memory *within* the [immaterial] soul." Draaisma, *The Metaphors of Memory*, 62. John Seelye's exhaustive history of Plymouth Rock as a physical relic notes that "the 'fame' of the Rock . . . almost certainly dates from the epochal moment in 1820 when it emerged from a local to a national eminence," a chronology congruent with the argument of the present study, which particularly sees mass self-conscious use of reliquary becoming popular among Americans (influenced by au courant physicalist memory theory) in the 1820s. John Seelye, *Memory's Nation: The Place of Plymouth Rock* (Chapel Hill: University of North Carolina Press, 2000), 1, and quoting Webster on 75; cf. 23, 32, and 67. David E. Stannard, in his still-important study of *The Puritan Way of Death*, showed that American Puritans commonly incorporated commemorative physical objects, such as mourning rings and tombstones, into their funereal rituals only from about 1650. Their use of such objects thereafter to mark death may have been harbingers of the still-more physicalist post-1790 American memory culture explicated in the present work. Yet, a comparison to what this book shows for the years after 1790 will reveal significant differences. Such use of physical memory props, as a reading of Stannard's study shows in pre-1790 American memory culture, appears to have been far less established, intense, pervasive, conscious, elaborated, physiognomic, popular, or science-oriented than what the present study demonstrates came into vogue after 1790. Some practices of memory treated by Stannard incorporated physical objects, but do not, from the evidence that he affords, appear to have been part and parcel of any sort of systematic view of memory as physical, to anything that might be labeled physicalism. David E. Stannard, *The Puritan Way of Death: A Study in Religion,*

Culture, and Social Change (New York: Oxford University Press, 1977), esp. 109–17.

12. Naturally, there were more enlisted men than officers among the veterans to begin with. By 1840, that disparity had magnified. For one reason, officers were generally older than privates (an average of six years older in this analysis). By 1840, only 7 of every 100 original officers still survived, while 24 of every 100 veterans in the already-larger cohort of enlisted men were still alive. As the number of veterans in a given community approached zero, those who remained to be honored as relics of the Revolution were increasingly apt to be privates, not elite members of the officer corps.

1. THE TAXIDERMIST

1. "Resolution of the American Philosophical Society," cited in Charles Coleman Sellers, *Portraits and Miniatures by Charles Willson Peale,* issued as vol. 42, pt. 1 of the *Transactions of the American Philosophical Society held at Philadelphia for Promoting Useful Knowledge* (Philadelphia: American Philosophical Society, 1952), 82.
2. Charles Willson Peale, cited in Sellers, *Portraits and Miniatures,* 82.
3. Sellers, *Portraits and Miniatures,* 82.
4. *The Selected Papers of Charles Willson Peale and His Family,* ed. Lillian B. Miller, vol. 1, *Charles Willson Peale: Artist in Revolutionary America, 1735–1791* (New Haven: Yale University Press, 1983), 563n12.
5. American Philosophical Society, "Certificate of Membership to Charles W. Peale," 21 July 1786, in *The Selected Papers of Charles Willson Peale and His Family,* ed. Miller, 1:449.
6. [Samuel Vaughan] to Sarah Vaughan, 20 April 1790, American Philosophical Society, Philadelphia. Samuel Vaughan's reportorial epistle to his wife about Franklin's death represents a particular genre of letter writing in the era. In the early national and antebellum periods correspondents often offered detailed descriptions of death scenes, probably in part to add to the pool of collective informal medical knowledge upon which people—in an era of uncertain professional medical care—drew to infer the prognoses of their own and their loved ones' ailments. Lewis O. Saum, "Death in the Popular Mind of Pre-Civil War America," *American Quarterly Review* 26 (1974): 481.
7. [Samuel Vaughan] to Sarah Vaughan, 23 April 1790, American Philosophical Society, Philadelphia.
8. Charles Willson Peale to John Beale Bordley, 26 April 1790, in *The Selected Papers of Charles Willson Peale and His Family,* ed. Miller, 1:585.

Arguing for a more muted contemporaneous national interest in, and reaction to, Franklin's death is Gordon S. Wood, *The Americanization of Benjamin Franklin* (New York: Penguin Press, 2004), 230–38.

9. *The Selected Papers of Charles Willson Peale and His Family*, ed. Miller, 1:586n1; on Franklin's being physically recognizable on an international scale even before the war, see, e.g., Harry S. Stout, "An Uncommon Friendship," in *The Divine Dramatist: George Whitefield and the Rise of Modern Evangelicalism* (Grand Rapids, MI: Eerdmans, 1991), 220–33; Dixon Wecter, *The Hero in America: A Chronicle of Hero-Worship* (Ann Arbor: University of Michigan Press, 1966), 67.

10. [Samuel Vaughan] to Sarah Vaughan, 20 April 1790.

11. Peale, broadside, "My Design in Forming This Museum," 1792, in *The Selected Papers of Charles Willson Peale and His Family*, ed. Lillian B. Miller, vol. 2, pt. 1, *Charles Willson Peale: The Artist as Museum Keeper, 1791–1810* (New Haven: Yale University Press, 1988), 12–15.

12. Charles Coleman Sellers, *Portraits and Miniatures by Charles Willson Peale*, issued as vol. 42, pt. 1 of the *Transactions of the American Philosophical Society held at Philadelphia for Promoting Useful Knowledge* (Philadelphia: American Philosophical Society, 1952), 82.

13. On contemporaneous comingling of art and science in Philadelphia, see generally R. W. Meyers, ed., *Art and Science in Philadelphia, 1740–1840* (New Haven: Yale University Press, 2011).

14. *The Selected Papers of Charles Willson Peale and His Family*, ed. Lillian B. Miller, vol. 5, *The Autobiography of Charles Willson Peale*, 116–17. These are techniques that Peale specified that he used for preserving various creatures, including small birds and "large creatures." Presumably, the techniques he would have used to embalm a human corpse would have been quite similar.

15. *The Selected Papers of Charles Willson Peale and His Family*, ed. Miller, 5:113; Charles Coleman Sellers, *Mr. Peale's Museum: Charles Willson Peale and the First Popular Museum of Natural Science and Art* (New York: W. W. Norton, 1980), 3.

16. "Peale's Museum: Announcement of Move to Philosophical Hall," *General Advertiser* (Philadelphia), 19 September 1794, in *The Selected Papers of Charles Willson Peale and His Family*, ed. Miller, vol. 2, pt. 1, 98.

17. Charles Willson Peale, "Address to the Corporation and Citizens of Philadelphia," 18 July 1816, in *The Selected Papers of Charles Willson Peale and His Family*, ed. Lillian B. Miller, vol. 3, *Charles Willson Peale: The Belfield Farm Years, 1810–1820* (New Haven: Yale University Press, 1983), 414, 417; "A Lover of Nature to the *Pennsylvania Packet*," in *The Selected*

Papers of Charles Willson Peale and His Family, ed. Miller, 1:582–83. For an overview of how Americans of the period employed physiognomic theories, see Christopher J. Lukasick, *Discerning Characters: The Culture of Appearance in Early America* (Philadelphia: University of Pennsylvania Press, 2011); on physiognomy as a transatlantic movement, see Lucy Hartley, *Physiognomy and the Meaning of Expression in Nineteenth-Century Culture* (Cambridge: Cambridge University Press, 2001).

18. J. C. Lavater, *Essays on Physiognomy; for the Promotion of the Knowledge and the Love of Mankind; Written in the German Language, Abridged from M. Holcroft's Translation* (Boston: David West, 1794), 24, 31, 33, 10, 230, 237–38.

19. Lavater, *Essays on Physiognomy*, 86.

20. Charles Willson Peale to General John Armstrong, 21 January 1809, in *The Selected Papers of Charles Willson Peale and His Family*, ed. Lillian B. Miller, vol. 2, pt. 2, *Charles Willson Peale: The Artist as Museum Keeper, 1791–1810* (New Haven: Yale University Press, 1983), 1172. Though Peale intended to make his museum accessible to the masses, David R. Brigham's study of its patronage concludes that primarily the well-heeled visited the establishment. David R. Brigham, *Public Culture in the Early Republic: Peale's Museum and Its Audience* (Washington, DC: Smithsonian Institution Press, 1995), 1. For a description of how the Peale family's exhibits became more commercialized over time see, generally, William T. Alderson, ed., *Mermaids, Mummies, and Mastodons: The Emergence of the American Museum* (Washington, DC: American Association of Museums, 1992).

21. *The Selected Papers of Charles Willson Peale and His Family*, ed. Miller, 5:327.

22. *The Selected Papers of Charles Willson Peale and His Family*, ed. Miller, 5:327–28.

23. *The Selected Papers of Charles Willson Peale and His Family*, ed. Miller, 5:327.

24. *The Selected Papers of Charles Willson Peale and His Family*, ed. Miller, 5:327.

25. *The Selected Papers of Charles Willson Peale and His Family*, ed Miller, 5:413. Peale's emphasis on the unity of the body paralleled the contemporaneous climate of opinion among physicians in Philadelphia. See Alexander Nemerov, *The Body and Raphael Peale: Life and Selfhood, 1812–1824* (Berkeley: University of California Press, 2001), 103. Nemerov also writes more generally of the existence of a significant discourse of "bodily thematics" in "early national Philadelphia" (8).

26. J. C. Lavater, *Essays on Physiognomy*, 218; *Aurora*, 28 December 1802, in *The Selected Papers of Charles Willson Peale and His Family*, ed. Miller, vol. 2, pt. 1, 478. Charles Willson Peale's son Raphael, with his father's encouragement, traveled extensively with a physiognotrace "making money . . . compensating for the loss of his professional standing [as a portraitist] in the vastness of his production—profiles by the hundreds of thousands." Milwaukee Art Center, *Raphael Peale, 1774–1825: Still Lifes and Portraits* (New York: M. Knoedler and Company, 1959), [3]. For an example of the evocative, sentimental significance of profiles in the period see Julia, "Address to a Miniature Profile," *New York Magazine, or Literary Repository* 2 (February 1791): 115.

27. Lavater, *Essays on Physiognomy*, 220; *The Selected Papers of Charles Willson Peale and His Family*, ed. Miller, vol. 2, pt. 2, 817n3.

28. Charles Willson Peale to Thomas Jefferson, 13 December 1806, in *The Selected Papers of Charles Willson Peale and His Family*, ed. Miller, vol. 2, pt. 2, 990. Peale believed that "a collection of profiles taken by" the physiognotrace would be a "feast to the physiognomist and philosopher." Charles Willson Peale, *Aurora*, 11 July 1803, cited in Edgar P. Richardson, Brooke Hindle and Lillian B. Miller, *Charles Willson Peale and His World* (New York: Harry N. Abrams, 1982), 223.

29. Charles Willson Peale to Select and Common Councils of Philadelphia, in *The Selected Papers of Charles Willson Peale and His Family*, ed. Miller, 3:442. On the sometimes conservative message in Peale's artistic expression—his generally-Jeffersonian political orientation notwithstanding—see Albert Boime, *Art in an Age of Counterrevolution, 1815–1848* (Chicago: University of Chicago Press, 2004), 519.

30. *The Selected Papers of Charles Willson Peale and His Family*, ed. Miller, vol. 2, pt. 2, 858.

31. William B. Fowle, "Boston Monitorial School," *American Journal of Education* 1 (February 1826): 78.

32. "Extracts from Dr. Samuel Annesley's Sermon on a Good Memory in Spiritual Things," *Mutual Rights and Methodist Protestant* 1 (November 1824): 158.

33. *Massachusetts Magazine* (July 1792): 440; "Life of Simonides," *New York Magazine, or Literary Repository* 1 (May 1796): 246.

34. Everard Home, "Observations on the Function of the Brain," *New-England Journal of Medicine and Surgery and Collateral Branches of Science* 4 (October 1815): 350; "Craniology," *Medical Repository of Original Essays and Intelligence, Relative to Physic, Surgery, Chemistry, and Natural History* (February–April 1808): 438–39.

35. "Use and Abuse of Memory," *American Annals of Education* 11 (1837): 491. On the tendency of intellectuals in the period to conflate—or at least strongly associate—natural and civil history, see Gilman M. Ostrander, *Republic of Letters: The American Intellectual Community, 1775–1865* (Lanham, MD: Rowman and Littlefield, 1999), 78–79.

36. Whitfield J. Bell, *A Cabinet of Curiosities: Five Episodes in the Evolution of American Museums* (Charlottesville: University Press of Virginia, 1967), 15–18, cited in Seth C. Bruggeman, *Here George Washington Was Born: Memory, Material Culture, and the Public History of a National Monument* (Athens: University of Georgia Press, 2008).

37. Rembrandt Peale to Thomas Jefferson, 8 January 8, 1824, in *The Selected Papers of Charles Willson Peale and His Family*, ed. Lillian B. Miller, vol. 4, *Charles Willson Peale and His Last Years, 1821–1827* (New Haven: Yale University Press, 1996), 355.

38. *The Selected Papers of Charles Willson Peale and His Family*, ed. Miller, 4:355.

39. Rembrandt Peale to Bushrod Washington, 12 January, 1824, in *The Selected Papers of Charles Willson Peale and His Family*, ed. Miller, 4:357.

40. See especially "A phrenology lecture in the hand of Rembrandt Peale . . . ," n.d., but probably 1839, Peale Family Papers, 1784–1864, Col. 396, box 2, Joseph Downs Collection of Manuscripts and Printed Ephemera, Winterthur Library; cf. Charles Colbert, *A Measure of Perfection: Phrenology and the Fine Arts in America* (Chapel Hill: University of North Carolina Press, 1997), 167. On Rembrandt Peale's general physiognomic interest see Lillian B. Miller, ed., *The Peale Family: Creation of a Legacy* (New York: Abbeville Press, 1996), 165. The Peales were certainly not alone in believing that Washington's character could be read physiognomically. For example, in 1807, the physician Richard Browne, in his treatise on physiognomy dedicated to Bushrod Washington, wrote, "When preeminent and striking qualities, whether good or bad, predominate in the mind, they are uniformly accompanied by some corresponding marks in the countenance. Was there ever . . . a Washington with a countenance, marked by weakness or clouded with guilt?" Richard Browne, *An Essay on the Truth of Physiognomy, and Its Application to Medicine* (Philadelphia: Thomas T. Stiles, 1807), 40; the dedication to Bushrod Washington is on p. 6. On Peale's *Patria Pater*, see also Wendy Bellion, *Citizen Spectator: Art, Illusion, and Visual Perception in Early National America* (Chapel Hill: Omohundro Institute and University of North Carolina Press, 2011), 296–303.

41. John van Wyhe, *Phrenology and the Origins of Victorian Scientific Naturalism* (New York: Routledge, 2016); Douwe Draaisma, *Metaphors of*

Memory: A History of Ideas About the Mind, trans. Paul Vincent (New York: Cambridge University Press, 2000), 78–82.

42. John D. Davies, *Phrenology: Fad and Science, a Nineteenth-Century American Crusade* (New Haven: Yale University Press, 1955), 8–9. On prevalent concern with the problem of the "confidence man" in nineteenth-century America and cross-pollinated contemporaneous interest in phrenology, see Karen Haltunnen, *Confidence Men and Painted Women: A Study of Middle-Class Culture in America, 1830–1870* (New Haven: Yale University Press, 1982), esp. 160, 206, and on the corresponding appeal of Lavaterian physiognomy, see 71 and 83.

43. On the etymology of "phrenology" see J. G. Spurzheim, *Outlines of Phrenology* (Boston: Marsh, Capen, and Lyon, 1832), 1. On the displacement of Calvinism in American theology by Arminianism, see Nathan O. Hatch, *The Democratization of American Christianity* (New Haven: Yale University Press, 1989); Hatch sums up the social, political, and religious "Crisis of Authority in Popular Culture" of the period in his chapter by that title, 3–16.

44. Colbert, *A Measure of Perfection,* 11. For early minutes of Philadelphia's phrenological society see "Constitution and Minutes of the Central Phrenological Society of Philadelphia," [19 February 1822–21 November 1827], Historical Society of Pennsylvania, Philadelphia.

45. Colbert, *A Measure of Perfection,* 30.

46. J. L. Pierce, "Remarks on Physical Education," *American Phrenological Journal and Miscellany* (Philadelphia) 2 (1840): 354; Cf. Spurzheim, *Outlines of Phrenology,* 95.

47. George Combe, cited in a review of *Essays on Phrenology, or an Inquiry into the Principles and Utility of the System of Drs. Gall and Spurzheim, and into the Objections Made against It, with Notes and Additions, Comprehending Memoirs on the Anatomy of the Brain, and on Insanity,* by George Combe, *Philadelphia Journal of the Medical and Physical Sciences* 4 (1822): 419.

48. Francis A. Yates, *The Art of Memory* (Chicago: University of Chicago Press, 1966), passim.

49. See, e.g., "Phrenological Theory of Memory," *Boston Pearl and Literary Gazette* 4, no. 27 (14 March 1835): 216.

50. "PHRENOLOGICAL ANALYSIS, Showing the Development of Brain, Power of Mind, Temperament, and Prominent Features of Character," 2 November 1836, American Philosophical Society.

51. J. M. Graves, *Phrenology, or the Doctrine of the Mental Phenomena, Explained, Illustrated, and Defended, in a Series of Lectures* (Norwich: M. B. Young, 1838), 116.

52. Amos Dean, *Lectures on Phrenology: Delivered before the Young Men's Association for Mutual Improvement, of the City of Albany* (Boston: Marsh, Capen, and Lyon, 1835), 201.

53. Dean, *Lectures on Phrenology,*162. On the extent to which physicalist assays of faculties, including memory, departed from prior soul-centered accounts of the faculties, see Dominik Perler, *The Faculties: A History* (New York: Oxford University Press, 2015), 255.

54. George Combe, *Notes on the United States of North America, 1838–1840,* 2 vols. (Edinburgh: Malachilan, Stewart & Co., 1841), 1:330.

55. See, e.g., Combe, *Notes on the United States of North America, 1838–1840,* 1:339.

56. Combe, *Notes on the United States of North America, 1838–1840,* 1:339.

57. "Rembrandt Peale's Lecture," newspaper clipping from Philadelphia *Public Ledger,* 26 January 1888, Peale Family Papers, 1784–1864, collection no. 396, box 2, folder 2, Joseph Downs Collection of Manuscripts and Printed Ephemera, Winterthur Library.

58. Johann Caspar Lavater, *Essays on Physiognomy; for the Promotion of the Knowledge and Love of Mankind,* trans. Thomas Holcroft (London: C. Whittingham, 1804), 12, 243; cf. [Johann Caspar Lavater], *The Pocket Lavater: The Science of Physiognomy: To Which Is Added, an Inquiry into the Analogy Existing between Brute and Human Anatomy, from the Italian of Porta* (New York: Van Winkle & Wiley, 1817), 32. Cf. "On a Lock of Hair," *Juvenile Port-Folio and Literary Miscellany* 4 (March 1816): 44, in which a lover describes a relic of hair taken from the beloved as the "faithful index of a mind, Pure as the new-born day."

59. "A phrenology lecture in the hand of Rembrandt Peale"; cf. Colbert, *A Measure of Perfection,* 167. Rembrandt Peale was no great anomaly for analyzing George Washington according to both broader physiognomic notions and phrenology. See, e.g., the frontispiece of Frederick Coombs's *Popular Phrenology,* published in 1841, which depicts George Washington between a "Phrenological Character" of him, and a "Physiognomical" analysis of him. Frederick Coombs, *Coombs's Popular Phrenology: Exhibiting the Exact Phrenological Admeasurements of Above Fifty Distinguished and Extraordinary Personages, of Both Sexes, with Skulls of the Various Nations of the World: Embellished with Above 50 Engravings and Poetical Descriptions of Beauty, Intellect, and Physiognomy* (Boston, 1841), frontispiece.

60. Joseph Delaplaine to Rubens Peale, 19 February 1818, in *The Selected Papers of Charles Willson Peale and His Family,* ed. Miller, 3:578n4; on 579 the editor points out that there is no evidence that any of the Peales responded to Delaplaine's request.

61. Joseph Delaplaine, *Delaplaine's Repository of the Lives and Portraits of Distinguished American Characters* (Philadelphia, 1816), preface, ii.

62. Delaplaine, *Delaplaine's Repository*, preface, iv.

63. The indispensable treatment of Buffon and other contemporaneous European critics of the New World environment remains Gilbert Chinard, "Eighteenth Century Theories on America as a Human Habitat," American Philosophical Society, *Proceedings* 91 (1947): 27–57. For exemplary European criticism see, e.g., N. C. Pitta, *A Treatise on the Influence of Climate on the Human Species: And on the Varieties of Men Resulting from It; Including an Account of the Criteria of Intelligence Which the Form of the Head Presents; And a Sketch of a Rational System of Physiognomy as Founded on Physiology* (London, 1812). For American reactions to such criticism see, e.g., Hugh Williamson, *Observations on the Climate in Different Parts of America, Compared with the Climate in Corresponding Parts of the Other Continent to Which Are Added Remarks on the Different Complexions of the Human Race; With Some Account of the Aborigines of America; Being an Introductory Discourse to the History of North-Carolina* (New York, 1811). For an illustration of American confidence in the idea that locality has an effect on the human body, see Robley Duglison, *Human Health; or, The Influence of Atmosphere and Locality* (Philadelphia: Lea and Blanchard, 1844).

64. Thomas Jefferson, as quoted in Chinard, "Eighteenth Century Theories," 42–43.

65. Thomas Jefferson, as quoted in Chinard, "Eighteenth Century Theories," 41.

66. Delaplaine, *Delaplaine's Repository*, preface, v.

67. Delaplaine, *Delaplaine's Repository*, introduction, vii–viii. One indication that Delaplaine took his *Repository* to be a contribution to memorialization as a science may have been his donation of a copy to the scientifically minded American Philosophical Society. [Joseph] Delaplaine to John Vaughan, 11 October 1816, American Philosophical Society.

68. Delaplaine, *Delaplaine's Repository*, introduction, viii; preface, iii.

69. Delaplaine, *Delaplaine's Repository*, introduction, iv, vii.

70. Delaplaine, *Delaplaine's Repository*, introduction, vii–viii.

71. Delaplaine, *Delaplaine's Repository*, introduction, iv–v.

72. To their own embarrassment, Americans often deemed it necessary to hire European artistic talent to produce quality nationalistic monuments for use in the United States. See, e.g., Pamela Savage Moore, *Diary of Pamela Savage Moore*, 15 December 1826, in *Pamela Savage of Champlain, Health Seeker in Oxford*, ed. Helen Harriet Salls (Raleigh:

North Carolina Division of Archives and History, 1952), 558, Alexander Street Press, "North American Women's Letters and Diaries: Colonial to 1950," http://alexanderstreet2.com/NWLDlive/index.html. For commendation of Delaplaine for using American engravers to produce his *Repository* in contradistinction to the Philadelphia publisher of Barlow's *Columbiad* several years before see "Delaplaine's Repository," *Literary and Musical Magazine* 3 (15 March 1819): 167.

73. Joseph Delaplaine, *Prospectus of Delaplaine's National Panzographia for the Reception of the Portraits of Distinguished Americans* (Philadelphia: William Brown, 1818), 12.

74. Delaplaine, *Delaplaine's Repository,* introduction, v.

75. Delaplaine, *Delaplaine's Repository,* introduction, v.

76. The essayist was particularly referencing physical monuments to the nation's heroes. "Edward," "On National Rewards," *Ladies' Literary Cabinet, Being a Repository of Miscellaneous Literary Productions, Both Original and Selected in Prose and Verse* 1 (1820): 69; cf. the claim in 1800, following Washington's death, that commercial medals with his likeness could be relied upon "to imprint on the Minds of All, especially of Youth, the Memory and important Services of him who bought our freedom" and were, for that purpose, ideal for "Children of all Classes." *Providence Gazette,* 15 February 1800, cited in Richard D. Brown, *Knowledge Is Power: The Diffusion of Information in Early America, 1700–1865* (New York: Oxford University Press, 1989), 257.

77. Delaplaine, *Delaplaine's Repository,* introduction, v.

78. Lucy Crawford claimed that in 1820, a group of seven men ascended the highest peak in the range. Naming it "Mount Washington," they proceeded to christen the others Mount Adams, Mount Jefferson, Mount Monroe, Mount Franklin, and Mount Clay. Next, they drank a home-made brew called "Oh-Be-Joyful," offering toasts "in honor to the great men." Morse Stearns, ed., *Lucy Crawford's History of the White Mountains* (Hanover, NH: Dartmouth Publications, 1966), 5–6. Crawford's account appears to have conflated naming of Mount Washington and naming of other peaks in the Presidential Range. Russell Lawson has argued that "Mount Washington" was so named "some time between 1785 and 1792," and that the appellation first appeared in print in Jeremy Belknap's *History of New-Hampshire.* Russell M. Lawson, *The American Plutarch: Jeremy Belknap and the Historian's Dialogue with the Past* (Westport, CT: Praeger, 1998), 99. Extant travelers' accounts suggest that Mount Washington was effective in evoking its namesake's memory. "Legend of the White Mountains," *Ladies' Magazine* 1 (March 1828):

135; "Sketches from Memory. No. I," *New England Magazine.* 9 (November 1835): 322–23. See also Angela Miller, *Empire of the Eye: Landscape Representation and American Cultural Politics, 1825–1875* (Ithaca, NY: Cornell University Press, 1993), 268, 270.

79. George Bancroft to Edward Everett, 25 July 1834, George Bancroft Papers, Massachusetts Historical Society.

80. Thomas Southgate to Charles Carroll, 28 March 1831, Charles Carroll Papers, item #1902, Maryland Historical Society; microfilm copy, David Library of the American Revolution, Washington Crossing, PA.

81. Robert C. Winthrop Scrapbook, Winthrop Papers, reel 44, Massachusetts Historical Society. The quotation here is from an address that Winthrop gave on 21 November 1834. For a still-helpful general history of place-naming in the United States, see George R. Stewart, *Names on the Land: A Historical Account of Place-Naming in the United States,* rev. ed. (Boston: Houghton Mifflin, 1958). Most useful for understanding how frequently Americans of the era used place-names to relocate nationalistic memory are statistics and charts concerning such practices in Wilbur Zelinsky, *Nation into State: The Shifting Symbolic Foundations of American Nationalism* (Chapel Hill: University of North Carolina Press, 1988), esp. 131–40.

82. "History of Concord," *North American Review* 42 (1836): 467.

83. "Bye-Gone Years," newspaper clipping from the *Washington Reporter,* John D. Shane scrapbook (c. 1835–45), Draper Collection, Kentucky MSS, Vol. 26 CC, Wisconsin State Historical Society. See Elizabeth A. Perkins, *Border Life: Experience and Memory in the Revolutionary Ohio Valley* (Chapel Hill: University of North Carolina Press, 1998), 20–21.

84. On early Americans' penchant for "portable relics" evoking memories of the young nation's Founders see Edward G. Lengel, *Inventing George Washington: America's Founder, in Myth and Memory* (New York: HarperCollins, 2011), 108.

85. "Delaplaine's Repository of the Lives and Portraits of Distinguished Americans," *The Portico, a Repository of Science & Literature* (October 1816): 283, 285.

86. "A Repository of the Lives and Portraits of Distinguished Americans," *Analectic Magazine, and Naval Chronicle* 8 (September 1816): 193.

87. "A Repository," 204; cf. "Delaplaine's Repository," 284.

88. Delaplaine, *Delaplaine's Repository,* 105–6.

89. "A Repository," 304.

90. *The Author Turned Critic, or the Reviewer Reviewed; Being a Reply to a Feeble and Unfounded Attack on Delaplaine's Repository, in the Analectic Magazine and Naval Chronicle, for the Month of September 1816* (1816): 21.

91. *The Author Turned Critic,* 16–17.

92. *The Author Turned Critic,* 16–17.

93. Joseph Delaplaine, *Prospectus of Delaplaine's National Panzographia for the Reception of the Portraits of Distinguished Americans* (Philadelphia: William Brown, 1818), 10–14.

94. "Delaplaine's National Gallery," *Literary and Musical Magazine* 3 (12 April 1819): 200.

95. On Delaplaine's personal expenditures in support of production of his ill-fated *Repository,* see Joseph Delaplaine to General Matthew Clarkson[?], 31 July 1816, Society Collection, case 19, box 39, Pennsylvania Historical Society. On Delaplaine's financial losses from the failure of the Panzographia, see Joseph Delaplaine to Ruben Haines III, 5 April 1824, ser. 2, box 18, folder 231, Wyck Papers, American Philosophical Society.

96. While numerous examples might be cited of Rembrandt Peale's tireless promotion of his own work as uniquely correct in its bodily representation of Washington, for a summation of his argument, see especially Rembrandt Peale, "Print of Washington. Alteration and Improvement of the Design," printed circular, n.d., William Baker, "Washington Biographical Sketches," scrapbook, Library Company of Philadelphia. For an enthusiastic report of endorsements of the accuracy of Rembrandt Peale's rendering see Jared Sparks to Timothy Pickering, 21 August 1826, Timothy Pickering Papers, Massachusetts Historical Society.

97. On efforts by those in the burgeoning middle class to use their growing consumer power to gain entrée into "refined" elite culture in the period, see especially Richard L. Bushman, *The Refinement of America: Persons, Houses, Cities* (New York: Random House, 1992).

98. E.g., Delaplaine imagined that the Panzographia would unite "different ranks in the same elegant pleasures," yet it seems clear that he was simultaneously signaling that the Panzographia would reinforce hierarchy: it would promote a "love or order," helping to "enforce submission to government"; the worthies whom Delaplaine identified as subjects of the Panzographia were all elites, and—as noted above—the presentation of their pictures would reflect a "careful discrimination of character." Joseph Delaplaine, "Delaplaine's National Panzographia," *The Academician, Containing the Elements of Scholastic Science and the Outlines of Philosophic Education, Predicated on the Analysis of the Human Mind, and Exhibiting the Improved Methods of Instruction* 1 (13 February 1819): 247, 250–51. On the pricing of the *Repository,* see "Domestic Literature and Science," *Analectic Magazine* 3 (June 1814): 523.

99. Rembrandt Peale, "Print of Washington." On Charles Willson Peale's care in pricing admission to his museum and his employment of the "physiognotrace," see above in the present chapter.

100. *The Selected Papers of Charles Willson Peale and His Family,* ed. Miller, 3:578n2. For a comparison of Delaplaine's gallery to Peale's museum that favors the former see "Delaplaine's Repository," *Literary and Musical Magazine* 3 (15 March 1819): 167.

101. Charles Coleman Sellers, *Mr. Peale's Museum: Charles Willson Peale and the First Popular Museum of Natural Science and Art* (New York: W. W. Norton, 1980), 2.

102. On the marketing of Heth, see especially Benjamin Reiss, *The Showman and the Slave: Race, Death, and Memory in Barnum's America* (Cambridge, MA: Harvard University Press, 2001).

103. Joseph Delaplaine to Ruben Haines III, 5 April 1824. In his letter to Haines, Delaplaine noted, that he was also writing to "Mr. Watson simultaneously," presumably a reference to Delaplaine's close friend, John Fanning Watson.

104. John F. Watson to John McAllister, June 12, 1847, Gratz mss., box 20, case 6, American Historians, folder for "Watson, John F.," Pennsylvania Historical Society.

105. John F. Watson, *Annals of Philadelphia and Pennsylvania,* rev. ed., 2 vols. (Philadelphia: Elijah Thomas, [1857]), 2:4. Cf. Gary B. Nash, *First City: Philadelphia and the Forging of Historical Memory* (Philadelphia: University of Pennsylvania Press, 2002), 208.

106. Watson, *Annals of Philadelphia and Pennsylvania,* 2:500.

107. Watson, *Annals,* 2:500.

108. Watson, *Annals,* 2:1; cf. "Local Attachment," *Weekly Visitant* 1, no. 43 (1806): 340; "Local Attachment," *The Polyanthos* 4 (March 1807): 281; "On the Influence of Local Attachment," *Lady's Magazine and Musical Repository* 3 (April 1802): 230–31.

109. Watson, *Annals,* 2:503; the list is dated "July, 1839."

110. Watson, *Annals,* 2:503.

111. John F. Watson, extra-illustrated original manuscript of *Annals of Philadelphia,* folder 42, 170, Library Company of Philadelphia.

112. Watson, extra-illustrated original manuscript of *Annals of Philadelphia,* Pennsylvania Historical Society.

113. On the creation of commercial objects to celebrate Lafayette's tour see Sarah J. Purcell, *Sealed with Blood: War, Sacrifice, and Memory in Revolutionary America* (Philadelphia: University of Pennsylvania Press, 2002), 181.

114. Richard N. Venable, Diary, 6 [June] and 7 [June] 1791, Virginia Historical Society.

115. Watson, *Annals,* 2:578.

116. Sarah M. Haines to "My Dear Cousin," 12 September 1824, ser. 2, box 28, folder 429, Wyck Papers, American Philosophical Society. The significance of such familiar bodily deportment toward Lafayette becomes even more evident when one recognizes that Americans of the period were inclined to emphasize Lafayette's social rank as a French nobleman, gaining satisfaction from the idea that a European aristocrat approved of their Revolution. Lloyd S. Kramer, "America's Lafayette, and Lafayette's America: A European and the American Revolution," *William and Mary Quarterly,* 3rd ser., 38, no. 2 (April 1981): 230.

117. Washington had died in 1799, Lafayette in 1834.

118. Watson, *Annals,* 2:580. Washington was not the only worthy whom Watson memorialized with hair. In 1836, the banker had a chair made of parts of another chair that William Penn had once owned, Penn's Treaty Elm, the supposed house of Columbus in Santo Domingo, trees outside Independence Hall, and fragments from the ships *Constitution* and *Pennsylvania.* Under glass, in a compartment of the chair's back, was preserved a lock of Chief Justice John Marshall's hair. Frank Sommer, "John F. Watson: First Historian of the American Decorative Arts," *Antiques* 83, no. 3 (March 1963): 303.

119. John F. Watson, "Excursion of 4 July 1835 to Trenton. N.J.," Joseph Downs Collection of Manuscripts and Printed Ephemera, no. 189, Watson Family Papers, folder 6, box 1, Winterthur Library.

120. See, e.g., Helen Diana Sheumaker, "'A Token That Love Entwines': Nineteenth-Century Hair Work and the American White Middle Class" (Ph.D. diss., University of Kansas, 1999). Sheumaker's account rarely broaches the epistemic issues with which this book is concerned, and primarily focuses upon the middle-to-late nineteenth century. Sheumaker does note that: "In the eighteenth century, the sentimental associations of hair were obliquely displayed; by the nineteenth century, hair work was openly worn for others to observe, and the sentimentality that it conveyed was explicitly presented" (167). For representative expressions of what hair meant as a sentimental personal memento from the body of someone beloved, see, e.g.: "A Lock of Hair," *Boston Weekly Magazine* 1 (15 September 1838): 12, in which it is asserted that "a lock of hair is far better than any picture," because "it is a part of the beloved object herself"; "My Museum," *The Hesperian; a Monthly Miscellany of General Literature, Original and Select* 3 (June 1839): 37; "I See Thee Still,"

Atkinson's Casket (January 1838): 11; "To a Lock of Hair," *The Knicker-bocker* 10 (December 1837): 504; J.N.B., "A Few Thoughts on Funerals," *The Knickerbocker; or, New York Monthly Magazine* 10 (September 1837): 229; J. Dogett Jr., "To a Lock of Hair," *Southern Literary Messenger* 2 (July 1836): 464; "The Lock of Hair They Sent Me," *Ladies' Magazine* 7 (January 1834): 37; A.P., "Wandering to the West," *American Monthly Magazine* 3 (June 1831): 175–78; "The Lock of Hair," *Atkinson's Casket* (February 1831): 1, implying that by knowledge of the beloved's hair, the lover might have been able to "read the mournful tale" of her death; "To 'Ganem' with a Lock of Hair," *Saturday Evening Post* 3 (25 September 1824): 1; "On a Lock of Hair," *Juvenile Port-Folio and Literary Miscellany* 3 (25 February 1815): 4.
121. Watson, *Annals*, 2:581.
122. "The Tomb of Washington," *The Knickerbocker; or, New York Monthly Magazine* 15, no. 5 (May 1840): 445.
123. The Struthers family is still in the monument business in the Philadelphia area; their tradition about John Struthers taking the lock of hair was summarized in their corporate webpage in 2004, as archived at https://web.archive.org/web/20040213092221/http://www.aaastefanmonuments.com/history/.
124. Watson, *Annals*, 2:581.
125. Jean B. Lee, "Historical Memory, Sectional Strife, and the American Mount Vernon, 1783–1853," *Virginia Magazine of History and Biography* 109, no. 3 (2001): 255–300. Lee asserts: "After Washington resigned command of the army in 1783, hundreds of people annually traveled to Mount Vernon. . . . Following his death and entombment there, the numbers swelled into the thousands" (256). For accounts of how visitors took away relics, see, e.g., 265 and 286. On how such visits contributed to emerging national identity, see especially 256–57. The proliferation of relics in the era pertaining to Washington's body may be considered as an illustration, or variation, of what C. M. Harris has aptly described as a process whereby "the first monuments to [Washington] were diffused in rhetoric and popular art." C. M. Harris, "Washington's Gamble, L'Enfant's Dream: Politics, Design, and the Founding of the National Capital," *William and Mary Quarterly*, 3rd ser., 56, no. 3 (July 1999): 564.
126. Letter from unidentified correspondent to "Uncle," dated Mount Vernon, Fairfax County, Virginia, 18 June 1822, Washington Family Papers, 1674–1853, Mount Vernon Ladies' Association of the Union, microfilm copy, David Library of the American Revolution.

127. Gary Laderman, *The Sacred Remains: American Attitudes toward Death, 1799–1883* (New Haven: Yale University Press, 1996), 17. Laderman's account is helpful on balance; see especially his description on p. 16 of how communities across the nation mourned Washington's death with simulated funeral processions that included empty coffins.

128. For typical Protestant criticism of Catholic use of relics see "Saints—Relics—Images," *Baltimore Literary and Religious Magazine* [2], no. 2 (February 1837): 86–89.

129. John Fanning Watson, "Account of New Settlers in the American Woods, also an Account of a Trip to Valley Forge and the Camp Hills, July 1828," Pennsylvania Historical Society.

130. "Valley Forge," *Freemasons Magazine and General Miscellany* 2 (October 1811): 47–48.

131. J. R. Murden, *The Art of Memory, Reduced to a Systematic Arrangement, Exemplified under the Two Leading Principles, Locality and Association* (New York: J. T. Murden, 1818), 19.

132. Murden, *The Art of Memory*, 24.

133. See, e.g., John Resch, *Suffering Soldiers: Revolutionary War Veterans, Moral Sentiment, and Political Culture in the Early Republic* (Amherst: University of Massachusetts Press, 1999), 96.

134. "Letter, printed, dated Fredericksburg, June 1, 1831; proposing a monument to the memory of the mother of George Washington," Virginia Historical Society; cf. Lawrence Lewis to George Washington Bassett, 5 May 1831, George Washington Bassett Papers, section I, Virginia Historical Society.

135. Watson, "Account of New Settlers in the American Woods," 9 and n.

136. Charles Griswold, *An Address in Commemoration of the Lives and Services of Ledyard and His Brave Associates, Who Fell at Groton Heights, Sept. 6, 1781, in Defence of Their Country, Delivered at Groton, (Conn.), September 6th 1826* (New London, CT: J. R. Clapp, 1826), 18–19.

137. Griswold, *An Address in Commemoration*, 18–19.

138. "An Address, Delivered at the Laying of the Corner Stone of the Bunker Hill Monument," *United States Literary Gazette* 2, no. 9 (1 August 1825): 332, 329.

139. "Bunker Hill Monument," newspaper clipping in John Newhall, Commonplace Book and Diary, 1825, Massachusetts Historical Society.

140. See, e.g., Ralph Waldo Emerson, "A Historical Discourse, Deliverd before the Citizens of Concord, 12th September 1835, on the Second Centennial Anniversary of the Incorporation of the Town," *American*

Historical Magazine 1, no. 6 (June 1836): 215; "Survivors of the Revolution," *Army and Navy Chronicle* 1, no. 43 (22 October 1835): 339.

141. Watson, "Account of New Settlers in the American Woods," 9n.
142. See figure on p. 5. The sample cohorts for this analysis were 120 randomly selected veteran officers of the Revolution and 120 randomly
selected veteran privates of the revolution for whom definite years of
death are listed in Daughters of the American Revolution, *DAR Patriot
Index: Centennial Edition*, 3 vols. (Washington, DC: National Society of
the Daughters of the American Revolution, 1990). Not surprisingly, officers tended to be older. The officers studied for the present analysis had
an average birth year of 1746, while the privates had an average birth
year of 1752.

2. THE ARCHIVIST

1. Jeremy Belknap to Ebenezer Hazard, 27 August 1790, printed in *Collections of the Massachusetts Historical Society,* ser. 5, vol. 3, *Belknap Papers*
(Boston: Massachusetts Historical Society, 1882), 231.
2. Massachusetts Historical Society, *"There is Nothing Like Having a Good
Repository": An Introduction to the Massachusetts Historical Society* (Boston: Massachusetts Historical Society, 1984), 1.
3. Jeremy Belknap to Ebenezer Hazard, 27 August 1790, in *Collections.*
4. Louis Leonard Tucker, *The Massachusetts Historical Society: A Bicentenni-
al History, 1791–1991* (Boston: Massachusetts Historical Society, 1991), 3;
John Thorton Kirkland, *A Sermon Delivered at the Internment of Jeremy
Belknap, D.D., Minister of the Church in Federal Street, Boston, June 22, 1798*
(Boston: Manning and Loring, [1798]), 15.
5. Jeremy Belknap, *The History of New Hampshire,* 3 vols. (Boston: Reprinted for the Author, 1784), 1:iv. On Belknap being an eyewitness to
the destruction of Prince's collection see *Proceedings of the Massachusetts
Historical Society, 1791–1835* (Boston: Massachusetts Historical Society,
1879), 1:viii; *Massachusetts Historical Society Collections* (hereafter, *MHS
Coll.*) (Boston: Massachusetts Historical Society, 1792), 1:2.
6. *MHS Coll.* (1792), 1:2.
7. On the elite social status of most founders of historical societies in the
early United States see Leslie W. Dunlap, *American Historical Societies,
1790–1860* (Philadelphia: Porcupine Press, 1974), 23.
8. George Richards Minot, *The History of the Insurrections in Massachusetts* (Worcester, MA: Isaiah Thomas, 1788), 28. On Minot's biases, and
why he tempered them in his narrative, see Daniel P. Szatmary, *Shays'*

Rebellion: The Making of an Agrarian Insurrection (Amherst: University of Massachusetts Press, 1980), xi–xii.

9. Jeremy Belknap to Josiah Waters, 24 September 1786, printed in 1886, *MHS Coll.*, 6th ser. (1891), 4:315.

10. On Belknap's nationalist vision for the Massachusetts Historical Society and his support of the new federal U.S. Constitution see William Charles Cole, "Jeremy Belknap: Pioneer Nationalist," *New England Quarterly* 10 (1937): 744.

11. Jeremy Belknap to Ebenezer Hazard, 4 February 1780, *MHS Coll.*, 5th ser. (1877), 2:255.

12. Jeremy Belknap to John Wentworth, 21 March 1791, *MHS Coll.*, 6th ser. (1891) 4:484.

13. Belknap was apparently influenced toward the Newtonian outlook by his mentor, Thomas Prince. David D. Van Tassel, *Recording America's Past: An Interpretation of the Development of Historical Studies in America, 1607–1884* (Chicago: University of Chicago Press, 1960), 22.

14. Jeremy Belknap, *Dissertations on the Character, Death, and Resurrection of Jesus Christ, and the Evidence of His Gospel; With Remarks on Some Sentiments Advanced in a Book Intitled 'The Age of Reason'* (Boston: Apollo Press, 1795), 108–9.

15. Jeremy Belknap to Ebenezer Hazard, 13 January 1784, *MHS Coll.*, 5th ser. (1877), 2:294; cf. the characterization of historical associations as offering "consistant records in the stead of vague traditions" in "Historical Associations—Louisana Society," *Commercial Review of the South and West* 3, no. 4 (April 1847): 353.

16. Russell M. Lawson, *The American Plutarch: Jeremy Belknap and the Historian's Dialogue with the Past* (Westport, CT: Praeger, 1998), 110.

17. Cf. Cole, "Jeremy Belknap: Pioneer Nationalist," 745; George B. Kirsch, *Jeremy Belknap: A Biography* (New York: Arno Press, 1982), 122. For Belknap's chart of "Remarkable Instances of Longevity" in New Hampshire's history see Belknap, *The History of New-Hampshire*, 3 vols. (Boston: Thomas & Andres, 1791), 2:250–52.

18. Jeremy Belknap to Ebenezer Hazard, 18 December 1780, *MHS Coll.*, 5th ser. (1877), 2:83; see also Jeremy Belknap to Ebenezer Hazard, 4 February 1780, *MHS Coll.*, 5th ser. (1877), 2:255.

19. On how Americans in the period conceived of the relationship between civil and natural history, see Brooke Hindle, *The Pursuit of Science in Revolutionary America* (Chapel Hill: University of North Carolina Press, 1956), 302–26, esp. 317–18.

20. Jeremy Belknap to Ebenezer Hazard, 19 August 1789, *MHS Coll.*, 5th ser. (1882), 3:159.

21. Of course, a cabinet of natural history specimens from a place was still not considered to be as instructive as actually visiting a place and examining its natural characteristics firsthand. "The mineralogist who laboriously ascends mountains, or visits the recesses of mines, for the purpose of improving the science to which he has devoted himself, possesses advantages far superior to the one who only travels from his room to a cabinet of curiosities, and who endeavours from one small specimen to form a conception of the grand geological construction." "The Landscape," *New-York Mirror, a Weekly Gazette of Literature and the Fine Arts* 1, no. 48 (26 June 1824): 378.

22. Margaret Heilbrun, "NYork, NCentury, N-YHS," *New-York Journal of American History* 65 (Spring 2003): 27. Note the similarly dismissive tone toward cabinets of curiosities taken by essayists in Walter M. Whitehill, ed., *A Cabinet of Curiosities: Five Episodes in the Evolution of American Museums* (Charlottesville: University of Virginia Press, 1967).

23. Robert Darnton, *The Great Cat Massacre and Other Episodes in French Cultural History* (New York: Basic Books, 1984), 5.

24. On the long history of cabinets of curiosities, see generally Patrick Mauries, *Cabinets of Curiosities* (London: Thomas and Hudson, 2002); Philipp Blom, *To Have and to Hold: An Intimate History of Collectors and Collecting* (New York: Overlook Press, 2003).

25. See generally Mauries, *Cabinets of Curiosities*; Blom, *To Have and to Hold*.

26. See "Natural Rights," in Daniel T. Rodgers, *Contested Truths: Keywords in American Politics Since Independence* (New York: Basic Books, 1987).

27. On Buffon, and similar European critics of the New World, see chapter 1.

28. "The Constitution of the Massachusetts Historical Society," 24 January 1791, as printed in *Proceedings of the Massachusetts Historical Society, 1791–1835*, 1:2.

29. William Bentley, *The Diary of William Bentley*, 2 vols. (Salem, MA: Essex Institute, 1905–14), 2:127.

30. *Proceedings of the Massachusetts Historical Society, 1791–1835*, 1:82.

31. William D. Jenks, "An Account of the Massachusetts Historical Society," *American Quarterly Register* 10, no. 2 (November 1837): 167.

32. "Buffon: American Degeneracy," Academy of Natural Sciences, Philadelphia, Pennsylvania, http://www.acnatsci.org/museum/jefferson /otherPages/degeneracy-02.html#degeneracy. See also Gaye Wilson, "Jefferson, Buffon, and the Mighty American Moose," *Monticello Newsletter* 13, no. 1 (Spring 2002): [1–3], https://www.monticello.org/sites /default/files/inline-pdfs/2002smse.pdf; Thomas Jefferson to Comte

de Buffon, 1 October 1787, online at the Library of Congress, American Memory Project, http://www.loc.gov/exhibits/jefferson/images/vc86p1.jpg.

33. Mss. of Massachusetts Historical Society minutes, 28 April 1836, Archives of the Massachusetts Historical Society (hereafter, MHS Archives).

34. "Biography of the Signers to the Declaration of Independence," *American Quarterly Review* 1, no. 2 (June 1827): 406; Elkanah Watson to James Sullivan, 14 April 1803, MHS Corresponding Secretary's Letterbook, 1800–1843, MHS Archives; David Humphreys to John Eliot, MHS Corresponding Secretary's Letterbook, 1792–1811, MHS Archives.

35. *Proceedings of the Massachusetts Historical Society, 1791–1835,* 1:15; Thomas Hall to the Corresponding Secretary of the MHS [John Elliot], 1 August 1802, MHS Corresponding Secretary's Letterbook, 1800–1843, MHS Archives.

36. Thomas Hall to the Corresponding Secretary of the MHS [John Elliot], 1 August 1802.

37. Jeremy Belknap to John Adams, 18 July 1789, Adams Papers, Microfilm Reel 372, Massachusetts Historical Society; Jeremy Belknap to Ebenezer Hazard, 5 June 1780, *MHS Coll.,* 5th ser. (1877), 2:56. In neither source is Belknap directly addressing the creation of historical societies, but he is colorfully expressing ideas that flow through the totality of his writings, and clearly applied in his thinking as he helped to begin the Massachusetts Historical Society.

38. Alexis de Tocqueville, "Of the Use Which the Americans Make of Public Associations in Civil Life," in *Democracy in America* (1839), bk. 2, ch. 5, trans. Henry Reeve, online at http://xroads.virginia.edu/~HYPER/DETOC/ch2_05.htm. Illustrating the general proliferation of associations, see L.B., "Enigmatical List of a Few of the Societies in This City," *New York Weekly Magazine; or, Miscellaneous Repository: Forming an Interesting Collection of Original and Select Literary Productions in Prose and Verse: Calculated for Instruction and Rational Entertainment—the Promotion of Moral and Useful Knowledge—and to Enlarge and Correct the Understandings of Youth* 1, no. 41 (13 April 1796): 323. For a contemporaneous comment on how useful association is in the context of noting the rise of historical societies in the new nation see Lewis Cass, *A Discourse Delivered at the First Meeting of the Historical Society of Michigan, September 18, 1829* (Detroit: Geo[rge] L. Whitney, 1830), 5–6.

39. "Act to Incorporate a Society by the Name of the Massachusetts Historical Society," reprinted in *Proceedings of the Massachusetts Historical Society, 1791–1835,* 1:62.

40. Cf. the definition of "corporation" from Edward D. Mansfield's *Political Grammar of the United States,* as reprinted in Lyman Cobb, *The North American Reader* (New York: Harper and Brothers, 1835), 475.

41. C.W., "Historical Associations," *Harvardiana* 1, no. 9 (1 May 1835): 269–70. On relevant legal changes in the period see Lawrence M. Friedman, *A History of American Law,* 2nd ed. (New York: Simon and Schuster, 1985), 198–200.

42. Jeremy Belknap to John Adams, 18 July 1789, Adams Papers, MHS; cf. Louis Leonard Tucker, *Clio's Consort: Jeremy Belknap and the Founding of the Massachusetts Historical Society* (Boston: Massachusetts Historical Society, 1990), xi.

43. *Proceedings of the Massachusetts Historical Society, 1791–1835,* 1:xx.

44. *Collections of the Massachusetts Historical Society,* 2nd ser. (Boston: Massachusetts Historical Society, 1814), 1:xviii, xvi. "Johnson" was probably a reference to Isaac Johnson, Massachusetts Bay Colony's first magistrate; "Cotton" could be the Reverend John Cotton, but plausibly could have been that more famous divine, Cotton Mather. I wish to thank L. J. Woolcock, assistant librarian at the Massachusetts Historical Society, for his generous help in puzzling out these referential possibilities.

45. *Collections of the Massachusetts Historical Society,* 2nd ser. (Boston: Massachusetts Historical Society, n.d.), 2:167n.

46. *Proceedings of the Massachusetts Historical Society, 1791–1835,* 1:433; *MHS Coll.,* 6th ser. (1891), 4:xvii.

47. Daniel Webster, *An Address Delivered at the Laying of the Cornerstone of the Bunker Hill Monument,* 4th ed. (Boston: Cummings, Hillard, and Company, 1825), 3; Lorenzo Samuel Knapp, *Memoir of General Lafayette with an Account of His Present Visit to This Country, and a Description of His Tour Through the United States; and a Detail of the Arrangements for the Celebration of the 17th June, and Laying the Cornerstone of the Bunker Hill Monument, With a Correct Likeness* (Boston: E. G. House, 1825), 23.

48. Jeremy Belknap to Ebenezer Hazard, 23 April 1781, as printed in *MHS Coll.,* 5th ser. (1877), 2:96; Jeremy Belknap to Ebenezer Hazard, 1 December [1783], as printed in *MHS Coll.,* 5th ser. (1877), 2:281.

49. *MHS Coll.,* (1792), 1:3.

50. H. A. Griswold to George Bancroft, no day and month, 1834, George Bancroft Papers, Massachusetts Historical Society.

51. George Bancroft to Edward Everett, 23 October 1833, George Bancroft Papers. Bancroft's posture of epistemic probity notwithstanding, he was subjected to intense pressure from agitators in the contemporary patriotic memory wars. For example, William Prescott, a lineal descendant

of a Patriot officer who fought at Bunker Hill, wrote to Bancroft: "One thing . . . for which you will be damned, I beg you to understand, (at least in this world) . . . is, if you do not render ample justice to the memory of my grandfather . . . who has had half his honors filched from him by gulls of historians whose eyes have been fascinated by the apparition of . . . [General] Warren, because he had the good luck of being shot on the battle field." William H. Prescott to George Bancroft, 16 March 1833, George Bancroft Papers.

52. Robert I. N. Phelps Stokes, *The Iconography of Manhattan Island*, 4 vols. (1915–28; reprint, New York: Arno Press, 1967), 1:386, 405.

53. Note in Pintard's own hand, dated 17 August 1821, on the reverse of an invitation from the British consul to John Pintard, John Pintard Papers, box 11, Misc. Mss., 182–44, folder 4, New-York Historical Society. On Pintard reinterrring family members' remains in "about 1830," see James Grant Wilson, *John Pintard, Founder of the New-York Historical Society: An Address Delivered before the New-York Historical Society [on] December 3, 1901* (New York: New-York Historical Society, 1902), 12.

54. "Reminiscences of the Early Life of John Pintard, either copied from his own manuscript or probably dictated to his daughter Louise at New York City about 1841," mss., John Pintard Papers, box 3, New-York Historical Society, 39–40.

55. "Reminiscences of the Early Life of John Pintard," 46–51.

56. John Pintard, Commonplace Book, mss., Pintard Papers, box 1, New-York Historical Society.

57. Circular from the New-York Historical Society to its members, 1828, Official Papers: 1805–46, Archives, New-York Historical Society.

58. Minutes of the New[-]York Historical Society, Volume 1, 1804–37 (bound mss.), Archives, New-York Historical Society; *Dictionary of American Biography* (1934), s.v. "Montgomery, Richard."

59. New-York Historical Society Circular, 11 March 1817, 1812–33 Corresponding Secretary Letterbook, Massachusetts Historical Society Archives.

60. George R. Stewart, *Names on the Land: A Historical Account of Place-Naming in the United States*, rev. ed. (Boston: Houghton Mifflin, 1958), 203.

61. Egbert Benson, *Memoir Read before the Historical Society of the State of New-York, 31st December 1816* (New York: William A. Mercein, 1817), 42.

62. [Joseph A. Scoville], *Biographical Sketch of John Pintard* ([New York?]: n.p., [c. 1863]), 24. The copy cited is in the print collections of the New-York Historical Society.

63. DeWitt Clinton, "A Discourse Delivered before the New-York Historical Society, at Their Anniversary Meeting, 6 December, 1811," in *Collections of the New-York Historical Society for the Year 1814* (New York: C. Van Winkle and Wiley, 1814), 39.

64. Samuel Mitchill, "A Discourse Delivered before the New-York Historical Society, at Their Anniversary Meeting, 6th December 1813: A Concise and Comprehensive Account of the Writings Which Illustrate the Botanical History of North and South America," in *Collections of the New-York Historical Society for the Year 1814*, 215. On the Hudson River School and patriotic American landscape painting of the era generally, see especially Angela L. Miller, *The Empire of the Eye: Landscape Representation and American Cultural Politics, 1825–1875* (Ithaca, NY: Cornell University Press, 1993).

65. For a useful chronological, if not especially analytical, history of the Historical Society of Pennsylvania, see Susan Stitt, "Pennsylvania," in *Historical Consciousness in the Early Republic: The Origins of State Historical Societies, Museums, and Collections, 1791–1861*, ed. H. G. Jones (Chapel Hill: North Caroliniana Society, 1995), 59–78. For evidence of the Historical Society of Pennsylvania juxtaposing artifacts of both American natural and civil history see "Donations for the Cabinet," *Transactions of the American Philosophical Society, Held at Philadelphia, for Promoting Useful Knowledge*, new ser., 32 (1818): 452–53.

66. Hampton L. Carson, *A History of the Historical Society of Pennsylvania*, 2 vols. (Philadelphia: Historical Society of Pennsylvania, 1940), 1:45.

67. Annals of Philadelphia, mss., John Fanning Watson Collection, Historical Society of Pennsylvania, 466. For an example of another badge retained as a memento of Lafayette's 1824 visit to Philadelphia see "Badge worn . . . in honor of Lafayette," 28 September 1824, Robert Hare Papers, American Philosophical Society.

68. Benjamin H. Coates, "Sketch of the Historical Society," *Memoirs of the Historical Society of Pennsylvania* (1826; reprint ed., Philadelphia: J. B. Lippincott, 1864), 1:x; cf. Susan Stitt, "Pennsylvania," 64.

69. *Memoirs of the Historical Society of Pennsylvania* (Philadelphia: M. Carty and David, 1826), 1:5, 17. The reader will recall that Watson's *Annals*, and his related invocations of the "local memory" tradition, in the context of its reification in Philadelphia by the likes of phrenologists, are detailed in chapter 1.

70. Annals of Philadelphia, mss., John Fanning Watson Collection.

71. Roberts Vaux to John Fanning Watson, 28 September 1824, mss., Letters and Communications to John Fanning Watson, 1823–29, Historical

Society of Pennsylvania; Joseph Delaplaine to Roberts Vaux, 5 March 1823, Vaux Papers, Pennsylvania Historical Society.

72. Roberts Vaux to John Fanning Watson, 22 July 1824, mss., Letters and Communications to John Fanning Watson, 1823–29, Historical Society of Pennsylvania.

73. Roberts Vaux to John Fanning Watson, 16 September 1824, mss., Letters and Communications to John Fanning Watson, 1823–29, Historical Society of Pennsylvania.

74. Roberts Vaux to John Fanning Watson, 26 July 1825, mss., Letters and Communications to John Fanning Watson, 1823–29, Historical Society of Pennsylvania.

75. John Fanning Watson, "Memorials of Country Towns and Places in Pennsylvania As Drawn Up by John F. Watson and Presented to the Historical Society of Pennsylvania. Read at a Meeting of the Council, Feb. 17, 1830," *Memoirs of the Historical Society of Pennsylvania*, 2, pt. 3 (Philadelphia: E. Littell, 1830), 182–83.

76. John Fanning Watson, "Memorials of Country Towns and Places in Pennsylvania," 182.

77. Deborah Norris Logan Diary, 15 February 1815, mss., Historical Society of Pennsylvania.

78. John F. Watson, *Annals of Philadelphia and Pennsylvania*, 2 vols., rev. ed. (Philadelphia: Elijah Thomas, 1857), 1:573.

79. John Fanning Watson to Abiel Holmes, Corresponding Secretary of the Massachusetts Historical Society, 13 February 1832, 1821–36 Corresponding Secretary Letterbook, Archives, Massachusetts Historical Society.

80. *Proceedings of the Massachusetts Historical Society, June 1861* (Boston: Massachusetts Historical Society, 1861), 209.

81. St. George Tucker to Jeremy Belknap, 9 August 1796, as printed in *MHS Coll.*, 5th ser., 3 (1882): 424.

82. George Tucker, remarks as redacted in William M. E. Rachal, ed., "Early Records of the Virginia Historical Society, 1831–33," *Virginia Magazine of History and Biography* 1, no. 67 (January 1959): 7.

83. "Address to the Public on the Views of the Society, October 1832," as reprinted in Rachal, ed., "Early Records of the Virginia Historical Society, 1831–33," 13.

84. On links between Virginia's decline and the founding of the society see especially Charles F. Bryan Jr., "Virginia," in *Historical Consciousness in the Early Republic*, ed. Jones, 81–83.

85. Francis Walker Gilmer to Peachy Gilmer, 22 February 1821 and 30 May 1822, Papers of Peachy Gilmer, Virginia Historical Society, Richmond.

86. George Tucker, *The Valley of the Shenandoah; or, Memoir of the Graysons,* 2 vols. (1824; facsimile ed., Chapel Hill: University of North Carolina Press, 1970), 1:1, 2:31.

87. [James Ewell Heath], *Edgehill; or, The Family of Fitzroyals,* 2 vols. (Richmond: T. W. White, 1828).

88. Thomas R. Gray, ed., *The Confessions of Nat Turner* (Richmond: T. W. White, 1832), 10.

89. Charles Henry Ambler, *The Life and Diary of John Floyd, Governor of Virginia* (Richmond: Richmond Press, 1918), 158.

90. Scot French, *The Rebellious Slave: Nat Turner in American Memory* (New York: Houghton, Mifflin, 2004), 2; see also 58–59.

91. Quoted in Erik S. Root, *Sons of the Fathers: The Virginia Slavery Debates of 1831–1832* (Lanham, MD: Lexington Books, 2010), 45–46.

92. Root, *Sons of the Fathers,* 56.

93. Root, *Sons of the Fathers,* 162.

94. Thomas R. Dew, *Review of the Debate in the Virginia Legislature of 1831 and 1832* (Richmond: T. W. White, 1832), 104.

95. See, e.g., C. L. Knapp, "Where Are Our Liberties?" *The Liberator* (Boston, MA), 13 February 1836, 26.

96. Robert Sutcliff, *Travels in Some Parts of North America, in the Years 1804, 1805, & 1806* (London: C. Peacock, 1811), 50.

97. "Remains of Washington," *Phoenix Gazette* (Alexandria, VA), 21 February 1832, 2.

98. "Washington's Remains," House of Representatives, 13 February 1832, in *Debates in Congress,* vol. 8, pt. 2, *Gales and Seaton's Register* (Washington, DC, 1832), 1785, 1799–1800.

99. Thomas W. Gilmer, "An Address Delivered before the Virginia Historical and Philosophical Society," *Southern Literary Messenger* 3 (February 1837): 101.

100. *Western Monthly Magazine and Literary Journal* 3 (November 1834): 610.

101. Charles F. Bryan Jr., "Virginia," in *Historical Consciousness in the Early Republic,* ed. Jones, 85.

102. *Daily Richmond Whig and Public Advertiser,* 24 January 1833, 2.

3. THE FREEDMAN

1. "Hamet Ackman [*sic*] Subscription List," 11 June 1827, Alden Partridge Records, Financial Records Box 10, June 1827 file, Norwich University Archives, Kreitzberg Library, Northfield, VT. On the geographic origins of cadets at the academy in the period see *Catalogue of the Officers and Cadets, Together with the Prospectus and Internal Regulations of the*

American Literary, Scientific, and Military Academy, at Middletown, Connecticut (Middletown, CT: Starr and Niles, 1826), 27. Susan Cifaldi, music librarian and assistant archivist for the Museum of Fife and Drum in Ivoryton, Connecticut, has suggested that the specific timing of the cadets' donation might have been prompted by sympathy for Achmet following the death of Achmet's wife—which according to source material that Cifaldi has consulted, reportedly occurred in late April of 1827. See Susan Cifaldi, "Hamet Achmet of Middletown, Connecticut: The Drummer Who Waited on Washington," www.moylan.info/bks/achmet/page1.html. I wish to acknowledge Cifaldi's generous assistance in procuring sources pertaining to Hamet Achmet.

2. Revealing and accounting for the physicalist and bodily turn in U.S. memory culture is the theme of chapter 1. For an exploration of the significance of bodies in collective American memory of the Civil War see Lisa Marie Herschbach, "Fragmentation and Reunion: Medicine, Memory, and Body in the American Civil War" (Ph.D. diss., Harvard University, 1997). No such detailed work has been done on bodies and memory of the Revolution. Though not as a subject of significant analysis, there is suggestive recognition of the significance of persistent war wounds as cues to remember the Revolution throughout John Resch's book, *Suffering Soldiers: Revolutionary War Veterans, Moral Sentiment, and Political Culture in the Early Republic* (Amherst: University of Massachusetts Press, 1999).

3. W. H. Prescott to George Bancroft, 17 June 1835, George Bancroft Papers, Massachusetts Historical Society.

4. The 1840 U.S. Census counted 17 slaves in Connecticut and 8,105 free Blacks. Bernard C. Steiner, *History of Slavery in Connecticut,* Johns Hopkins University Studies in Historical and Political Science, 11th ser., 9–10 (Baltimore: Johns Hopkins University Press, 1893), 84. On the tendency among northerners in the period to "forget" their region's historical involvement with slavery, and to persecute free Blacks in their midst, see generally Joanne Pope Melish, *Disowning Slavery: Gradual Emancipation and "Race" in New England, 1780–1860* (Ithaca, NY: Cornell University Press, 1998).

5. Cf. Patricia Bradley, *Slavery, Propaganda and the American Revolution* (Jackson: University Press of Mississippi, 1998), 60–61; Charles Patrick Neimeyer, *America Goes to War: A Social History of the Continental Army* (New York: New York University Press, 1996), 83. With the post–Revolutionary War patriotic memory culture that it explicates, this chapter concentrates on memory of Black Patriots who fought in

that conflict; on African Americans who fought as Loyalists, see especially Alan Gilbert, *Black Patriots and Loyalists: Fighting for Emancipation in the War for Independence* (Chicago: University of Chicago Press, 2012).

6. Parker Pillsbury to William C. Nell, 24 April 1851, printed in William C. Nell, *Services of Colored Americans in the Wars of 1776 and 1812* (Boston: Robert F. Wallcutt, 1852), 17; see also Sidney Kaplan and Emma Nogrady Kaplan, *The Black Presence in the Era of the American Revolution* (Amherst: University of Massachusetts Press, 1989), 56.

7. William Anderson, quoted in William H. Harris, *The Battle of Groton Heights*, rev. and enlarged by Charles Allyn (New London, CT: Charles Allyn, 1882), 285.

8. "A Veteran of the Revolution," *Atkinson's Saturday Evening Post* 15 (8 October 1836): 2. According to an editorial note, the item was reprinted from the *New York Journal*.

9. "Hammet Achmet," *New York Observer*, 27 July 1893, clippings file, Middlesex County [CT] Historical Society; William C. Nell, *The Colored Patriots of the American Revolution, With Sketches of Several Distinguished Colored Persons: To Which Is Added a Brief Survey of the Condition and Prospects of Colored Americans* (Boston: Robert G. Wallcutt, 1855), 134, "Hammet Achmet," n.d., clippings file, Middlesex County [CT] Historical Society (hereafter MCHS); "Gen[.] George Washington's Hair Given to Mrs. S. A. Hart in 1840 by his servant—Hamet Achmet," artifact of hair in a gold-colored frame, with n.d. newspaper clipping on the reverse, collections of the MCHS; Emilie T. Stedman, *Hammet Achmet: A Servant of George Washington*, 2d ed. (Middletown, CT: n.p., [1900]). The extant sources do not agree on the timeline, nor on some of the details, of Achmet's history prior to his time in Middletown from the 1820s. See also, e.g.: "Washington's Servant," *Natchez Weekly Courier* (Natchez, Mississippi), 13 September 1839, 3; "Wm. Larned Overseer Complaint against Certain Blacks Oct 9th, 1806," *Providence Town Papers*, ser. 3, vol. 60, MSS 214, sg. 1, no. 008728; cf. Gabriel Loiacono, "Poor Laws and the Construction of Race in Early Republican Providence, Rhode Island," *Journal of Policy History* 25, no. 2 (2013): 264–87; Gabriel Loiacono, "William Larned, Overseer of the Poor: Power and Precariousness in the Early Republic," *New England Quarterly* 88, no. 2 (2015): 223–51.

10. "Hammet Achmet," *New York Observer*, 27 July 1893.

11. "Hammet Achmet," *New York Observer*, 27 July 1893. The sword in question is referenced as well in Peter Snooks to the editors of *American*

Union (Concord, NH), 31 June 1851, as printed in "Letter from New Hampshire," *American Union* (Boston, MA), 5 July 1851, 2. Snooks reports that it is in the cabinet of curiosities of William Prescott, 2nd, that it was purportedly worn by George Washington at his wedding, and given to Achmet by Bushrod Washington, among other particulars. By the terms of his "Last Will and Testament," William Prescott 2nd, at his death in 1875, left the sword to his son, William Prescott, 3rd., Will of William Prescott, Probate Records, Wills, vol. 56 (1875–1880), 96, *New Hampshire, U.S., Wills and Probate Records, 1643–1982*, [Ancestry.com online database], Ancestry.com Operations, https://www.ancestrylibrary.com/imageviewer/collections/8996/images/007133287_00365?usePUB=true&_phsrc=Eol745&_phstart=successSource&usePUBJs=true&pId=218253, accessed 19 February 202.

12. Nell, *The Colored Patriots of the American Revolution*, 134.
13. Hamet Achmet, Pension Application S3810, United States, National Archives and Record Administration, Revolutionary War Pension Application and Bounty Land Warrant Files, microfilm copy, David Library of the American Revolution.
14. Hamet Achmet, Pension Application S3810.
15. Richard Alsop, *A Poem Sacred to the Memory of George Washington, Late President of the United States, and Commander in Chief of the Armed Forces of the United States, Adapted to the 22d of Feb. 1800* (Hartford, CT: Printed by Hudson and Goodwin, 1800), 5.
16. *Journal of a Tour, of a Detachment of Cadets: From the A.L.S. & M. Academy, Middletown, to the City of Washington, in December 1826* (Middletown, CT: W. D. Starr, 1827), 89–91.
17. Henry Luce III Center for the Study of American Culture, *Perspectives on the Collections of the New-York Historical Society* (New York: New-York Historical Society, 2000), 120.
18. "The Nation's Guest," *Niles' Weekly Register*, 16 October 1824, 103.
19. "The Nation's Guest," 103; [George Washington Parke Custis], *Oration by Mr. Custis of Arlington; with an Account of the Funeral Solemnities in Honor of the Lamented Gen. James M. Lingan* (Washington City, 1812), 7, 34.
20. On Silliman's evangelical religious beliefs, see George Park Fisher, *Life of Benjamin Silliman, M.D., LL.D., Late Professor of Chemistry, Mineralogy, and Geology in Yale College: Chiefly from His Manuscript Reminiscences, Diaries, and Correspondence*, 2 vols. in 1 (New York: Charles Scribner, 1866), 1:78–86. For a standard Protestant criticism of Catholicism for venerating relics see, e.g., "Saints—Relics—Images," *Baltimore Literary and Religious Magazine* [2], no. 2 (February 1837): 86–89.

21. "La Fayette's Progress," *Saturday Evening Post* 3 (28 August 1824): 2.
22. Thus, he supplied a relic seeker with "the flannel morning gown which was worn by my uncle," George Washington, "to the time of his death," admitting, "I have constantly used it since, so that it is not only old but perhaps tattered," but allowing, that for its service as "a memento, however, these defects will not, I am sure, be considered as objections." Bushrod Washington to Captain [illegible] Bliss, 24 December 1811, Sol Feinstone Collection, no. 1513, David Library of the American Revolution, on deposit at the American Philosophical Society.
23. Washington heir Nelly Custis understood the iconographic value of a waistcoat worn by General Washington, and gave "a scrap of one of George Washington's waistcoats . . . to Harriet Huntres [?] in 1820," inscription on paper found with fragment of George Washington's waistcoat, Henry Luce III Center for the Study of American Culture, item number Z. 1848, New-York Historical Society.
24. Unidentified aide of General Washington to Miss Kitty [Livingston], Valley Forge, 18 March 1778, film 228, reel 1, Washington Family Papers, 1674–1853; Mount Vernon Ladies' Association of the Union, microfilm copy, David Library of the American Revolution.
25. George Washington to Major Andrew Billings, 17 June 1783, digitized online version of George Washington, *The Writings of George Washington from the Original Manuscript Sources*, 39 vols, ed. John Clement Fitzpatrick (Washington, DC: U.S. Government Printing Office, 1931–44), "George Washington Resources at the University of Virginia Library," http://etext.lib.virginia.edu/washington/, accessed 3 June 2003. Washington was not the only Founder to leave hair to admirers and loved ones. For example, in 1812, Abigail Adams sent intertwined locks of her own and her husband's hair to Mercy Otis Warren. One of Warren's friends later wrote of that historian and sister of proto-Revolutionary James Otis: "Her little hands, which are still fair and almost transparent, were adorned with rings, chiefly mourning ones; but one which she has lately received from the former President Adams, with his and his wife's hair, she seems to value most highly." Abigail Smith Adams to Mercy Otis Warren, 30 December 1812, in *Correspondence between John Adams and Mercy Warren*, ed. Charles Francis Adams (Boston: Massachusetts Historical Society, 1878), 195, Alexander Street Press, "North American Women's Letters and Diaries: Colonial to 1950," http://alexanderstreet2.com/NWLDlive/index .html, accessed 27 May 2003; Mercy Otis Warren to Abigail Adams, 26 January 1813, in *Correspondence between Adams and Warren*, 503;

Sarah Cary to Henry Cary, 10 October 1814, in *The Cary Letters*, ed. Caroline G. Curtis (Cambridge, MA: Riverside Press, 1891), 335, Alexander Street Press, "North American Women's Letters," accessed 27 May 2003.

26. Tobias Lear, Diary, 17 December 1799, photocopy, Historical Society of Pennsylvania. The relic became a precious heirloom among Lear's descendants, displayed along with accompanying poetry about the hair written by Tobias Lear's mother. "Flotsam," *Historical Magazine, and Notes and Queries Concerning the Antiquities, History, and Biography of America* 3, no. 2 (February 1874): 115.

27. Timothy Bigelow, *An Eulogy on the Life, Character and Services of Brother George Washington, Deceased—Pronounced before the Fraternity of Free and Accepted Masons, by Request of the Grand Lodge, at the Old South Meeting House, Boston, on Tuesday, February 11, 1800. Being the Day Set Apart by Them to Pay Funeral Honors to Their Deceased Brother. By Brother Timothy Bigelow, to Which Are Added, Two Addresses to the Deceased, When President of the United States, and His ANSWERS; Together with—The Letters of Condolence of the Grand Lodge to Mrs. Washington, and Her Answer* (Boston: I. Thomas and E. T. Andrews, [1800]), 26.

28. "Mrs. Lewis" to Mrs. James Gibson, 24 November 1824, film 228, reel 3, Washington Family Papers, 1674–1853.

29. "Jackson and Lafayette," newspaper clipping in John Newhall, Commonplace Book and Diary, 1825, Massachusetts Historical Society.

30. *Middlesex Gazette* (Middletown, CT), 4 October 1826.

31. Lock of George Washington's Hair, Object Inventory #150, Library Company of Philadelphia.

32. "Association," *The Polyanthos* 4 (1807): 88–89.

33. "Animal Magnetism," *American Ladies' Magazine* 12 (December 1835): 693.

34. On Peter A. Browne's beliefs about the scientific value of his hair collection see Kettall [illegible] to Peter A. Browne, 2 February 1852, P. A. Browne's Collection of Pile, Academy of Natural Sciences of Philadelphia; cf. "On Genius As Dependent on the Color of the Human Hair," *Atkinson's Casket* (January 1829): 20; "Human Hair," *The Observer* (6 January 1811): 50; "The Hair," *Journal of Health* 1 (14 April 1830): 235–37, especially the claim that hair is a racial marker, inasmuch as the "hue of the hair corresponds, pretty uniformly, with the colour of the skin" (236); "On the Human Hair," *Family Magazine* 3 (1835–36): 313–14, especially the drawing on p. 314 of hair as seen through a microscope. For a satire on popular belief in physiognomy in general, and of the physiognomic

significance of hair, see E.M.I., "Elements of Physiognomy," *Boston Weekly Magazine* 3 (5 December 1840): 9. For a brief introduction to Browne's collection that includes numerous full-page color photographs of hair samples, see Robert McCracken Peck, *Specimens of Hair: The Curious Collection of Peter A. Browne* (New York: Blast Books, 2018).

35. P. A. Browne, *The Classification of Mankind by the Hair and Wool of Their Heads, With an Answer to Dr. Pritchard's Assertion, That 'The Covering of the Head of the Negro Is Hair, Properly So Termed, and Not Wool,' Read before the Ethnological Society, Nov. 3, 1849* (Philadelphia: A. Hart, 1850), 4, 20.

36. Elizabeth Parke Custis to Gideon Snow, 18 October 1828 [date of uncertain legibility], film 228, reel 3, Washington Family Papers, 1674–1853; Mount Vernon Ladies' Association of the Union, microfilm copy, David Library of the American Revolution.

37. "Hammet Achmet," *New York Observer,* 27 July 1893.

38. Perry Miller, "The Garden of Eden and the Deacon's Meadow," reprinted in Byron Dobell, comp., *A Sense of History: The Best Writing from the Pages of American Heritage* (Boston: Houghton Mifflin, 1985), 114.

39. Judges 13–16.

40. "Hammet Achmet," *New York Observer,* 27 July 1893.

41. Cf. *Rawlings v. Boston* 3 H. & McH. 139 (1793, Md.); *Renney v. Mayfield,* 5 Tenn. 165 (1817); *Vaughan v. Phebe,* 8 Tenn. 5 (1827); *Gregory v. Baugh,* 29 Va. 665 (1831); *Miller v. Denman,* 16 Tenn. 233 (1835); *Thomas v. Beckman,* 40 Ky. 29 (1840); *Watkins v. Carlton,* 37 Va. 560 (1840). All cases cited as per LexisNexis Uni, https://www.lexisnexis.com.

42. James Otis, as excerpted in Bernard Bailyn, ed., *Pamphlets of the American Revolution, 1750–1765,* vol. 1, *1750–1765* (Cambridge, MA: Belknap Press of Harvard University Press, 1965), 439–40.

43. *Hudgins v. Wrights,* 11 Va. 1 (Hen. and M.), 139–41 (1806). Ariela Gross has pointed out that, in rendering his opinion in *Hudgins,* Tucker expressed greater confidence in reading race from bodies than did Judge Roane who, in his own seriatim opinion in the case, expressed doubt that such physical markers as hair were always such legible evidences of race as Tucker's opinion seemed to suppose. See Ariela J. Gross, "Litigating Whiteness: Trials of Race Determination in the Nineteenth-Century South," *Yale Law Journal* 108 (October 1998): 129–30. For an extended examination of the *Hudgins* case in comparison to the earlier, celebrated "Quock Walker Cases" in Massachusetts, see Keith Beutler, "'Let Justice Be Done Though the Heavens Fall!': Emancipation Cases

in the Early American Republic" (M.A. thesis, University of Tennessee, Knoxville, 1999).

44. *Hudgins v. Wrights,* 11 Va. 1 (Hen. and M.), 141.
45. Achmet's self-portrait adorns a request for release of his pension funds, and is in the collection of the Middlesex County [CT] Historical Society.
46. Shane White and Graham White, "Slave Hair and African American Culture in the Eighteenth and Nineteenth Centuries," *Journal of Southern History* 61 (February 1995): 45–76.
47. Henry Bibbs, *Narrative of the Life and Adventures of Henry Bibb, an American Slave, Written by Himself* (New York: Published by the Author, 1849), 27, electronic edition, University of North Carolina at Chapel Hill, "Documenting the American South," 2000, http://docsouth.unc.edu/neh/bibb/menu.html, accessed 16 February 2004.
48. "Hamet Achmet," *New York Observer,* 27 July 1893.
49. Hamet Achmet, Pension Application S3810.
50. For a helpful overview of Sutphen's story, see William Schleicher and Susan Winter, "Patriot and Slave: The Samuel Sutphen Story," *New Jersey Heritage Magazine* 1, no. 1 (Winter 2002): 30–43; Samuel Sutphen Pension Application R10321, United States, National Archives and Record Administration, Revolutionary War Pension Application and Bounty Land Warrant Files, microfilm copy, David Library of the American Revolution.
51. Samuel Sutphen Pension Application R10321.
52. Samuel Sutphen Pension Application R10321.
53. Samuel Sutphen Pension Application R10321.
54. Samuel Sutphen Pension Application R10321.
55. Charles Caldwell, quoted in William Stanton, *The Leopard's Spots: Scientific Attitudes toward Race in America, 1815–59* (Chicago: University of Chicago Press, 1960), 6; [Benjamin Smith Barton], "Account of Henry Moss, a White Negro," *Philadelphia Medical and Physical Journal* 2 (1806): 3; J.W., "Remarkable Change of an African's Complexion," *Wonderful Magazine and Extraordinary Museum* 1 (1808): 61; Review of *The Variety of Complexion and Figure in the Human Species,* by Samuel Stanhope Smith, *The Port-Folio* 4, no. 3 (September 1814): 252–71; B[enjamin] Rush, "Reasons for Ascribing the Colour of Negroes to Leprosy," *Monthly Magazine and American Review* 2, no. 4 (April 1800): 298–301; Samuel Stanhope Smith, *An Essay on the Causes of the Variety of Complexion and Figure in the Human Species,* ed. Winthrop D. Jordan (1787, rev. 1810; reprint, Cambridge, MA: Harvard University Press,

1965), 52, 58–59, 174; John Wood Sweet, *Bodies Politic: Negotiating Race in the American North, 1730–1830* (Baltimore: Johns Hopkins University Press, 2003), 271–86. See also Ronald T. Takaki, *Iron Cages: Race and Culture in Nineteenth-Century America* (New York: Alfred A. Knopf, 1979), 31–33. On the possible impact of the Moss affair on American literature in the period see Leland S. Person, "Poe's Philosophy of Amalgamation: Reading Racism in the Tales," in *Romancing the Shadow: Poe and Race,* ed. J. Gerald Kennedy and Lillian Weissberg (Oxford: Oxford University Press, 2001), 209–10; Jared Gardner, *Master Plots: Race and the Founding of an American Literature, 1787–1845* (Baltimore: Johns Hopkins University Press, 1998), 72.

56. Solomon Northup, *Twelve Years a Slave: Narrative of the Life of Solomon Northup, a Citizen of New-York Kidnapped in Washington City in 1841, and Rescued in1853 from a Cotton Plantation Near the Red River, in Louisiana* (Auburn, NY, 1853), 79–80.

57. Samuel Sutphen Pension Application R10321.

58. Andrew Ferguson Pension Application S32243, Revolutionary War Pension Application and Bounty Land Warrant Files, Microfilm copy, David Library of the American Revolution.

59. Sipeo/Sip Watson, Widow's Pension Application, 18240, Revolutionary War Pension Application and Bounty Land Warrant Files, microfilm copy, David Library of the American Revolution.

60. "The President's Tour," *Niles' Weekly Register* (Baltimore), 19 July 1817, 327; cf. Daniel Webster's boast as speaker a political dinner in Maine in 1835 that a "soldier of the revolution who sits near me, on being introduced to me, grasped me by the hand and conjured me to stand fast by my country." "The Past," *Niles' Weekly Register* (Baltimore), 17 October 1835, 106. On Monroe's visit to Fort Groton, and his interaction with Park and Avery, see *A Narrative of a Tour of Observation Made during the Summer of 1817, by James Monroe, President of the United States, Through the North-Eastern and North-Western Departments of the Union: With a View to the Examination of Their Several Military Defences* (Philadelphia: S. A. Mitchell and H. Ames, 1818), 84. There is evidence that in the early nineteenth century another minority veteran of sorts, celebrated female Revolutionary War soldier Deborah Sampson, displayed her scars to buttress her public accounts of her service in the Revolution, and—also consistent with physicalist understandings of memory—passed on material relics evocative of herself to her surviving relatives. See Alfred F. Young, *Masquerade: The Life and Times of Deborah Sampson, Continental Soldier* (New York: Alfred A. Knopf, 2004), 17, 193, and 288.

61. Sipeo/Sip Watson, Widow's Pension Application, 18240.

62. Quork Martrick, Pension Application S11039, Revolutionary War Pension Application and Bounty Land Warrant Files, National Archives and Records Administrations, Microfilm copy, David Library of the American Revolution.

63. Quork Martrick, Pension Application S11039.

64. For a useful anthology examining the long history of orality in African and African American cultures see Ronald B. Jackson II and Elaine B. Richardson, eds., *Understanding African American Rhetoric: Classical Origins to Contemporary Innovations* (New York: Routledge, 2003). For useful reflections on the transplantation of African oral tradition to the New World in the context of the Caribbean see Lucie Pradel, *African Beliefs in the New World: Popular Literary Traditions of the Caribbean*, trans. Catherine Bernard (Trenton, NJ: Africa World Press, 1998), 127–237.

65. Walter J. Ong, *Orality and Literacy: The Technologizing of the Word* (New York: Methuen, 1988), 67. On the concern within Yoruba oral tradition to judge and indicate the epistemic veracity of sources of the information being conveyed, see especially Barry Hallen, "Yoruba Moral Epistemology," in *A Companion to African Philosophy*, ed. Kwasi Wiredu (Malden, MA: Blackwell, 2004), esp. 298–303.

66. Cf. Ong, *Orality and Literacy*, 67–68; Alistair Thomson, "Fifty Years On: An International Perspective on Oral History," *Journal of American History* 85 (September 1998): 593. Note too Lee M. Brown's instructive generalization about how traditional African ontologies differ from western ontological outlooks where personal identity is concerned. In Brown's words, "the western concept of the person is essentially dualistic, while the traditional African concept of person is not. Within western thought, persons can be differentiated as physical or nonphysical entities." Such differentiation from a traditional African perspective is impossible. "In both Akan and Yoruba, a human that is a person is" an undifferentiated "composite of body and spirit (mind), and without either, there is no corresponding person." Lee M. Brown, "Understanding and Ontology in Traditional African Thought," in *African Philosophy: New and Traditional Perspectives*, ed. Lee M. Brown (Oxford: Oxford University Press, 2004), 163.

67. *Boston Journal*, 17 August 1859, clipping as enclosed in Robert Babcok, Pension Application R343, Revolutionary War Pension Application and Bounty Land Warrant Files, National Archives and Records Administrations, microfilm copy, David Library of the American Revolution.

68. Cf. Ong, *Orality and Literacy*, 32.

69. "Hammet Achmet," *New York Observer,* 27 July 1893. As John W. Blassingame once noted, "because of his traditional fascination with the written word, the American historian, when confronted with . . . oral lore" often lacks applicable "methodological tools." John W. Blassingame, *Slave Testimony: Two Centuries of Letters, Speeches, Interviews, and Autobiographies* (Baton Rouge: Louisiana State University Press, 1977), xliii.

70. "Hammet Achmet," *New York Observer,* 27 July 1893.

71. Quork Martrick, Pension Application S11039.

72. Charles Barnett/Barny, Pension Application, S8048, United States, National Archives and Record Administration, Revolutionary War Pension Application and Bounty Land Warrant Files, microfilm copy, David Library of the American Revolution.

73. Primus Babcock, Pension Application, S37.698, United States, National Archives and Record Administration, Revolutionary War Pension Application and Bounty Land Warrant Files, microfilm copy, David Library of the American Revolution.

74. Calvin Goddard, as quoted in Nell, *Services of Colored Americans,* 15.

75. Unidentified newspaper clipping in Oliver Cromwell, Pension Application, S34.613, United States, National Archives and Record Administration, Revolutionary War Pension Application and Bounty Land Warrant Files, microfilm copy, David Library of the American Revolution.

76. Elizabeth Parke Custis to Gideon Snow, 18 October 1828 [date of uncertain legibility], film 228, reel 3, Washington Family Papers, 1674–1853; Mount Vernon Ladies' Association of the Union, microfilm copy, David Library of the American Revolution; Elisabeth Parke Custis to John Lutz, 14 April 1828, Lutz Papers, Historical Society of Pennsylvania. For further illustrations of contemporaneous interest in autographs as harbingers of character see: "The Autograph Hunter," *New-York Mirror: A Weekly Gazette of Literature and the Fine Arts* 13, no. 50 (11 June 1836): 395; "A Rare Autograph," *Southern Rose* 7, no. 19 (11 May 1839): 289; "Autography: Number Two," *Southern Literary Journal and Magazine of Arts* 3, no. 6 (June 1838): 445, which compares autography and phrenology; for specific reference to Washington's autograph in the context of considering veneration of relics, including hair relics, see William E. Burton, "A Rummage in My Old Bureau," *Burton's Gentleman's Magazine and American Monthly Review* 5, no. 3 (September 1839): 156. Exemplifying interest in the autographs of the Founders generally see "Another Day among the Autographs," *Southern Rose* 5, no. 23 (8 July 1837): 177–78.

77. William Coff, Pension Application, S39.347, United States, National Archives and Record Administration, Revolutionary War Pension Application and Bounty Land Warrant Files, microfilm copy, David Library of the American Revolution.

78. Primus Hall, Pension Application, W751, United States, National Archives and Record Administration, Revolutionary War Pension Application and Bounty Land Warrant Files, microfilm copy, David Library of the American Revolution.

79. Nell, *Services of Colored Americans*, 12.

80. Paul Jennings, *A Colored Man's Reminiscences of James Madison* (Brooklyn, NY: George C. Beadle, 1865), 20.

81. Evidences demonstrate beyond a reasonable doubt—and with a degree of certitude uncommon in historical analysis—that Jefferson did impregnate Hemings, and was, in fact, probably the father of *each of* her children. For analysis and compilation of the relevant evidence, see Annette Gordon-Reed, *Thomas Jefferson and Sally Hemings: An American Controversy* (Charlottesville: University Press of Virginia, 1997); and Thomas Jefferson Memorial Foundation, *Thomas Jefferson and Sally Hemings* (Charlottesville: Thomas Jefferson Memorial Foundation, 2000). On the statistical correlation between Jefferson's visits to Monticello and the likely dates of conception of Sally Hemings's children see Fraser D. Neiman, "Coincidence or Causal Connection? The Relationship between Thomas Jefferson's Visits to Monticello and Sally Hemings's Conceptions," *William and Mary Quarterly*, 3rd ser., 57 (January 2000): 198–210. For evidence that Jefferson distanced himself emotionally from his slave children see the published 1873 interview with Madison Hemings, "Life among the Lowly, No. 1," *Pike County [Ohio] Republican*, 13 March 1873, as reprinted in Gordon-Reed, *Thomas Jefferson and Sally Hemings*, 247. For an overview of the evidence for the Hemings-Jefferson sexual relationship, and of its implications for scholarship bearing on Jefferson, see Jan Ellen Lewis and Peter S. Onuf, eds., *Sally Hemings and Thomas Jefferson: History, Memory, and Civic Culture* (Charlottesville: University Press of Virginia, 1999). Madison Hemings recalled in his 1873 interview, "I learned to read by inducing the white children to teach me the letters." Gordon-Reed, *Thomas Jefferson and Sally Hemings*, 247.

82. Gordon-Reed, *Thomas Jefferson and Sally Hemings*, 247.

83. Gordon-Reed, *Thomas Jefferson and Sally Hemings*, 247.

84. See, e.g., Lucia Stanton and Dianne Swann-Wright, *Getting Word: The Monticello African-American Oral History Project* (Charlottesville: Thomas

Jefferson Foundation, 2002); Lucia Stanton, *Slavery at Monticello* (Charlottesville: Thomas Jefferson Memorial Foundation, 1996); Lucia Stanton, *Free Some Day: The African-American Families of Monticello* (Charlottesville: Thomas Jefferson Foundation, 2000).

85. Stanton, *Free Some Day,* 102–3; Lucia Stanton and Dianne Swann-Wright, "Bonds of Memory: Identity and the Hemings Family," in *Sally Hemings and Thomas Jefferson,* ed. Lewis and Onuf, 176.

86. On national reaction to the deaths of Jefferson and Adams see especially Andrew Burstein, *America's Jubilee* (New York: Alfred A. Knopf, 2001).

87. Stanton, *Slavery at Monticello,* 10–11.

88. Isaac Jefferson, "Memoirs of a Monticello Slave: The Reminiscences of Isaac Jefferson about Life at Monticello recorded by Charles Campbell," mss., ca. 1847, Alderman Library, Special Collections, University of Virginia, 9, 12, and 16.

89. One can infer, too, that he thought that Washington was handsomer than Thomas Jefferson, and one wonders if he did mean to thus criticize Thomas Jefferson, if Isaac Jefferson was indirectly hinting at something else: that he respected Washington more than Thomas Jefferson for having done notoriously what Thomas Jefferson did not do: provide for the freeing of his slaves after his death. Cf., below, in this chapter, the discussion of "signifying" in African American oral culture.

90. "Hammet Achmet," *New York Observer,* 27 July 1893.

91. Founders Online, "George Washington's Last Will and Testament, 9 July 1799," https://founders.archives.gov/documents/Washington/06-04-02 -0404-0001.

92. Nonetheless, most verified former slaves of Washington, unlike Achmet, appear to have left no evidence of having conspicuously identified themselves as his ex-slaves. Lucia Greene Medford has observed, "It is perhaps no coincidence that none of those who registered as free people in Fairfax and Alexandria in the decades before the Civil War chose to embrace the most famous name in the area" by taking "Washington" as a surname. Edna Greene Medford, "Beyond Mount Vernon: George Washington's Emancipated Laborers and Their Descendants," in *Slavery at the Home of George Washington,* ed. Philip J. Schwarz (Mount Vernon, VA: Mount Vernon Ladies' Association, 2001), 153–54. For a press report in the mid 1830s on Washington's negative view of slavery see, e.g., "Washington's Opinions of Slavery," *African Repository and Colonial Journal* 12, no. 2 (1836): 48–50. Offering thoughtful speculation about the spread of knowledge about Washington's emancipation clauses in his will to African Americans at the time of Washington's death is

Richard D. Brown, *Knowledge Is Power: The Diffusion of Information in Early America, 1700–1865* (New York: Oxford University Press, 1989), 257.

93. For a masterful satire on the commonality of press reports in the nineteenth century about surviving putative slaves of George Washington see Mark Twain, "The Negro Body-Servant of General Washington," *The Galaxy* (New York) 5 (February 1868): 154–56. For an example of a bodily description of Washington that relies upon a Black servant's recollections, note the description of Washington when he was courting his future wife, Martha, in "Courtship and Marriage of Washington," *Ladies' Companion, a Monthly Magazine; Devoted to Literature and the Fine Arts* (December 1835): 59.

94. On the Heth affair, see generally Benjamin Reiss, *The Showman and the Slave: Race, Death, and Memory in Barnum's America* (Cambridge. MA: Harvard University Press, 2001). For representative contemporaneous accounts drawing attention to Heth's aged body, including gnarled fingers said to resemble "the talons of a bird of prey," and highlighting her claim to have been physically proximate to baby George Washington, nursing him, and putting his first set of clothes on him right after his birth, see "The Nurse of Washington," *Western Examiner, a Journal Embodying a Full and Impartial Enquiry into the Truth or Falsity of the Christian Religion; Whether Philosophically or Historically Viewed* 2 (1 October 1835): 295; "Joice Heth—Washington Family, &c.," *Army and Navy Chronicle* 1, no. 37 (10 September 1835): 290–91.

95. "Hammet Achmet," *New York Observer*, 27 July 1893.

96. Samuel J. May, *Some Recollections of Our Antislavery Conflict* (Boston: Fields Osgood & Co., 1869), 41.

97. May, *Some Recollections*, 40.

98. May, *Some Recollections*, 40.

99. Early Lee Fox, *The American Colonization Society, 1817–1840* (Baltimore: John Hopkins University Press, 1919), 79. Fox's work has been superseded as the standard overview of its subject by P. J. Staudenraus, *The African Colonization Movement, 1816–1865* (New York: Columbia University Press, 1961).

100. May, *Some Recollections*, 42; Edmund Fuller, *Prudence Crandall: An Incident of Racism in Nineteenth-Century Connecticut* (Middletown, CT: Wesleyan University Press, [1971]), 22.

101. Illustrative of how Crandall's school became a matter of common discussion throughout New England is William Lloyd Garrison to Helen E. Benson, 8 March 1834, in *The Letters of William Lloyd Garrison*, vol. 1, *I*

Will Be Heard! 1822–1835, ed. Walter M. Merrill (Cambridge, MA: Harvard University Press, 1971), 289.

102. Maria L. Child, *An Appeal in Favor of Americans Called Africans* (New York: Arno Press, 1968), 200, facsimile of an 1836 edition of the work, which was first printed in 1833; Jennifer Lee James, "Jehiel C. Beman: A Leader of the Northern Free Black Community," *Journal of Negro History* 82, no. 1 (Winter 1997): 136, 150–51; also valuable for understanding Beman is Kathleen Housley, "'Yours for the Oppressed': The Life of Jehiel C. Beman," *Journal of Negro History* 77, no. 1 (Winter 1992): 17–29.

103. "Miss Prudence Crandall," *Evangelical Magazine and Gospel Advocate,* 4, no. 18 (4 May 1833): 142.

104. Susan Strane, *A Whole-Souled Woman: Prudence Crandall and the Education of Black Women* (New York: W. W. Norton, 1990), 79; May, *Some Recollections,* 71.

105. May, *Some Recollections,* 52.

106. May, *Some Recollections,* 67. Owing to a hung jury in her first trial, Crandall actually endured two trials. See May, *Some Recollections,* 68–69.

107. Strane, *A Whole-Souled Woman,* 102.

108. *Report of the Arguments of Counsel, in the Case of Prudence Crandall, plff. in error, vs. State of Connecticut: before the Supreme Court of Errors, at Their Session at Brooklyn, July 1834, by a Member of the Bar* (Boston: Garrison & Knapp, 1834), 15–16, Library of Congress, "American Memory," online archive, http://hdl.loc.gov/loc.rbc/rbcmisc.lst0089.

109. *Report of the Arguments of Counsel, in the Case of Prudence Crandall,* 22.

110. *Report of the Arguments of Counsel, in the Case of Prudence Crandall,* 6.

111. *Report of the Arguments of Counsel, in the Case of Prudence Crandall,* 24. As transcribed on the same page, Crandall also argued that contemporaneous debates among antislavery advocates and supporters of forced Black repatriation to Africa properly had no bearing on Crandall's case.

112. *Report of the Arguments of Counsel, in the Case of Prudence Crandall,* 30. On the overall valences of arguments in the period from Black service in the Revolution, particularly with reference to questions of citizenship, see Gary B. Nash, *The Forgotten Fifth,* Nathan I. Huggins Lectures (Cambridge, MA: Harvard University Press, 2006), esp. ch. 3, "Race and Citizenship in the New Republic," 123–170; Douglas R. Edgerton, *Death or Liberty: African Americans and Revolutionary America* (Oxford: Oxford University Press, 2009), 247.

113. *Report of the Arguments of Counsel, in the Case of Prudence Crandall,* 34.

114. On the work of colonizationists in Middletown in the 1820s, see Staudenraus, *The African Colonization Movement, 1816–1865*, 127. See also "Mr. Editor . . . ," *Colored American* (New York), 20 November 1841.

115. "Hammet Achmet," *New York Observer*, 27 July 1893.

116. "Washington's Slave," *Colored American* (New York), 14 September 1839; "APPEAL of Forty Thousand Citizens, Threatened with Disfranchisement, to the People of Pennsylvania," *Colored American* (New York), 3 May 1838; "War between England and America, No. 3," *Colored American* (New York), 27 February 1841; "Varieties," *Colored American* (New York), 15 June 1827; "Episcopal Religious Papers," *Colored American* (New York); 17 June 1837; "Good—Very Good," *Colored American* (New York), 4 April 1840. Cf. Jeremy Belknap to Ebenezer Hazard, 13 January 1784, in *Massachusetts Historical Society Collections*, 5th ser. (Boston: Massachusetts Historical Society, 1877), 2:294; John Pintard, Commonplace Book, mss., Pintard Papers, box 1, New-York Historical Society, esp. where Pintard copied the maxim: "Trust not everything to memory; half a word taken on the spot, is worth a cartload of recollection"; cf. Noah Webster to Samuel Lee, 20 December 1824, Noah Webster Papers, New York Public Library. On sales of the *Colored American* in Middletown, see *Colored American* (New York), 23 May 1840. See generally Elizabeth McHenry, *Forgotten Readers: Recovering the Lost History of African-American Literary Societies* (Durham, NC: Duke University Press, 2002), 85; Carla Peterson, *"Doers of the Word": African-American Women Speakers and Writers in the North (1830–1880)* (New Brunswick, NJ: Rutgers University Press, 1995), 13.

117. Daniel Alexander Payne, *Recollection of Seventy Years* (1888; reprint, New York: Arno Press, 1968), 11, 93, 107; Daniel Alexander Payne, *History of the African Methodist Episcopal Church* (Nashville: Publishing House of the AME Sunday School Union, 1891), iv–vii.

118. Payne, *Recollections*, 11.

119. Jeremiah Asher, *An Autobiography: With Details of a Visit to England, and Some Account of the History of the Meeting Street Baptist Church, Providence, R.I, and of the Shiloh Baptist Church, Philadelphia, P.A.* (Philadelphia: Published by the Author, 1862), 3; Gad Asher, Pension File, S17244, United States, National Archives and Record Administration, Revolutionary War Pension Application and Bounty Land Warrant Files, microfilm copy, David Library of the American Revolution.

120. Asher, *An Autobiography*, 1–4.

121. W. E. B. Du Bois, *The Souls of Black Folks*, ed. David W. Blight and Robert Gooding-Williams, Bedford Series in History and Culture (1903; reprint, Boston: Bedford Books, 1997), 38–39.

122. Asher, *An Autobiography*, 5–6.

123. For a comprehensive, vivid study of Black Revolutionary War veterans, drawing upon 500 pension applications by racial minorities, and ably tracing veterans' political and cultural legacies, see Judith Van Buskirk, *Standing in Their Own Light: African American Patriots in the American Revolution* (Norman: University of Oklahoma Press, 2017).

124. "Hammet Achmet," *New York Observer,* 27 July 1893.

125. "Hammet Achmet," *New York Observer,* 27 July 1893; Hamet Achmet, Pension Application S3810.

126. E.g., "Hamet. General Washington's Slave," *Wetumpka Argus* (Alabama), 18 September 1839, 1. On "Atlantic Creoles," see, e.g.: Ira Berlin, *Many Thousands Gone: The First Two Centuries in North America* (Cambridge, MA: Harvard University Press, 1998), esp. 25, and 381n1; Ira Berlin, *Generations of Captivity: A History of African-American Slaves* (Cambridge, MA: Harvard University Press, 2003), 32; Jane G. Landers, *Atlantic Creoles in the Age of Revolutions* (Cambridge, MA: Harvard University Press, 2010); on the culture genealogy of "Atlantic Creoles," see Linda M. Heywood and John K. Thornton, *Central Africans, Atlantic Creoles, and the Foundation of the Americas, 1585–1660* (New York: Cambridge University Press, 2007).

4. THE EVANGELICAL

1. "Owns Six Hairs of Washington," *Spokesman-Review* (Spokane, WA), 21 February 1932, 5. On Downey's matriculation at Wesleyan University, see also "Downey, Charles Gibbs" in Matthew Simpson, ed., *Cyclopedia of Methodism*, 5th ed. (Philadelphia: Louis Everts, 1883), 309.

2. Since "evangelical" is a central concept in the present analysis, it is worth noting that the working definition of "evangelical" being employed here comes from British historian David W. Bebbington. In *Evangelicalism in Modern Britain: A History from the 1730s to the 1980s,* Bebbington highlighted four key aspects of evangelical religion, a "quadrilateral of priorities" as he termed them: "*conversionism,* the belief that lives need to be changed; *activism,* the expression of the gospel in effort; *biblicism,* a particular regard for the Bible; and what may be called *crucicentrism,* a stress on the sacrifice of Christ on the cross." D. W. Bebbington, *Evangelicalism in Modern Britain: A History from the 1730s to the 1980s* (London: Unwin Hyman, 1989), 3. Those same emphases were already defining

for "Christians of all the evangelical denominations in the United States" during the early national and early antebellum eras. Robert Baird, *Religion in the United States of America* (Glasgow: Blackie and Son, 1844), 414; cf. 499.

3. "Owns Six Hairs of Washington," *Spokesman-Review* (Spokane, WA), 21 February 1932, 5.

4. "History of George Washington's hair in possession of Charles Downey," https://digital.palni.edu/digital/collection/archives/id/140437, accessed 6 September 2019.

5. Accession no. 1991.175, Carter Collections Center, Strawbery Banke Museum, Portsmouth, NH. According to the museum's accession file, "letters are worked in long and short stitches in a combination of hair and probably linen thread, the former twisted around and held by the latter." Cf. Charles W. Brewster, *Rambles About Portsmouth: Sketches of Persons, Localities, and Incidents of Two Centuries*, 2nd ser. (Portsmouth, NH: Brewster and Son, 1859), 266–67.

6. John 1:14 (NASB).

7. Willbur Fisk, *Travels in Europe: Viz., in England, Ireland, Scotland, France, Italy, Switzerland, Germany, and the Netherlands*, 4th ed. (New York: Harper & Bros., 1839), 373–74.

8. Fisk, *Travels*, 77, 530, 560, 619; 2 Kings 2:1–15 (KJV); "Methodist Relics," *Quarterly Review of the Methodist Episcopal Church, South* (Nashville, TN), (April 1880): 372; Fisk, *Travels*, 273.

9. Joseph Holdich, *The Life of Willbur Fisk, D.D.: The First President of the Wesleyan University* (New York: Harper & Bros., 1842), 367, 335, 32, 156–58, 348, 454; J. B. Wakeley, *Lost Chapters Recovered from the Early History of Methodism* (New York: Carlton and Porter, 1858), 119–20.

10. J[oseph] Holdich, *True Greatness: A Discourse on the Character of Rev. Willbur Fisk* (Middletown, CT: E. Hunt, 1839), 35–36.

11. David B. Potts, *Wesleyan University, 1831–1910: Collegiate Enterprise in New England* (Hanover, NH: Wesleyan University Press, 1999), 24–25.

12. Years later, in 1866, speaking in New York at a church service celebrating the "Centenary Jubilee of Methodism," Heman delightedly brandished relics of Methodist church history before the audience. *New-York Tribune*, 19 June 1886, 8.

13. "Death of Hammet Achmet," *New-England Weekly Review* (Hartford, CT), 3 December 1842; "Connecticut, Town Marriage Records, pre-1870 (Barbour Collection)," in "Ancestry Library," https://www.ancestrylibrary.com, accessed 14 September 2019; for further information about the location of Achmet's house, see "Some Memories of

Middletown: The Washington Hotel Which Became the Jarvis Mansion, Lafayette and Other Visitors," *Historiographer of the Episcopal Diocese of Connecticut,* no. 121 (September 1982): 4, which places Achmet's "little hut" at the "southwest corner of the old Washington Street graveyard on Vine Street," and relates a story of Lafayette recognizing Achmet on a visit to Middletown, a tale remarkably similar to Lafayette's purported encounter with a Black man named "Robert" on a visit to Philadelphia, as recounted in "Origin of the 'Bones,'" *Greensboro Patriot* (Greensboro, NC), 5 September 1846, 3. An apparent residence is visible in the southwest corner of the "Burial Ground," the cemetery at what had been Washington and Vine in R. Whitford, "Map of the City of Middletown" (Philadelphia: Richard Clark, 1851). From the conjunction of these evidences, a likely location of Achmet's house is 41°33'23.6"N 72°39'39.0"W. Achmet's wife at the time of his death, Mary Ann, married an Andrew P. Folio, who is buried in the Washington Street Cemetery. "Andrew P. Folio," Find A Grave, https://www.findagrave.com/memorial/24675354/andrew-p-folio, accessed 12 November 2019. In the year of his death, 1875, Folio (sometimes spelled "Foleo") lived on "Vine, east of Cemetery," probably referring to Middletown's Indian Hill Cemetery; see *Middletown City Directory for 1875–6* (N.p.: Fitzgerald and Dillon, [1875]), 26. Folio's house is marked in the "Middletown" inset map in [Henry Francis Walling], "Map of Middlesex County, CT" (New York: H. & C. T. Smith, 1859).

14. See, e.g.: Roger Finke and Roger Starke, "How the Upstart Sects Won America: 1776–1850," *Journal for the Scientific Study of Religion* 28, no. 1 (1989): 27.

15. Nathan Bangs, *A History of the Methodist Episcopal Church,* vol. 3, *From the Year 1816 to the Year 1828* (1840; reprint, New York: T. G. Lane & C. B. Tipett, 1845), 323.

16. Mark P. Fackler and Charles H. Lippy, eds., *Popular Religious Magazines of the United States* (Westport, CT: Greenwood Press, 1995), 101; Gaylord P. Albaugh, *History and Annotated Bibliography of American Religious Periodicals and Newspapers Established from 1730 Through 1830* (Worcester, MA: American Antiquarian Society, 1994), xiv; Everett Hermann, "Nathan Bangs: Apologist for American Methodism" (Ph.D. diss., Emory University, 1973), 128n61.

17. "Extraordinary Subscription," *Atkinson's Saturday Evening Post* 10 (19 November 1831): 3.

18. Albaugh, *History and Annotated Bibliography of American Religious Periodicals,* xiv.

19. Abel Stevens, *Life and Times of Nathan Bangs, D.D.* (New York: Carlton and Porter, 1863), 244.

20. George Bancroft to Edward Everett, 11 July 1834, George Bancroft Papers, Massachusetts Historical Society.

21. Fackler, and Lippy, eds., *Popular Religious Magazines of the United States,* 101.

22. Whitney R. Cross, *The Burned-Over District: The Social and Intellectual History of Enthusiastic Religion in Western New York, 1800–1850* (1950; reprint, New York: Harper & Row, 1956), 3; Jon Butler, "Toward the Antebellum Spiritual Hothouse," in *Awash in a Sea of Faith: Christianizing the American People* (Cambridge, MA: Harvard University Press, 1990), chap. 8, 225–56.

23. "Memory," *Christian Advocate* (hereafter, *CrAd*), 6 May 1836.

24. James Floy, "The Judgment Register," *Methodist Magazine and Quarterly Review* 20, no. 2 (April 1838): 166. The rendering of Revelation 20:12 here is as printed in the article in the *Methodist Magazine,* which was slightly edited, and that without notation, from the full text of that verse in the Authorized Version of the Bible. Bangs edited the *Methodist Magazine* from 1820 to 1828. Edmund S. Janes, *Sermon on the Death of Nathan Bangs, D.D., May 6, 1862* (New York: Carlton and Porter, [1862?]), 22.

25. Floy, "The Judgment Register," 166–76; cf. William T. Hamilton, *Memory after Death: A Sermon Delivered in the Government Street Church, Mobile* (Mobile, AL: T. H. Cooper, 1838), 7, 15.

26. *CrAd,* 19 September 1828, as cited in Hermann, "Nathan Bangs: Apologist for American Methodism," 125. In its focus on anecdotes useful for supporting its teleological outlook, the *Advocate* typified evangelical publications of the period. Cf. the explication of "use-oriented" evangelical printed material in Candy Gunther Brown, *The Word in the World: Evangelical Writing, Publishing, and Reading in America, 1789–1880* (Chapel Hill: University of North Carolina Press, 2004), 80.

27. See, e.g., "Biographical Department," *CrAd,* 3 April 1835.

28. "Miscellaneous," *CrAd,* 24 January 1840.

29. On the Elizabethan-era development in Britain of confidence that England was central in God's plans to usher in millennial utopia, see William Haller, *Foxe's Book of Martyrs and the Elect Nation* (London: Jonathan Cape, 1963). On the importation and adaptation into American culture of such beliefs see James F. Maclear, "The Republic and the Millennium," in *Religion in American History: Interpretive Essays,* ed. John M. Mulder and John F. Wilson (Englewood Cliffs, NJ: Prentice-Hall, 1978), 181–98;

and Robert T. Handy, *A Christian America: Protestant Hopes and Historical Realities* (New York: Oxford University Press, 1971), 7.

30. Nathan O. Hatch, *The Sacred Cause of Liberty* (New Haven: Yale University Press, 1977). On transatlantic millenarianism in the Revolutionary era, see Susan Juster, *Doomsayers: Anglo-American Prophecy in the Age of Revolution* (Philadelphia: University of Pennsylvania Press, 2003). See also Lee Tuveson, *Redeemer Nation: The Idea of America's Millennial Role* (Chicago: University of Chicago Press, 1968); Jonathan D. Sassi, *A Republic of Righteousness: The Public Christianity of the Post-Revolutionary New England Clergy* (Oxford: Oxford University Press, 2001), at, e.g., 3–5, 11, 150–53.

31. Lyman Beecher, *A Plea for the West* (Cincinnati: Truman and Smith, 1835), 8–9; cf. Lyman Beecher, *The Memory of Our Fathers: A Sermon Delivered at Plymouth, On the Twenty-second of December, 1827,* 2d ed. (Boston: T. R. Marvin, 1828), 6–7, wherein Beecher offers essentially the same millennial characterization of the United States, broadening New England's Puritan calling to the nation.

32. "Female Patriotism," *CrAd,* 9 October 1835.

33. Lyman Beecher, quoted in J. Earl Thompson Jr. and Elwyn A. Smith, "The Reform of the Racist Religion of the Republic," in *The Religion of the Republic,* ed. Elwyn A. Smith (Philadelphia: Fortress Press, 1971), 277.

34. G. V. H. Forbes, "Address in Behalf of the American Colonization Society, Delivered in Bromfield-street Church, Boston, July 4th," *CrAd,* 31 July 1829.

35. See, e.g.: David L. Jeffrey, *People of the Book: Christian Identity and Literary Culture* (Grand Rapids, MI: Eerdmans, 1996); "William Tyndale," *Methodist Quarterly Review* (New York) (April 1884): 231.

36. "Life of George Washington, Hannah More, and Conversations on the S.S.M.," *CrAd,* 14 February 1840, 101.

37. Gabriel P. Disoway, "Oration Delivered on the 4th Instant in the Methodist Church," *CrAd,* 10 July 1829, 181.

38. See, e.g., "Washington's Papers," *CrAd,* 2 June 1827, 155 and 159; "Sparks' Life of Franklin," *CrAd,* 24 April, 1840, 143; "The Person and Character of Washington," *CrAd,* 14 February 1840, 104; cf. the positive reference to consulting Sparks in "Life of George Washington, Hannah More, and Conversations on the S.S.M.," 101.

39. "Dr. Franklin's Opinion of Church Libraries in Preference to Bells and Steeples," *CrAd,* 3 February 1827, 87.

40. "The Asbury Historical Society," *CrAd,* 8 November 1839, 45; "Formation of Historical Societies, Dr. Bangs' History of the Methodist E. Church,

Life of Thomas Ware, &c," *CrAd*, 27 December 1839, 73; See also "Connecticut Historical Society," *CrAd*, 10 April 1840.

41. "Keep Your Newspapers," *CrAd*, 1 January 1836, 75.

42. Nathan Bangs, *A History of the Methodist Episcopal Church*, 12th ed., vol. 1, *From the Year 1766 to the Year 1792* (New York: Carlton and Porter, 1860), 1:1.

43. Suffice it to say, the iterations of such substance dualism have been many. See, e.g., Carsten Colpe, Dietrich Ritschl, and Martin Haller, s.v. "Soul," *Encyclopedia of Christianity* (Grand Rapids, MI: Eerdmans, 2008), 5:127–28.

44. "Development of the Mind," *CrAd*, 30 January 1835, 92.

45. Stevens, *Life and Times of Nathan Bangs, D.D.*, 17.

46. A Soldier of the American Revolution, *Letter in Answer to the Speech of the Rev. Dr. Mason at the Thirteenth Annual Meeting of the British and Foreign Bible Society, Printed in the "Christian Herald," Vol. III, Saturday, September 6, 1817, No. 24* (Elizabeth-Town, NJ: Shepard Kollock, 1818), 2, 8–9.

47. Bangs, *A History of the Methodist Episcopal Church*, 1:121, 138.

48. Bangs, *A History of the Methodist Episcopal Church*,12th ed., 1:122.

49. Christine Leigh Heyrman, *Southern Cross: The Beginnings of the Bible Belt* (Chapel Hill: University of North Carolina Press, 1997), 243–44.

50. "Extracts from Address Delivered in Brooklyn," *CrAd*, 6 July 1827, 175.

51. Dee E. Andrews, *The Methodists and Revolutionary America, 1760–1800: The Shaping of an Evangelical Culture* (Princeton, NJ: Princeton University Press, 2002), 228; *Autobiography of A. C. Morehouse: An Itinerant Minister of the New York and New York East Conferences of the Methodist Episcopal Church* (New York: Tibbals Book Company, 1895), 149.

52. Bangs, *A History of the Methodist Episcopal Church*, 6th ed., vol. 2, *From the Year 1793 to the Year 1816*, 2:286.

53. See figure on p. 5.

54. On the Second Great Awakening and social class see Paul E. Johnson, *A Shopkeeper's Millennium*, rev. ed. (New York: Hill and Wang, 2004), 141; Catherine A. Brekus, *Strangers and Pilgrims: Female Preaching in America, 1740–1845* (Chapel Hill: University of North Carolina Press, 1998), 132; David W. Kling, *A Field of Wonders: The New Divinity and Village Revivals in Northwestern Connecticut, 1792–1822* (University Park: Pennsylvania State University Press, 1993), 191; John H. Wigger, *Taking Heaven by Storm: Methodism and the Rise of Popular Christianity in America* (New York: Oxford University Press, 1998), 5.

55. "Celebration of American Independence," *Susquehanna Democrat* (Wilkes-Barre, PA), 7 July 1826, 3.

56. James Hall, Pension Application W25741, United States, National Archives and Record Administration, Revolutionary War Pension Application and Bounty Land Warrant Files.

57. Deposition of John Anderson, 30 December 1835, in William Spain Pension Application W6148, United States, National Archives and Record Administration, Revolutionary War Pension Application and Bounty Land Warrant Files.

58. John Fisher to "The Secretary of War," 24 April 1818, in Patrick Connolly Pension Application S35861, United States, National Archives and Record Administration, Revolutionary War Pension Application and Bounty Land Warrant Files.

59. John Crawford Pension Application R2472, United States, National Archives and Record Administration, Revolutionary War Pension Application and Bounty Land Warrant Files. According to depositions in the file, Crawford was believed to have been a lieutenant in the war, but his papers, including his commission, had been destroyed.

60. James Adams Pension Application S16306, United States, National Archives and Record Administration, Revolutionary War Pension Application and Bounty Land Warrant Files The characterization of Riley is in a deposition by Adams.

61. Thomas J. Barret deposition in Benjamin Burch Pension Application W23743, United States, National Archives and Record Administration, Revolutionary War Pension Application and Bounty Land Warrant Files.

62. "Captain Josiah Cleveland," *Hartford Courant* (Hartford, CT), 6 July 1843, 2, reprinting a piece from "the Boston Atlas of the 4th."

63. For an example of the general currency of the phenomenon in contemporaneous evangelical culture see William Burke, *Memoir of William Burke, Soldier of the Revolution, Reformed from Intemperance, and For Many Years a Consistent and Devoted Christian, Carefully Prepared from a Journal Kept by Himself, to Which Is Added an Extract from a Sermon Preached at His Funeral, by Rev. Nathaniel Miner* (Hartford, CT: Case, Tiffany, and Company, 1837).

64. "The Soldier's Mite," *CrAd*, 27 July 1828. Another example of an item in the *Advocate* conjoining a discussion of the war record of a low-ranking Revolutionary War veteran who converted to evangelicalism after the Revolution and an explication of his piety is Ezra Kellog to [the Editor], 2 December 1830, as printed in *CrAd*, 31 December 1830.

65. "A Visit to the Capitol at Washington," *CrAd*, 18 January 1833.

66. W[ilia]m. Staughton, "To Whom It May Concern," 11 April 1828, as printed in Andrew Sherburne, *Memoirs of Andrew Sherburne: A Pensioner*

of the Navy of the Revolution (Providence, RI: H. H. Brown, 1831), viii; cf. xii.

67. James M. Dalzell, *John Gray of Mount Vernon; The Last Soldier of the Revolution* (Washington, DC: Gibson Brothers Printers, 1868), 9, 13.

68. James McCormick Dalzell, *Private Dalzell, His Autobiography, Poems, and Comic War Papers[,] Sketch of John Gray, Washington's Last Soldier, Etc.* (Cincinnati: Robert Clarke & Co., 1888), 198–201.

69. Dalzell, *John Gray of Mount Vernon,* 9.

70. Dalzell, *John Gray of Mount Vernon,* 9–10.

71. Jean B. Lee, "Historical Memory, Sectional Strife, and the American Mount Vernon, 1783–1853," *Virginia Magazine of History and Biography* 109 (2001): 293.

72. See, e.g., Mark A. Noll, *The Old Religion in a New World: A History of North American Christianity* (Grand Rapids, MI: Eerdmans, 2002), 49; Mark A. Noll, *A History of Christianity in the United States and Canada* (Grand Rapids, MI: Eerdmans, 1992), 132–34.

73. The term is from Mark A. Noll, *America's God: From Jonathan Edwards to Abraham Lincoln* (Oxford: Oxford University Press, 2002), ch. 9, "The Evangelical Surge," 161–86.

74. Benjamin Franklin, *The Autobiography of Benjamin Franklin,* ed. Louis P. Masur (New York: Bedford Books, 1993), 70. On Franklin's religious journey, see especially Thomas S. Kidd, *Benjamin Franklin: The Religious Life of a Founding Father* (New Haven: Yale University Press, 2017).

75. Franklin, *Autobiography,* 109.

76. Benjamin Franklin to Ezra Stiles, in *The Complete Works of Benjamin Franklin,* ed. John Bigelow, 10 vols. (New York: G. P. Putnam's Sons, 1887–88), 10:194.

77. Mason L. Weems, *The Life of Benjamin Franklin* (Philadelphia: M. Carey, 1817), 202–2; on Weems's affinity for Methodism, see, e.g.: George Burwell Utley, *The Life and Times of Thomas John Claggett: First Bishop of Maryland and the First Bishop Consecrated in America* (Chicago: R. R. Donnelley, 1913), 51. On Weems in the wider context of Protestant print culture and patriotic myth-making, but with particular reference to his better-known popular biographies of Washington, see especially François Furstenberg, *In the Name of the Father: Washington's Legacy, Slavery, and the Making of a Nation* (New York: Penguin Press, 2006), 105–45.

78. Weems, *The Life of Benjamin Franklin,* 202–3; Acts 26:29 (KJV).

79. "Mason L. Weems to Thomas Jefferson, 31 July 1815," *Founders Online,* National Archives, https://founders.archives.gov/documents /Jefferson/03-08-02-0513. Original source: *The Papers of Thomas*

Jefferson, Retirement Series, vol. 8, *1 October 1814 to 31 August 1815,* ed. J. Jefferson Looney (Princeton, NJ: Princeton University Press, 2011), 633–634

80. AMs., "Remarks on the Life of Franklin: Priorities and Principles Worthy of Imitation," January 1813, box 10, folder 11, Willbur Fisk Papers, Special Collections and Archives, Olin Library, Wesleyan University. See, e.g.: "Extract of a letter from the Rev. Rome Elton to the Hon. Abner Forbes," *CrAd,* 24 March 1827, 114; "The Time to Study," *CrAd,* 14 September 1827, 8; "Perseverance," *CrAd,* 5 October 1827, 20, "Good Advice," *CrAd,* 7 December 1827, 56; "Carrying the Head Too High," *CrAd,* 6 August 1830; "Early Rising," *CrAd,* 22 July 1831, 188; "The American Aquatic," *CrAd,* 12 August 1831, 200; "Walking," *CrAd,* 9 September 1831, 8; "Wesleyan University," *CrAd,* 2 November 1832, 37; "Hints to Mechanics and Working Men," *CrAd,* 7 December 1832, 40; "Industry and Application," *CrAd,* 19 June 1835, 172; "Dr. Franklin's Moral Code," *CrAd,* 17 June 1836, 172; "Youth," *CrAd,* 17 February 1837, 104; "Longevity of Our Forefathers," *CrAd,* 22 December 1837, 72; "Lectures on the Book of Proverbs," *CrAd,* 24 January 1840, 92; "Thoughts on Poverty and Riches," *CrAd,* 24 April 1840, 143.

81. "Dr. Franklin and Thomas Paine," *CrAd,* 18 July 1828. On the provenance of the letter see the editorial note at "From Benjamin Franklin to ———, [13 December 1757]," *Founders Online,* National Archives, accessed September 29, 2019, https://founders.archives.gov/documents/Franklin/01-07-02-0130. Original source: *The Papers of Benjamin Franklin,* vol. 7, *October 1, 1756 through March 31, 1758,* ed. Leonard W. Labaree (New Haven: Yale University Press, 1963), 293–95.

82. Jonathan Elliot, ed., *The Debates in the Several State Conventions, on the Adoption of the Federal Constitution, As Recommended by the General Convention at Philadelphia in 1787* [*Elliot's Debates*], *Debates on the Adoption of the Federal Constitution in the Convention Held at Philadelphia in 1787; With a Diary of the Debates of the Congress of the Confederation as Reported by James Madison, a Member and Deputy from Virginia, Revised and Newly Arranged by Jonathan Elliot* (Washington, DC: Author, 1845), 5:253–54. On the significance to evangelicals of the Franklin prayer story, see also Mark A. Noll, "Evangelicals in the American Founding and Evangelical Political Mobilization Today," in *Religion and the New Republic: Faith in the Founding of America,* ed. James H. Hutson (Lanham, MD: Rowman and Littlefield, 2000), 137–38; John G. West Jr., *The Politics of Revelation and Reason: Religion and Civic Life in the New Nation* (Lawrence: University Press of Kansas, 1996), 11–12; Steven K. Green, *Inventing a Christian America:*

The Myth of the Religious Founding (New York: Oxford University Press, 2015), 215–16; John Fea, *Was America Founded as a Christian Nation?*, rev. ed. (Louisville, KY: John Knox Press, 2016), 151–53.

83. "Dr. Franklin on Prayer," *CrAd*, 17 February 1827, 96; see also Benjamin Franklin, "Speech to the Constitutional Convention, June 28, 1787," Holograph manuscript. Manuscript Division, Library of Congress (145), http://www.loc.gov/exhibits/religion/vc006642.jpg, accessed 28 October 2019.

84. "Dr. Franklin," *CrAd*, 16 April 1830, 129.

85. "Interesting Historical Anecdote," *CrAd*, 13 April 1832, 129–30.

86. "Dr. Franklin's Infidelity," *CrAd*, 15 January 1836.

87. "Thomas S. Hinde to James Madison, 20 August 1832," James Madison Papers at the Library of Congress, accessed February 28, 2021, https://www.loc.gov/item/mjm021136/. See also, e.g.: "Interesting Historical Anecdote," *CrAd*, 13 April 1832, 129; "Youth's Department," *CrAd*, 9 November 1832; "Wesleyan University," *CrAd*, 2 November 1832, 37; Harmon Kingsbury, *The Sabbath: A Brief History of Laws, Petitions, Remonstrances and Reports* (New York: Robert Carter, 1840), 266.

88. Benjamin Franklin, "Codicil," in *The Writings of Benjamin Franklin,* ed. Albert Henry Smith, 10 vols. (New York: Macmillan, 1905–7), 10:508.

89. Thomas S. Kidd, *George Whitefield: America's Spiritual Founding Father* (New Haven: Yale University Press, 2014), 256.

90. "The Tomb of Whitefield," *CrAd*, 23 August 1832, 205.

91. James P. Byrd, *Sacred Scripture, Sacred War: The Bible and the American Revolution* (New York: Oxford University Press, 2013), 17.

92. J. T. Headley, *Chaplains and Clergy of the Revolution* (New York: Charles Scribner, 1864), 92–93.

93. Minton Thrift, *Memoir of the Rev. Jesse Lee[,] With Extracts from His Journals* (New York: N. Bangs and T. Mason; Myers and Smith, 1823), 156.

94. [Abel Stevens], *Sketches and Incident; or, A Budget from the Saddle-Bags of a Superannuated Itinerant* (New York: Carlton and Phillips, 1853), 7, 120.

95. Richard Hofstadter, *America at 1750: A Social Portrait* (New York: Vintage Books, 1973), 292.

96. Noll, *A History of Christianity in the United States and Canada,* 91; Barnett goes further than Noll, seeing parallels in the material remembrance of Washington and Whitefield. Teresa Barnett, *Sacred Relics: Pieces of the Past in Nineteenth-Century America* (Chicago: University of Chicago Press, 2013), 37 and 40.

97. Robert Philip, *The Life and Times of George Whitefield, M.A.* (London: R. & C. Childs, 1838), 447.

98. Phillis Wheatley, "An Elegaic Poem on the Death of . . . George White-field," as reprinted in "Variants of Published Poems," in *Complete Writings*, ed. Vincent Carretta (New York: Penguin Books, 2001), 115.

99. "Enclosure: Poem by Phillis Wheatley, 26 October 1775," *Founders Online*, National Archives, accessed September 29, 2019, https://founders.archives .gov/documents/Washington/03-02-02-0222-0002. Original source: *The Papers of George Washington*, Revolutionary War Series, vol. 2, *16 September 1775–31 December 1775*, ed. Philander D. Chase (Charlottesville: University Press of Virginia, 1987), 242–44; see also "To George Washington from Phillis Wheatley, 26 October 1775," *Founders Online*, National Archives, accessed September 29, 2019, https://founders.archives.gov /documents/Washington/03-02-02-0222-0001. Original source: *The Papers of George Washington*, 2:242; "From George Washington to Lieutenant Colonel Joseph Reed, 10 February 1776," *Founders Online*, National Archives, accessed September 29, 2019, https://founders.archives.gov/ documents/Washington/03-03-02-0209. Original source: *The Papers of George Washington*, Revolutionary War Series, vol. 3, *1 January 1776–31 March 1776*, ed. Philander D. Chase (Charlottesville: University Press of Virginia, 1988), 286–91.

100. *Massachusetts, Town and Vital Records, 1620–1988* [Ancestry.com online database], Ancestry.com Operations, 2011, https://search.ancestrylibrary .com/cgi-bin/sse.dll?gl=allgs&new=1&rank=1&msT=1&gsfn= Whitefield+Washington&gsfn_x=1&catbucket=rstp&MSAV=0&uidh= eqi&gss=angs, accessed 10 March 2018.

101. "George Whitefield, and George Washington," *New York Evangelist*, 6 June 1840, 91.

102. On Washington's religious journey, see especially Mary V. Thompson, *"In the Hands of a Good Providence": Religion in the Life of George Washington* (Charlottesville: University of Virginia Press, 2008); see also Paul F. Boller Jr., *George Washington and Religion* (Dallas: Southern Methodist University Press, 1963), esp. 68–74.

103. Marked-up copy in the Free Library of Philadelphia of *The New-England Primer Enlarged: For the More Easy Attaining the True Reading of English: to Which Is Added, Several Chapters and Sentences of the Holy Scriptures: Also Mr. Roger's [sic] Verses, &c.* (Germantown, [PA]: Printed by Christopher Sower, 1771), frontmatter. Special thanks are due to Cornelia S. King, legendary librarian extraordinaire, at the Book Company of Philadelphia, for bringing this object to my attention and to my colleague, computer expert James F. West, for his invaluable help in enhancing and deciphering a high-resolution photograph of the frontispiece. See

also David Hackett Fischer, *Liberty and Freedom: A Visual History of America's Founding Ideas* (New York: Oxford University Press, 2005), 179. On printers of the primer eventually replacing George III's image with Washington's, see Nila Banton Smith, *American Reading Instruction* (Newark, DE: International Reading Association, 2002), 57. For an argument that such juxtapositions of George Washington and George III reflected a long half-life in America for popular emotional attachment to aspects of monarchy, see Brendan McConville, *The King's Three Faces: The Rise and Fall of Royal America, 1688–1776* (Chapel Hill: University of North Carolina Press, 2006), esp. 315. When Hewson died in 1821, he parceled out, through his will, several other depictions of Washington to his children. John Hewson Will, photocopy, Coll. #203, Winterthur Library.

104. "To George Washington from ——, 10 June 1798," *Founders Online*, National Archives, accessed September 29, 2019, https://founders.archives .gov/documents/Washington/06-02-02-0246. Original source: *The Papers of George Washington*, Retirement Series, vol. 2, *2 January 1798–15 September 1798*, ed. W. W. Abbot (Charlottesville: University Press of Virginia, 1998), 319.

105. Gerald E. Kahler, *The Long Farewell: Americans Mourn the Death of George Washington* (Charlottesville: University of Virginia Press, 2008).

106. See, e.g.: Richard Furman, *Humble Submission to Divine Sovereignty, the Duty of a Bereaved Nation. A Sermon [on Ps. xxxix. 9] Occasioned by the Death of . . . General George Washington, etc. United States* (Charleston: W. P. Young, 1800), 13; John R. Johnson, *Eulogy on General George Washington[,] A Sermon* (Albany: L. Andrews, 1890), 7.

107. "A Trip to Washington," *CrAd*, 5 May 1841, 152.

108. William Parker Cutler, et al., *Life[,] Journals and Correspondence of Rev. Manasseh Cutler, L.L.D.*, 2 vols. (Cincinnati: Robert Clarke, 1888), 2:57–58.

109. C. E. Gadsden, *An Essay on the Life of the Right Reverend Theodore Dehon, D.D.* (Charleston, SC: A. E. Miller, 1833), 238–39.

110. Samuel Melancthon Worcester, *The Life and Labors of Rev. Samuel Worcester, D.D.* (Boston: Crocker and Brewster, 1852), 2:418–19.

111. T[ruman] A[ugust] Post, *Truman Marcellus Post, D.D.* (Boston: Congregational Sunday-School and Publishing Society, 1891), 175 and 228; John 11:25–26 (AV).

112. Olive Alden Taylor, *Memoir of the Rev. Oliver Alden Taylor of Manchester Massachusetts* (Cleveland, OH: Jewett, Proctor, and Worthington, 1854), 313.

113. Nathan S. S. Beman, *The Western Continent, A Discourse Delivered in the First Presbyterian Church, Troy, July Fourth, 1841* (Troy, NY: N. Tuttle, 1841), 26.

114. "The Methodists," *Buffalo Commercial Advertiser* (Buffalo, NY), 26 April 1884, 2; see also Matthew Ryan Costello, "'The Property of the Nation': Democracy and the Memory of George Washington, 1799–1865" (Ph.D. diss., Marquette University, 2016), 122.

115. Richard Snowden, *The American Revolution: Written in Scriptural or Ancient Historical Style* (Baltimore: W. Pechin, 1796), 38.

116. G. J. Hunt, *The Historical Reader . . . in the Scriptural Style*, 3rd ed. (New York: Daniel D. Smith, 1819), 9.

117. Nathan Bangs, *Errors of Hopkinsianism Detected and Refuted* (New York: John C. Totten, 1815), 35.

118. Nathan Bangs, *An Original Church of Christ* (New York: T. Mason and G. Lane, 1837), 135–36. For other examples of theological discussants illustrating polemical points with references to George Washington, see, e.g.: Jeremiah Chaplin, *The Greatness of Redemption, A Sermon . . . Delivered before the Baptist Missionary Society in Massachusetts* (Boston: Manning and Loring, 1808), 23; "Review of Reviews," *Panoplist and Missionary Magazine United* (Boston) (June 1810): 26; "Religious Communication," *Baptist Missionary Magazine* (Boston) (March 1823): 48; William Pierce, "The Law a Shadow," *Religious Magazine* 1 (Boston) (1834): 158; [Benjamin Parsons], *The Christian Layman; or, The Doctrine of the Trinity, Fully Considered* (Mobile, AL: Doubleday and Sears, 1840), 14, 58, 87, and 104; "Scriptural Illustrations," *Gospel Anchor* (Troy, NY), 27 July 1833, 54; S. S. Schmucker, *Elements of Popular Theology* (Andover, MA: Gould and Newman, 1834), 53–54; "Editorial Items," *New Church Repository* (New York) (February 1849): 100; "Theophilus," *A Biblical Trinity* (Hartford, CT: Edwin Hunt, 1850), 72 and 296.

119. "Astounding and Disgraceful Facts," *Niles' Weekly Register* 38, no. 9 (24 April 1830): 174; "Grand Masonic Ceremonies and Visit to the Tomb of Washington," *Masonic Mirror* (Boston), 24 April 1830, 1; Steven C. Bullock, *Revolutionary Brotherhood: Freemasonry and the Transformation of the American Social Order, 1730–1840* (Chapel Hill: University of North Carolina Press, 1996), 177–78.

120. "Washington's Church," *CrAd*, 19 February 1830, 100.

121. "Mr. Wellford, et al., to Charles Carroll of Carrollton, 19 February 1831," Papers of Charles Carroll of Carrolton, film 20, reel 3, item 1900, microfilm copy, David Library of the American Revolution. By that time, Presbyterian churches had generally embraced evangelical theology;

see, e.g., William G. McLoughlin, ed., *The American Evangelicals: 1800–1900* (New York: Harper & Row, 1968), 5–6. For Washington family reactions to the Presbyterians' plan to honor Mary Washington see George Washington Bassett to unidentified correspondent, 29 March 1831, George Washington Bassett Papers, Virginia Historical Society, in which Bassett complains that to turn Mary Ball Washington's body over to Presbyterians would only be "forcing a connexion in death with those whose rites and ceremonies she agreed not with in life." When a rival committee in Fredericksburg, rather than the Presbyterians, did begin a monument to Mary Ball Washington that same year, the Rev. E. C. M'Guire, himself a Washington relative by marriage, and an erstwhile defender of George Washington in evangelical terms, gave the formal opening prayer at the monument's dedication, which was attended by President Andrew Jackson. Susan Rivière Hetzel, *The Building of a Monument: A History of the Mary Washington Association and Their Work* (Lancaster, PA: Press of Wickersham, 1903), 11; "Visit of the President of the United States to Fredericksburg," *New-York Mirror,* 8 June 1833, 385. For an example of contemporaneous interest in Mary Ball Washington in the *Christian Advocate* see "The Mother of Washington," *CrAd,* 14 October 1831; continued in *CrAd,* 31 October 1831.

122. "Washington Hill; Not Horse-Hill," *CrAd,* 12 December 1834, 64.
123. "Interesting Relic," *Farmer's Cabinet* (Amherst, NH), 6 January 1848, 3.
124. "Dr. Franklin's Opinion of Church Libraries in Preference to Bells and Steeples," *CrAd,* 3 February 1827, 87.
125. "General Washington," *Wyoming Republican and Farmer's Herald* (Kingston, PA), 10 January 1838.
126. *Catholic Telegraph,* 11 September 1835; see also Anonymous, *Letters Addressed to a Protestant Friend by a Catholic Priest* (Philadelphia: Peter F. Cunningham, 1870), 87–93.
127. Frances Wright, *Address, Containing a Review of the Times, As First Delivered, in the Hall of Science, New York. On Sunday, May 9, 1830* (New York: Office of the Free Enquirer, 1830), 10–11; on angry reaction to Wright's voicing her claim that Washington was not a Christian see Frances Trollope, *Domestic Manners of the Americans,* ed. Donald Smalley (1832; reprint, New York: Alfred A. Knopf, 1949), 363, esp. n5.
128. E. C. M'Guire, *The Religious Opinions and Character of Washington* (New York: Harper & Bros., 1836), 75.
129. Review of *Religious Opinions and Character of Washington* by E. C. M'Guire, *New York Review* 1, no. 1 (March 1837): 237.

130. For commentary on Owen's reference to Willson, see Boller, *George Washington and Religion,* 16–18. Boller's work, however, regularly confuses the Rev. James R. Willson and Bird Wilson, another New York clergyman of the period. Presumably it is Boller's conflating of the two, coupled with the otherwise deserved influence of Boller's book, that has led historians to overlook J. R. Willson's important role in antebellum controversies over memory of the religious beliefs of the Founders. Apparently Boller was misled by the misspelling of "Willson" as "Wilson" in *Albany Daily Advertiser,* 29 October 1831; cf. Boller, *George Washington and Religion,* 197n46. Bird Wilson was not even preaching in Albany in 1831, as Boller supposed. See Thomas Longworth, *Longworth's American Almanac, New-York Register, and City Directory for the Fifty-sixth Year of American Independence* (New York: Thomas Longworth, 1831), 693, s.v. "Wilson, Bird"; *The National Cyclopædia of American Biography* (1899), s.v. "Wilson, Bird." Owen, for obvious reasons delighted with reports of Willson's sermon, went to see the clergyman personally. According to Owen, Willson privately explained that he had "inquired himself, he said, of Madison what were his opinions on religion, and Madison 'evaded any expression whatever of his religious faith.'" Concerning his controversial sermon, Willson told Owen: "As I conceive that truth is truth, whether it makes out for us or against us, I will not conceal from you any information on this subject, even such as I have not yet given to the public." Origen Bacheler and Robert Dale Owen, *Discussion of the Existence of God and the Authenticity of the Bible,* 2 vols. in 1 (London: J. Watson, 1840), 2:231n; cf. 2:232–35.

131. *Journal of the Assembly of the State of New York* (28 January 1832): 165; *Albany Argus,* 30 January 1832; *Albany Journal,* 27 January 1832; *Albany Journal,* 30 January 1832. The office of chaplain was itself somewhat controversial in the legislature, with one member opposing it on the grounds that "contrary to the provisions of the constitution" it amounted to a "connexion between government and religion however remote." *Albany Argus,* 5 January 1832.

132. On the burning of Willson in effigy, Samuel Carlisle, "A Paper of the History of the Reformed Presbyterian Church, in the Vicinity of Newburgh, and on the Life of Rev. James R. Willson, D.D.," n.d., 4, "Willson, James Renwick" clippings file, Presbyterian Historical Society, Philadelphia; James R. Willson, *Prince Messiah's Claims to Dominion Over All Governments: and the Disregard of His Authority by the United States in the Federal Constitution* (Cincinnati: Smith and Chipman, 1848), 3; "Partialist Toleration," *Evangelical Magazine and Gospel*

Advocate, 3, no. 10 (10 March 1832): 79. For an atypical tempered reaction to Willson's sermon see "A Professor of Christianity" to the Editor, *Albany Daily Advertiser*, 1 November 1831. Willson, in spite of the furor occasioned by his sermon, was unrepentant, writing sarcastically in a private entry in late January of 1832: "In this Christian land, the legislature of this state refuse[s] to have prayer from one who pleads for the royal prerogatives of the Lord Jesus Christ." James Renwick Willson, Commonplace Book, 28 January 1832, box 35, Papers of James Renwick Willson, Library, Reformed Presbyterian Theological Seminary, Pittsburgh, PA. Willson also maintained "[t]hat a very distinguished man," such as Washington was, "should not have left him behind him," which he did not, "distinct evidense [*sic*] of his faith, is proof almost positive that he had none. Who doubts that he was a warrior and a statesman[?]" James Renwick Willson in his Commonplace Book, 14 February 1832. In Willson's opinion, the Founders, especially Washington, were being viewed idolatrously by many Americans. The clergyman complained privately that a writer in the "Daily Advertiser . . . says[,] 'The child,' meaning Washington, 'increased in wisdom, in stature, favoured by heaven and beloved of men.' Thus, he applies to Washington what the evangelist applies to Christ," and, in the conclusion of the same article essentially "prays to" Washington, "the titular saint." James Renwick Willson in his Commonplace Book, 22 February 1832. For an example of a clergyman several years later seeming to pray to Washington in public, see C. G. M'Lean, *Address Delivered on the Anniversary of Washington's Birthday, February 22d, 1838* (Gettysburg, PA: H. C. Ninstedt, 1838), 22, in which M'Lean addresses the "Spirit of our father," Washington.

133. See, e.g.: Miles King to James Madison, 29 June 1816, *Founders Online*, National Archives, accessed September 29, 2019, https://founders.archives.gov/documents/Madison/99-01-02-5225; and especially Madison's response: James Madison to Miles King, 5 September 1816, *Founders Online*, National Archives, accessed September 29, 2019, https://founders.archives.gov/documents/Madison/99-01-02-5425.

134. "To James Madison from James R. Willson, 1 June 1813," *Founders Online*, National Archives, accessed September 29, 2019, https://founders.archives.gov/documents/Madison/03-06-02-0341 Original source: *The Papers of James Madison*, Presidential Series, vol. 6, *8 February–24 October 1813*, ed. Angela Kreider, J.C.A. Stagg, Jeanne Kerr Cross, Anne Mandeville Colony, Mary Parke Johnson, and Wendy Ellen Perry (Charlottesville: University of Virginia Press, 2008), 361–62.

135. "Thomas S. Grimké to James Madison, 30 January 1833," *Founders Online*, National Archives, accessed 11 April 2019, https://founders.archives .gov/documents/Madison/99-02-02-2672; "Thomas S. Grimké to James Madison, 21 August 1833," *Founders Online*, National Archives, accessed 11 April 2019, https://founders.archives.gov/documents/Madison/99-02 -02-2820.

136. "James Madison to Thomas S. Grimké, 6 January 1834," *Founders Online*, National Archives, accessed 11 April 2019, https://founders.archives .gov/documents/Madison/99-02-02-2904.

137. "James Madison to Thomas S. Grimké, 15 August 1827," *Founders Online*, National Archives, accessed 11 April 2019, https://founders.archives.gov /documents/Madison/99-02-02-1097.

138. "James Madison to Thomas S. Grimké, 10 August 1833," *Founders Online*, National Archives, accessed 11 April 2019, https://founders.archives.gov /documents/Madison/99-02-02-2811.

139. "Thomas S. Grimké to James Madison, 21 August 1833," *Founders Online*, National Archives, accessed 11 April 2019, https://founders.archives.gov /documents/Madison/99-02-02-2820.

140. "James Madison to Jared Sparks, 8 April 1831," *Founders Online*, National Archives, accessed 11 April 2019, https://founders.archives.gov/ documents/Madison/99-02-02-2323; "James Madison to Thomas S. Grimké, 6 January 1834," *Founders Online*, National Archives, accessed 11 April 2019, https://founders.archives.gov/documents/Madison/99-02 -02-2904.

141. "Thomas S. Grimké to James Madison, 25 March 1834," *Founders Online*, National Archives, accessed 11 April 2019, https://founders.archives .gov/documents/Madison/99-02-02-2958.

142. William Meade, *Old Churches, Ministers, and Families of Virginia*, 2 vols. (1857; reprint, Philadelphia: J. B. Lippincott, 1910), 2:227–28. Meade would soon have his own relic of Washington. In 1839, George Washington's heirs presented him with "a staff cut from the tomb of the Father of his Country." J. Johns, *A Memoir of the Life of the Right Rev. William Meade, D.D.* (Baltimore: Innes, 1867), 461.

143. John Benson Lossing, *The Pictorial Field-Book of the Revolution; or, Illustrations, by Pen and Pencil, of the History, Biography, Scenery, Relics, and Traditions of the War for Independence*, 2 vols. (New York: Harper, 1850), 2:213–15; John Benson Lossing, *Mount Vernon and Its Associations: Descriptive, Historical, and Pictorial* (Cincinnati: Yorston, 1883), 91–93; see also: "Pohick Episcopal Church: The History of Pohick Church, Pre–Civil War," http://www.pohick.org/history.html, accessed 22 October 2019;

"A Foot-Jaunt in Virginia—No. 10," *New York Evening Post*, 16 November 1848, 1.

5. THE SCHOOLMISTRESS

A version of this chapter was previously published by University of Massachusetts Press, and the author wishes to thank that press for being allowed to retain the publishing rights to the chapter, and to reprint from it here.

1. A. W. Fairbanks, ed., *Emma Willard and Her Pupils; or, Fifty Years of Troy Female Seminary, 1822–1872* (New York: Mrs. Russell Sage, 1898), 3.
2. Fairbanks, *Emma Willard and Her Pupils*, 73.
3. Emma Willard, *History of the United States; or, Republic of America: Exhibited in Connexion with Its Chronology and Progressive Geography; By Means of a Series of Maps*, 2d ed. (New York: White, Gallaher & White, 1829), vi.
4. Scrapbook in the Elizabeth Emerson Atwater Papers, Natural History Collections and Archives, box 4, series 2: Collecting (1809–1875, n.d.), sub-series 2: Ethnographic, Chicago Academy of Sciences/Peggy Notebaert Nature Museum,; see also "Correspondence of Elizabeth Atwater and G. W. Clinton," in *Res Botanica*, ed. P. M. Eckel, (St. Louis: Missouri Botanical Garden, August 6, 2003), http://www.mobot.org/plantscience/ResBot/hist/corrauth/AtwaterClinton/IntroAtwater.htm.
5. Fairbanks, ed., *Emma Willard and Her Pupils*, 148–49.
6. Lawrence A. Cremin, *American Education: The National Experience, 1783–1876* (New York: Harper & Row, 1980), 390–91.
7. Emma Willard, "Preface," in William Channing Woodbridge, *A System of Universal Geography, on the Principles of Comparison and Classification*, 8th ed. (Hartford, CT: John Beach, 1838), xi. For the engraved picture of a monument see the book's unpaginated front matter.
8. Willard, "Preface," xi; Willard, *History of the United States*, vi, x.
9. Willard, *History of the United States*, x.
10. Willard, *History of the United States*, ix; cf. Susan Schulten, *Mapping the Nation: History and Cartography in Nineteenth-Century America* (Chicago: University of Chicago Press, 2012), 18–40.
11. Willard, *History of the United States*, xv.
12. Bernard Wishy, *The Child and the Republic: The Dawn of Modern American Child Nurture* (Philadelphia: University of Pennsylvania Press, 1968), vii; cf. "The Teacher; or, Moral Influence Employed in the Education of the Young," *North American Review* 4, no. 104 (July 1839): 246. For an excellent summary of the history of beliefs about mind and body in early America with a concentration on how changes in such beliefs

influenced pedagogues in the 1820s and 1830s a still-useful article is John R. Betts, "Mind and Body in Early American Thought," *Journal of American History* 54, no. 4 (March 1968): 787–805.

13. H. Humphrey, *Domestic Education* (Amherst, MA: J. S. & C. Adams Publishers, 1840), 63; see also Wishy, *The Child and the Republic*, 38.

14. "Development of the Mind," *Christian Advocate and Journal* 9, no. 23 (30 January 1835): 92.

15. William H. Brooks, "On the Education of the Five Senses," in *The Introductory Discourse and the Lectures Delivered before the American Institute of Instruction, in Boston, August 1831* (Boston: Hillard, Gray, Little, and Wilkins, 1832), 110; cf. M. Winship, *Thoughts on Teaching* (Boston: J. Howe, 1831), 3; Walter B. Johnson, "On the Utility of Visible Illustrations," in *The Introductory Discourse*, 67, 77. The conviction that sight is the most memorable of the senses reflects the fact that, according to work that has been done on the "history of the senses," in the period, sight was gaining in the epistemic importance ascribed to it relative to the other senses. Even Richard Cullen Rath, in a work focusing on sound in early America, has noted the gradual privileging of sight in American culture from about 1750 and continuing through the nineteenth century. Richard Cullen Rath, *How Early America Sounded* (Ithaca, NY: Cornell University Press, 2003), 178. For a similar recognition in another history of sound, see Mark M. Smith, *Listening to Nineteenth-Century America* (Chapel Hill: University of North Carolina Press, 2001), 318n2. Cf. "On the Part Performed by the Sympathetics in the Functions of the Senses," *Monthly Journal of Foreign Medicine* (January 1828): 65–68; "The Senses," *Ladies' Magazine and Literary Gazette* 4 (May 1831): 209–16.

16. Y, "The Origin and Value of 'the Picture System,'" *American Annals of Education* 10, no. 4 (October 1834): 475.

17. See, e.g., "Machinery of Education," *Mechanics' Magazine and Journal of the Mechanics' Institute* 2, no.2 (August 1833): 93.

18. Cf. "Machinery of Education," 93; X, "Influence of the 'Picture System' of Education," *American Annals of Education* 4, no. 5 (May 1834): 206; Y, "The Origin and Value of 'the Picture System,'" 474; Edward Mansfield, *Lecture on the Qualifications of Teachers* (Cincinnati: N. S. Johnson, 1837), 13.

19. Y, "On the Use of Pictures in School Books," *American Annals of Education* 4, no. 11 (November 1834): 513; cf. Willard, "Preface," xi. Woodbridge, in the context of addressing controversy over the "Picture System," explained that he had planned publication of the pictures that made it into his geography even before his affiliation with Willard, but she articulated

similar "principles and methods." [William Channing Woodbridge], "The Rudiments of Geography and the Picture System," *American Annals of Education* 4, no. 12 (December 1834): 581.

20. William Maclure, "An Epitome of the Improved Pestalozzian System of Education," *American Journal of Science and Arts* 10 (3 January 1825): 145, 151. On phrenologists' physicalist epistemologies, particularly with reference to memory, see especially chapter 1. On the concern of phrenologists with education see, e.g., J. G. Spurzheim, *Philosophical Catechism of the Natural Laws of Man*, 2d ed. (Boston: Marsh, Capen, and Lyon, 1832), 44–45.

21. In the 1820s, Amos Eaton and Lincoln Phelps taught biology at Troy Female Seminary with Pestalozzian methods. Elizabeth B. Keeney, *The Botanizers: Amateur Scientists in Nineteenth-Century America* (Chapel Hill: University of North Carolina Press, 1992), 59–60; Anne Firor Scott, "The Ever-Widening Circle: The Diffusion of Feminist Values from the Troy Female Seminary, 1822–1872," *History of Education Quarterly* 19, no. 1 (Spring 1979): 8. William Woodbridge, Willard's sometime coauthor, became a devoted Pestalozzian. W. S. Monroe, *History of the Pestalozzian Movement in the United States* (Syracuse, NY: C. W. Bardeen, 1907), 141–43. On the teaching of Combe's phrenological theories at Willard's seminary see "Troy Female Seminary," *American Ladies' Magazine* 8, no. 12 (December 1835): 703; for an endorsement of Willard's pedagogy by Combe see "Mrs. Willard on Female Education," *American Lady's Magazine* 7, no. 4 (April 1834): 163–73.

22. Willard, *History of the United States*, vi.

23. Willard, *History of the United States*, 416; emphasis added.

24. Fairbanks, *Emma Willard and Her Pupils*, 17, 113; Alma Lutz, *Emma Willard: Pioneer Educator of American Women* (Boston: Beacon Press, 1964), 52–53.

25. Annie McDowell, as quoted in Fairbanks, *Emma Willard and Her Pupils*, 78.

26. Arabella M. Pearson, as quoted in Fairbanks, *Emma Willard and Her Pupils*, 89.

27. Emma Hart Willard to Almira H. Phelps, 14 May 1831, in *Journal and Letters from France and Great Britain* (Troy, NY: N. Tuttle, 1833), 391, "North American Women's Letters and Diaries: Colonial to 1950" Alexander Street Press, http://alexanderstreet2.com/NWLDlive/index .html, accessed 8 October 2004. Emma Hart Willard to Almira H. Phelps, 2 June 1831, in *Journal and Letters,*365. For other examples of Willard reminiscing, or reporting nostalgic or historically evocative

experiences on her European sojourn in language then associated with physicalist theories of memory see, e.g., Emma Hart Willard to [unidentified correspondent], 14 May 1831, in *Journal and Letters*, 292; and Emma Hart Willard, Diary, in *Journal and Letters*, 353.

28. Emma Hart Willard to [unidentified correspondent], 14 February 1831, in *Journal and Letters*, 198; Emma Hart Willard to Almira H. Phelps, 2 June 1831, in *Journal and Letters*, 374–75; Emma Hart Willard to Almira H. Phelps, 4 November 1830, in *Journal and Letters*, 36.

29. Emma Hart Willard, Diary, December 1830, in *Journal and Letters*, 121.

30. Emma Hart Willard, Diary, December 1830, in *Journal and Letters*, 126; Emma Hart Willard to Almira H. Phelps, 4 November 1830, in *Journal and Letters*, 42; Emma Hart Willard to Almira H. Phelps, 7 December 1830, in *Journal and Letters*, 88–89.

31. John F. Watson, *Historical Tales of Olden Time: Concerning the Early Settlement and Progress of Philadelphia and Pennsylvania* (Philadelphia: E. Littell and Thomas Holden, 1833), vii; John F. Watson, *Historical Tales of the Olden Time: Concerning the Early Settlement and Progress of New-York City and State* (New York: Collins and Hannay, 1832), v, 187–88.

32. [Samuel G. Goodrich], *The First Book of History[;] For Children and Youth[;] By the Author of Peter Parley's Tales[;] With Sixty Engravings and Sixteen Maps* (Boston: Richardson, Lord and Holbrook, 1831), iv; Samuel G. Goodrich, *Recollections of a Lifetime; or, Men and Things I Have Seen: in a Series of Familiar Letters to a Friend, Historical, Biographical, Anecdotical, and Descriptive*, 2 vols. (New York: Auburn and Miller, 1856), 2:308 and 310–11.

33. Goodrich, *Recollections of a Lifetime*, 1:102; cf. 105.

34. Goodrich, *Recollections of a Lifetime*, 1:107.

35. Goodrich, *Recollections of a Lifetime*, 1:23.

36. Goodrich, *Recollections of a Lifetime*, 1:22.

37. Goodrich, *Recollections of a Lifetime*, 1:27–29.

38. [Goodrich], *The First Book of History*, iv.

39. [Goodrich], *The First Book of History*, iv, 25, 58, 105, 112; cf. [Samuel G. Goodrich], *The Tales of Peter Parley About America[;] With Engravings*, 2d. ed. (Boston: S. G. Goodrich, 1829), 10.

40. [Goodrich], *The First Book of History*, 121.

41. John A. Nietz did write ambiguously in his history of American textbooks that a "considerable number of authors," of textbooks, "particularly the earlier ones, commented" that "the study of history would help improve the memory." However, Nietz's, like subsequently written histories by other scholars, is not attentive either to detailed enunciations of

memory theory in early American textbooks, or to how the physicalist outlooks on memory itself that the textbooks endorsed may have influenced their reportage of acts of contemporaneous patriotic American commemoration. John A. Neitz, *Old Textbooks* (Pittsburgh: University of Pittsburgh Press, 1961), 239.

42. Besides references in prefaces of Willard's and Goodrich's textbooks as already cited above, see, e.g., John Frost, *A History of the United States for the Use of Schools and Academies,* rev. ed. (Philadelphia: Edward C. Biddle, 1837), 6.

43. George Merriam, *The American Reader: Containing Extracts Suited to Excite a Love of Science and Literature, to Refine the Taste, and to Improve the Moral Character* (Boston: Pierce and Williams, 1828), 9 and 138. For another textbook allusion to the intellectual principle of "contiguity" as it relates to the association of ideas see [Jacob and Gorham Drummer?], *The Mount Vernon Reader: A Course of Reading Lectures Designed for Senior Classes* (Boston: William Crosby, 1840), 258.

44. William Sullivan, *The Poetical Class Book: Intended to Instruct the Higher Classes in Schools in the Origin, Nature, and Use of Political Power* (Boston: Lord and Hollbrook, 1830), 15.

45. H. G. Otis as excerpted in Ebenezer Bailey, *The Young Ladies' Class Book* (Boston: Lincoln and Edmands, 1831), 160–61. For a poetic excerpt on the relation of memory to place see [Samuel] Rodgers, as excerpted in Anna Barbauld, *The Female Speaker; or, Miscellaneous Pieces in Prose and Verse* (Boston: Wells and Lilly, 1824), 80.

46. J. L. Blake, *The School Reader: Designed for a First-Class Book* (Boston: William Hyde, 1832), 91–92.

47. Moses Severance, *The American Manual* (Cazenovia, NY: S. H. Henry, 1835), 69.

48. James Hall, *The Western Reader* (Cincinnati: Copley and Fairbank, 1834), 32.

49. Ebenezer Porter, *The Rhetorical Reader,* 6th ed. (Andover, MA: Flagg, Gould and Newman, 1833), 159.

50. John Hall, *The Reader's Guide* (Hartford, CT: Canfield and Robins, 1836), 305.

51. "Dr. Thacher," quoted in [S. G. Goodrich], *The Life of George Washington* (Philadelphia: Thomas, Cowperthwait and Co., 1840), 171; cf. 174. Though Samuel Goodrich disclaimed authorship of this volume, the copyright names "S. G. Goodrich" as author; cf. the cataloging note at Indiana State University, Walker Collection, online catalog, https://web .archive.org/web/20051216215316/http:/library.indstate.edu/level1.dir /cml/rbsc/walker/walker-g.html.

52. [James Jones Wilmer], *The American Nepos* (Baltimore: G. Douglas, 1805), 368–71. Notice too, on 377–81, how Wilmer's textbook devotes space to tracing George Washington's connection to a box of relic wood, to which there is evidence that he was actually indifferent, passed on to him by an admiring member of the British aristocracy.

53. Joseph Richardson, *The American Reader* (Boston: Lincoln and Edmunds, 1810), 116.

54. Richardson, *The American Reader,* 203.

55. A. M. Blake, *The Historical Reader* (Concord, NH: Horatio Hill, 1830), 300.

56. [Goodrich], *The First Book of History,* 121.

57. Sybilla M[iriam Peale] Simmons to Elizabeth [De Peaster Peale] Patterson, 6 October 1824, Peale-Sellars Papers, American Philosophical Society.

58. "Address by the Bunker Hill Monument Association to the Selectmen of the Several Towns in Massachusetts, Boston, October 1st, 1824," transcription in Solomon Willard Papers (1823–1844), Massachusetts Historical Society.

59. Willard, *History of the United States,* 417.

60. President John Quincy Adams as quoted in C. B. Taylor, *A Universal History of the United States of America* (Buffalo, NY: Ezra Strong, 1833), 413.

61. Emma Willard, as excerpted in "Mrs. Willard on Female Education," *American Ladies' Magazine* 7, no. 4 (April 1834): 168, 172, and cf. 173.

62. Emma Willard, "Principles Contained in Stewart's Philosophy of the Mind, Applied to Show the Importance of Cultivating the Female Mind," *American Ladies' Magazine* 9, no. 1 (January 1836): 43–44. On a physicalist, "mechanical" view of human memory, and reflecting the commonplace belief in the era that memories physically laid down in youth are most enduring see "On Memory," *The Pastime; A Literary Paper* 1, no. 24 (1 December 1807): 185; cf. "On Memory," *Weekly Visitor* (12 May 1810): 6. For an exhortation to mothers to teach with sensate pedagogy, "giving the united assistance of the eye and the ear to the memory," and to particularly instruct their children in history, see "Maternal Instruction," *American Journal of Education* 3, no. 11 (November 1827): 653. As if to suggest that her own knowledge, especially of the American Revolution, was traceable to the unique effectiveness of mothers as teachers, Willard dedicated her *History* to her mother with a poem stressing her mother's firsthand experience of the American Revolution. Willard, *History of the United States,* n.p. Cf. Nina Baym, "Women and the Republic: Emma Willard's Rhetoric of History," *American Quarterly* 43 (March 1991): 11.

63. "Mary, the Mother of Washington," *Christian Watchman* 6 (June 1833): 266–69.

64. "The Mother of Washington," *Ladies' Magazine and Literary Gazette* 4 (September 1831): 384.

65. See, e.g., "The Mother of Washington," *Saturday Evening Post* 5, no. 33 (19 August 1826): 1–2.

66. George Washington Parke Custis, as cited in "The Mother of Washington," *Ladies' Magazine and Literary Gazette*, 393.

67. [Lydia H.] Sigourney, as excerpted in Ebenezer Bailey, *The Young Ladies' Class Book* (Boston: Lincoln and Edmands, 1831), 160–61; cf. [Lydia H.] Sigourney, as excerpted in Samuel Worcester, *A Fourth Book of Lessons for Reading* (Boston: Carter, Hendee, and Company, 1835), 97–100.

68. "Mary, the Mother of Washington," 269. On Emma Willard's enlistment in the 1840s cult of Mary Washington see Baym, "Women and the Republic," 12.

69. "Letter, printed, dated Fredericksburg, June 1, 1831; proposing a monument to the memory of the mother of George Washington," Virginia Historical Society; cf. Lawrence Lewis to George Washington Bassett, 5 May 1831, George Washington Bassett Papers, Section I, Virginia Historical Society.

70. "Mother of Washington," *Workingman's Advocate* 2 (4 June 1831): 1. For a personal recollection of Mary Washington doing so, given as part of an argument for the propriety of building a monument on the site of her burial, see Lawrence Lewis to George Washington Bassett, 15 May 1831, George Washington Bassett Papers, Section I, Virginia Historical Society. Cf. Lydia H. Sigourney's hope that, in the wake of the monument's construction, American mothers would undertake pilgrimages to the site, which would impress them with their own power to "impress" the rising generation. L[ydia] H. S[igourney], "The Mother of Washington," *Southern Literary Messenger* 1, no. 1 (August 1834): 6.

71. On linkage of religion and nationalism in textbooks of the era, but with too little attention to the role of historical memory in that process, see J. Merton England, "The Democratic Faith in American Schoolbooks, 1783–1860," *American Quarterly* 15 (Summer 1963): 196.

72. Redding S. Sugg Jr., *Motherteacher: The Feminization of American Education* (Charlottesville: University Press of Virginia, 1978), 36.

73. John Hubbard, *The American Reader: Containing a Selection of Narratives, Harangues, and Addresses*, 2d ed. (Bellows Falls, VT: Bill Blake, 1820), 52–55.

74. *The Progressive Reader or Juvenile Monitor* (Concord, NH: Hoag and At-wood, 1831), 78.

75. Noah Webster, *History of the United States: To Which Is Prefixed a Brief Historical Account of Our Ancestors from the Dispersion of Babel to Their Migration to America and of the Conquest of South America by the Span-iards* (New Haven: Durrie and Peck, 1832): 1, v, and 310–11.

76. Noah Webster to Thomas [illegible], 28 December 1808; Noah Webster to Thomas [illegible], 23 February 1809, reel 1, Noah Webster Papers, Manuscripts and Archives Division, New York Public Library. On how Webster's religious views changed over time, see generally Richard M. Rollins, *The Long Journey of Noah Webster* (Philadelphia: University of Pennsylvania Press, 1980).

77. [Charles Prentiss], *History of the United States of America: With a Brief Account of Some of the Principal Empires & States of Ancient and Modern Times* (Keene, NH,: John Prentiss, 1820), 4.

78. Samuel Williams, *A History of the American Revolution: Intended as a Reading-Book for Schools* (New Haven: W. Stores, 1824), v.

79. Willard, *History of the United States,* ix.

80. Pauline Maier, *American Scripture: Making the Declaration of Indepen-dence* (New York: Alfred A. Knopf, 1997).

81. Willard argued that the position on memory and memorization that she and Woodbridge took in their textbook was such as to "abridge the labor of mind, and to enable the memory to lay up the most in the smallest compass" by classifying "particulars under general heads," and she as-serted that: "Capacity of mind is acquired by those habits of study, which cultivate the powers of abstraction and generalization." Willard, "Pref-ace," xii. See other examples of polemicists deriding rote memorization of particulars for their own sake, rather than for bringing to mind more general insights, principles, and understanding in, e.g.: "Common Educa-tion," *American Journal of Education* 2 (March, 1827): 162; "Of Memory," *Philadelphia Repository and Weekly Register* 5 (27 April 1805): 130; "Abuse of Catechisms," *American Sunday School Magazine* 6 (June 1829): 167; "Rules for Composing Catechisms for Children," *American Sunday School Magazine* 2 (September 1825): 264; "General Rules for the Improve-ment of Knowledge," *Columbian Magazine; Comprehending Ecclesiastical History, Morality, Religion, and Other Useful Matter* 1, no. 5 (July/August 1806): 160–61; William B. Fowle, "Use and Abuse of Memory," *American Annals of Education* 7, no. 11 (November 1837): 490–91; "Education," *East-ern Magazine* 1, no. 2 (July 1835): 49; "Hints to Young Teachers," *Amer-ican Annals of Education* 4, no. 5 (May 1834): 217; "Elementary Books,"

Western Academician and Journal of Education and Science 1 (September 1837): 361–63; "How to Teach Little Children," *American Annals of Education* 7 (July 1837): 306. Cf. representative examples of contemporaneous claims that assert that memory must thus be selective, such as, e.g.: "Austin's Life of Gerry," *North American Review* (January 1829): 38; "On the Improvement of Memory," *Universal Asylum and Columbian Magazine* 2 (July 1792): James Floy, "The Judgment Register," *Methodist Magazine and Quarterly Review* (April 1838): 165–76; "Education," *The Floriad* 1, no. 14 (22 November 1811): 421. Notice especially George Mifflin Dallas's address to college students on "memory" in which he celebrates the "moral influence of memory" that "arises as well from what is *ejected* as from what is *retained*." George Mifflin Dallas, "An Oration on the Moral Influence of Memory, Delivered at Nassau College, Princeton, on the Evening Preceding the Commencement of 1809," *The Port-Folio* 3, no. 5 (May 1810): 399. See also Neitz, *Old Textbooks*, 239; and Bernard Wishy's observation that, between 1830 and 1860, it was increasingly asserted that schools ought to prepare students to "acquire knowledge as they needed it, and not to be loaded like 'beasts of burden.'" with facts that lack practical value. Wishy, *The Child and the Republic*, 70–71.

82. John Quincy Adams, *An Address Delivered at the Request of a Committee of the Citizens of Washington on the Occasion of the Reading of the Declaration of Independence, on the Fourth of July 1821* (Washington, DC: Davis and Force, 1821), 20–21. For a work that announces in its title its argument that there should be a transition to teaching principles of the Revolution from its history, and away from merely teaching the history of the Revolution per se, see [Anonymous], *The Principles and Practice of the Patriots of the Revolution; Being an Appeal to Reason and Common Sense* (Philadelphia: S. Roberts, 1819), esp. viii. 1–2, 31. Note especially the frontispiece citing Maubreuil: "Man may disappear; principles alone . . . are imperishable," a poignant, prescriptive allusion in an era when Americans were anxiously observing the passing away of the United States' Founding generation. For a humorous gem from an 1835 work of fiction portraying a student wrenching the Declaration of Independence out of its historical context to argue from its principles against his teachers' classroom governance see Michael Kammen, *A Season of Youth: The American Revolution and the Historical Imagination* (New York: Alfred A. Knopf, 1978), 260–63.

83. Willard, *History of the United States*, ix.

84. Theodore Stanton and Harriet Stanton Blatch, eds., *Memoir of Elizabeth Cady Stanton*, in *Elizabeth Cady Stanton, as Revealed in Her Letters, Diary,*

and Reminiscences, vol. 1(New York: Harper & Row, 1922), 17, "North American Women's Letters and Diaries: Colonial to 1950," Alexander Street Press, http://alexanderstreet2.com/NWLDlive/index.html.

85. Stanton and Blatch, *Memoir of Elizabeth Cady Stanton,* 37.

86. Emma Willard, *History of the United States,* ix; Miriam Gurko, *The Ladies of Seneca Falls: The Birth of the Woman's Rights Movement* (New York: Macmillan, 1974), 96.

87. Elisabeth Griffith, *In Her Own Right: The Life of Elizabeth Cady Stanton* (New York: Oxford University Press, 1984), 54.

EPILOGUE

1. On Edmond's painting, see Glen Wallach, *Obedient Sons: The Discourse of Youth and Generations in American Culture, 1630–1860* (Amherst: University of Massachusetts Press, 1997), 109–10.

2. Abraham Lincoln, "Address to the Young Men's Lyceum," 27 January 1838, in *Abraham Lincoln, Speeches and Writings,* vol. 1, *1832–1858,* ed. Don E. Fehrenbacher, Library of America (New York: Literary Classics of the United States, 1989), 28, 33, and 36. Evidence that as a young lawyer Lincoln took seriously prevailing ideas about physiognomy of the sort that, the present book has shown, become important in the "physicalist" memory culture of the day is the fact that he paid attention to the physiognomy, including hair and eye color, of potential jurors during jury selection for trials with which he was professionally involved. Alan Spiegel, "Abraham Lincoln, Esquire," Organization of American Historians, *Talking History,* online radio program, 12 April 2004, http://www.oah.org/site/assets/talkinghistory/2004/Lincoln.mp3, from 18 min. and 37 secs. to 19 min. and 1 sec.

3. Oliver Wendell Holmes, "The Last Leaf," in *The Early Poems of Oliver Wendell Holmes* (New York: T. Y. Crowell and Company, 1899), 91–93.

4. E. B. Hillard, *Last Men of the Revolution: Containing a Photograph of Each from Life* (1864; reprint, William D. Garrett, ed., intro. by Archibald MacLeish [Barre, MA]: Barre Publishers, 1968), 56; Hillard also took pleasure in seeing a lock of hair from the head of still-living Revolutionary War veteran Samuel Downing: Hillard, *Last Men of the Revolution,* 41. For a recent reappraisal of Hillard's use of evidence, see Don H. Hagist, *The Revolution's Last Men: The Soldiers behind the Photographs* (Yardley, PA: Westholme, 2016).

5. Abraham Lincoln, "Address at Gettysburg, Pennsylvania, 19 November 1863," in *Abraham Lincoln, Speeches and Writings,* vol. 2, *1859–1865,* ed.

Don E. Fehrenbacher, Library of America (New York: Literary Classics of the United States, 1989), 536.

6. Wayne Fields, *Union of Words: A History of Presidential Eloquence* (New York: Free Press, 1996), 285–93.

7. For examples of scholarship on the construction of post–Civil War memory of that conflict that emphasizes reliance upon monuments and relics, see, e.g., Kirk Savage, *Standing Soldiers, Kneeling Slaves: Race, War, and Monument in Nineteenth-Century America* (Princeton, NJ: Princeton University Press, 1997); Thomas A. Desjardin, *These Honored Dead: How the Story of Gettysburg Shaped American Memory* (Cambridge, MA: De Capo Press, 2003); David W. Blight, *Race and Reunion: The Civil War in American Memory* (Cambridge, MA: Harvard University Press, 2001). On former Confederate and Union troops exchanging locks of hair at a reunion at Gettysburg in 1887, see David W. Blight, *Beyond the Battlefield: Race, Memory, and the American Civil War* (Amherst: University of Massachusetts Press, 2002), 179.

8. "Gen. Wilson Tells Personal Stories of Famous Men," *St. Louis Post Dispatch*, 30 April 1913, 6.

9. Abraham Lincoln, "Speech in United States House of Representatives: The War with Mexico," in *Collected Works*, ed. Roy P. Basler, with Marion Dolores Pratt and Lloyd A. Dunlap, 9 vols. (New Brunswick, NJ: Rutgers University Press, 1953–55), http://name.umdl.umich.edu/lincoln1, accessed 5 March 2013.

10. "Laying the Cornerstone of the Boston Post Office," *Frank Leslie's Illustrated Newspaper*, 4 November 1871. For a recollection of Washington's hair being preserved during a fire at the Mason's facility, see "Chase Remembers Cows on Common," *Boston Globe*, 9 November 1919, 6. "Gen. Wilson Tells Personal Stories of Famous Men," 6; cf. James Wilson, *Washington—Lincoln and Grant* (New York: New York Society of the Order of the Founders and Patriots of America, 1903), 26; "Hair of Famous Men for Art Museum—Numerous Relics Are Offered to New York Institution by General Wilson's Will," *Ogden Examiner* (Ogden, UT), 19 March 1914. Two years later, an appraiser reportedly doubting the authenticity of Wilson's relics rated them as of little economic value. "Lincoln's Hair Is Valueless as Relic Appraisal Reveals," *Pittsburgh Press*, 12 April 1916, 16.

11. Richard B. McCaslin, *Lee in the Shadow of Washington* (Baton Rouge: Louisiana State University Press, 2001), 214; see also, 30; Old, hair, jet. Measurements; L 2.1, W 1.2cm, Arlington House, Robert E. Lee Memorial, ARHO 5024, Museum Management Program, National Park Service,

Department of the Interior, http://www.nps.gov/museum/exhibits/arho /exb/Family/ARHO5024_Buttons-%26-Hair.html, accessed 5 March 2013.

12. Robert W. Rydell, *All the World's A Fair: Visions of Empire at American International Expositions, 1876–1916* (Chicago: University of Chicago Press., 1984), 35.

13. On the presence of Washington's hair, see, e.g.: George Frederick Kunz and Charles Hugh Stevenson, *The Book of the Pearl; the History, Art, Science, and Industry of the Queen of Gems* (New York: Century Co., 1908), 438; on how the self-congratulatory ethos of the affair ignored the plight of African Americans, see Eric Foner, *Reconstruction: America's Unfinished Revolution, 1863–1877* (New York: Harper & Row, 1988), 564–65.

14. Foner, *Reconstruction: America's Unfinished Revolution, 1863–1877,* 581.

15. Ring, catalog number 1914.808.1, Rutherford B. Hayes Collection. Provenance note: "This ring contains the hair of George Washington. It was given by George Washington to Mrs. Alexander Hamilton, who gave it to her son, Honorable James A. Hamilton. He in turn gave it to John Hay, who then gave it to President Hayes on February 22, 1877." Rutherford B. Hayes Presidential Center online catalog, http://rbhayes.pastperfect -online.com/31794cgi/mweb.exe?request=record;id=86920B2A-A409 -45E0-9B5E-844764881780;type=101, accessed 11 March 2013.

16. Charles Richard Williams, ed., *Diary and Letters of Rutherford Birchard Hayes: 1834–1860,* 5 vols. (Columbus: Ohio State Archeological and Historical Society, 1922), 1:15–25; "Russel House," Middlesex County Historical Society outdoor marker, at the intersection of High Street and Washington Street in Middletown, CT, on the campus of Wesleyan University; cf. "Some Memories of Middletown: The Washington Hotel Which Became the Jarvis Mansion, Lafayette and Other Visitors," *Historiographer of the Episcopal Diocese of Connecticut,* no. 121 (September 1982): 4.

17. "Locks of Hair from Presidents," "Lynched," and "Burned at the Stake," *Weekly Wisconsin* (Milwaukee, WI), 28 April 1884, all on 6.

18. "A Lock of George Washington's Hair," and "Gag Law Applied to a Fire Eater," *Broome Republican* (Binghamton, NY), 1 December 1906, both on 4. See also "White Men Better Clay," *Evening Telegram* (St. John's, Newfoundland), 8 December 1906, 5, http://news.google.com/newspapers ?id=2p0jAAAAIBAJ&sjid=YDsDAAAAIBAJ&pg=2762%2C2549171, accessed 11 March 2013.

19. Mark Twain (Samuel Clemens) and Charles Dudley Warner, *The Gilded Age: A Tale of Today* (Hartford, CT: American Publishing Company, 1874).

20. Twain and Warner, *The Gilded Age*, 221–22.
21. Mark Twain [Samuel Clemens] to J. H. Twitchell, 4 November 1904, in *Mark Twain's Letters*, ed. Albert Bigelow Paine, 2 vols. (New York: Harper & Row, 1917), 2:761–62. Though Twain, of course, could not have foreseen it, in 1954, when the Greenwich Village, New York, Chamber of Commerce began soliciting a fundraiser to save the "Mark Twain House" from demolition, a putative lock of George Washington's hair was reportedly among the early donations. "Fund Drive Falling Short," *Waterloo Daily Courier* (Waterloo, IA), 20 January 1954; see also *Mark Twain Journal* 20, no. 2 (Summer 1980): 14.
22. Warren Zimmerman, *First Great Triumph: How Five Americans Made Their Country a World Power* (New York: Farrar, Straus, and Giroux, 2002), 82–83; Michael R. Beschloss, *Presidential Courage: Brave Leaders and How They Changed America, 1789–1989* (New York: Simon and Schuster, 2007), 154; Patricia O. Toole, *The Five of Hearts: An Intimate Portrait of Henry Adams and His Friends, 1880–1918* (New York: Simon and Schuster, 1900), 288–89.
23. "France at the Fair," *Weekly Missoulian* (Missoula, MT), 23 August 1893, 7.
24. "State Buildings at World's Fair," *Autumn Leaves* 6, no. 11 (November 1848): 486.
25. "At the Fair," *Sacramento Daily Union* [Sacramento, CA], 13 June 1893, http://cdnc.ucr.edu/cdnc/cgi-bin/cdnc?a=d&cl=search&d=SDU18930613.2.58&srpos=2&e=13-06-1893-13-06-1893--en--20--1--txt-TI-%22at+the+fair%22+----, accessed 23 March 2013.
26. "Nannie" Williams to "Aunt Lucy," 4 July 1893, as reprinted in "Minnie and Nannie," *The Democrat* (McKinney, TX), 29 November 1894, 1.
27. "Its Climax at Night," *Chicago Tribune*, 5 July 1893, Last Edition, 1.
28. John Madden, M.D., "Herman W. Mudgett[,] alias H. H. Holmes," letter to the editor, 20 August 1896, printed in *Journal of the American Medical Association* 27, no. 9 (29 August 1896): 500.
29. "Minnie and Nannie," 1.
30. Erik Larson, *The Devil in the White City: Murder, Magic, and Madness at the Fair That Changed America* (New York: Random House, 2004), 290–96. Larson's account is a gripping one, but must be used with evidential caution as it maintains its appeal at the price of some literary license. On Holmes and murder as a science, see, e.g., "Progressive Art of Murder," *Scranton Tribune* (Scranton, PA), 27 July 1895, Library of Congress, "Chronicling America," http://chroniclingamerica.loc.gov/lccn/sn84026355/1895-07-27/ed-1/seq-5/, accessed 20 March 2013; see also "Had Twenty Victims [—] Holmes Confesses How He Reduced

Murder to a Science," *Indiana State Journal* (Indianapolis, IN), 8 April 1896, issue 15; col F.

31. Henry Adams, *The Education of Henry Adams: An Autobiography* (New York: Houghton Mifflin, 1918), 342.

32. Adams, *The Education of Henry Adams*, 343.

33. In 1902 Henry wrote to his brother Brooks Adams, "I apprehend for the next hundred years an ultimate cosmic collapse; but not on any of our old lines. My belief is that science is to wreck us. . . . This is however, a line of ideas wholly new and very repugnant to our contemporaries. You will regard it with mild contempt. I owe it only to my having always had a weakness for science mixed with metaphysics. I am a dilution of a mixture of Lord Kelvin and St. Thomas Aquinas." Henry Adams to Brooks Adams, in *The Letters of Henry Adams*, Vol. 5, *1899–1905*, ed. J. C. Levenson, Ernest Samuels, et al. (Cambridge, MA: Belknap Press of Harvard University Press, 1988), 399; see also 141 and 420.

34. Henry Adams, *The Degradation of the Democratic Dogma* (New York: Macmillan, 1920), 17 and 108. See also 13–21, wherein Henry Adams elaborates upon what he takes to have been Washington's system, the relation of that system to John Adams's and John Quincy Adams's politics, and Washington's death as the de facto end of the system. Henry Adams partly blames the failure of what he represents as John Quincy Adams's effort to revive and fulfill Washington's plans upon Adams's relying too fully upon his own "profound scientific mind," while not realizing that "science might defeat its own intended end" (20).

35. Adams, *The Degradation of the Democratic Dogma*, 84.

36. Adams, *The Education of Henry Adams*, 266.

37. Adams, *The Degradation of the Democratic Dogma*, 85. Adams had a tortured intellectual relationship with scientific and scientistic thought. The view of history that he developed was thoroughly scientistic. For a useful evaluation of Henry Adams's alternating repulsion and attraction to scientism, see Wilfred M. McClay, *The Masterless: Self and Society in Modern America* (Chapel Hill: University of North Carolina Press, 1994), 34–36.

38. Adams, *The Education of Henry Adams*, ch. 25, "The Dynamo and the Virgin," 379–90; Henry Adams, *Letters to a Niece and Prayer to the Virgin of Chartres* (New York: Houghton and Mifflin, 1920), 127. See also Jackson Lears, *Rebirth of a Nation: The Making of Modern America, 1877–1920* (New York: HarperCollins, 2009), 274.

39. Henry Adams to Charles Francis Adams Jr., London, 11 April 1862, excerpted in Louis P. Masur, *The Real War Will Never Get in the Books:*

Selections from Writers during the Civil War (New York: Oxford University Press, 1993), 7.

40. "A Pendant Containing . . . ," *Clay County News* (Spencer, IA), 30 June 1904, 2.

41. Adams, *The Education of Henry Adams*, 46. On Hay giving out Washington's hair to patrons, see Ring, catalog number 1914.808.1, Rutherford B. Hayes Collection; Zimmerman, *First Great Triumph*, 82–83; Beschloss, *Presidential Courage*, 154. When Henry Adams's close relative Elizabeth Coombs Adams died in 1903, a lock of Washington's hair was among the effects she reportedly left behind in her home.

42. Adams, *The Education of Henry Adams*, 466.

43. "Man Could Build Civilization Again from This Record," *St. Louis Post-Dispatch*, 30 April 1904, 2.

44. "Are You Civilized?" *St. Louis Post-Dispatch*, 23 May 1904, 5.

45. "Generals to Meet Old Foes," *St. Louis Post-Dispatch*, 9 August 1904, 4; "McGee: The Overlord of the Savage World," *St. Louis Post-Dispatch*, 17 July 1904, A10; "Mysterious Little Primitives Come to the World's Fair," *St. Louis Post-Dispatch*, 17 April 1904, B5; "Can Test Your Brain Power: Remarkable Instruments in the Building of Anthropology," *St. Louis Post-Dispatch*, 21 May 1904, 1; "Missourians Top Mankind in Stature, Says Professor WJ McGee," *St. Louis Post-Dispatch*, 27 March 1904, A3B; "Put Men under the Microscope: Novel World's Fair Plan a Scientific Study of the Races," *St. Louis Post-Dispatch*, 10 February 1904, 7; "Igorrotes in Dress Parade Omit Clothes," *St. Louis Post-Dispatch*, 19 June 1904, A4; "Igorrotes Now Use 'Hello Box': Wires Have Thus Far Stood Strain of Conversation in Dialect of Anthropoids," *St. Louis Post-Dispatch*, 29 July 1904, 2; "Why Clothes Are Worn: Questions with Igorrotes," *St. Louis Post-Dispatch*, 18 May 1904, 9; "Igorrote Tom-Tom Throbs Defiance to Scouts' Band, and War Is Imminent," *St. Louis Post-Dispatch*, 24 May 1904, 2.

46. *Alexandria Gazette* (Alexandria, VA), 10 May 1887, 4, Library of Virginia, Richmond, VA, http://virginiachronicle.com/cgi-bin/virginia?a=d&d=AG18870510.1.2#, accessed 28 April 2013. For a more sympathetic account of the queen receiving the hair, see "Washington's Indian Girl," *Boston Daily Globe*, 10 May 1887, 2. See also State of Hawaii, Office of Hawaiian Affairs, Washington, DC, Bureau, and Ke Ali'i Maka'ainana Hawaiian Civic Club, *Ali'i Diplomatic Missions and Other Business Travel to Washington, D.C.[:] Phase 2 Research* (Honolulu, HI: Office of Hawaiian Affairs, 2009), 20, http://haunaniapoliona.org/pdfs/Alii_Diplomatic_Missions_2009.pdf, accessed 27 April 2013; "Queen 'Lil' Has But Seven Trunks," *St. Louis Post-Dispatch*,

10 May 1904, 1; "Queen Lil Is Ill; Will Hurry Home," *St. Louis Post-Dispatch*, 11 May 1904, 7; Liliuokalani, *Hawaii's Story by Hawaii's Queen, Liliuokalani* (Boston: Lee and Shepard, 1898), 125–27; Neil Thomas Proto, *The Rights of My People: Liliuokalani's Enduring Battle with the United States, 1893–1917* (New York: Algora Publishing, 2009), 54, 163–64.

47. "Present to Lord John Russell," *New-Bedford Mercury* (New-Bedford, MA), 10 February 1837, 4; "Kossuth in Philadelphia," *New York Times*, 25 December 1851; Béla Vassady Jr., "The 'Tochman Affair': An Incident in the Mid-Nineteenth-Century Hungarian Emigration to America," *Polish Review* (1980): 21 and n49; "George Washington's Hair: A Lock of It among the Presents Received by Bismarck," *Knoxville Journal* (Knoxville, TN), 1 April, 1895, 1.

48. The best-known surviving document, both to Americans in 1904 and today, wherein Washington had argued for a restrained foreign policy was his 1796 "Farewell Address," asking, e.g., "Why quit our own to stand upon foreign ground?" George Washington, "Farewell Address (1796)," Avalon Project, Yale Law School, http://avalon.law.yale.edu /18th_century/washing.asp, accessed 20 April 2013. On Gilded Age anti-imperialists' arguments from Washington's Farewell Address, and American-imperialists' counter arguments in the same era, see Matthew Spalding and Patrick J. Garrity, *A Sacred Union of Citizens: George Washington's Farewell Address and the American Character* (Lanham, MD: Rowman and Littlefield, 1996), 155–57.

49. "If But a Single Lock . . . ," *Ironwood News Record* (Ironwood, MI), 26 June 1909, 4.

50. "The Exhibit of the Historical Society of Pennsylvania," *Pennsylvania Magazine of History and Biography* 42, no. 4 (1918): 353 and 356.

51. "Washington's Hair Red; Was Weak Speller," *Evening News* (San Jose, CA), 23 February 1922, 1; "Washington's Hair," *Spokesman Review* (Spokane, WA), 12 April 1922, 4; "Washington's Hair Was Hazel Brown," *New York Times*, 1 March 1922, 3; "Washington's Hair Was White," *Indiana Evening Gazette* (Indiana, PA), 24 February 1922, 4; "The Color of Washington's Hair," *Youngstown Daily Vindicator* (Youngstown, OH), 8 March 1922, noting the concern about race underlying the debate about Washington's hair color, and appealing to science as an adjudicator showing lack of correlation between race and red hair.

52. "Willed a Lock of Washington's Hair," *Delphos Daily Herald* (Delphos, IA), 2 August 1902, [3]; "Hair of Famous Men for Art Museum—Numerous Relics Are Offered to New York Institution by General Wilson's Will," *Ogden Examiner* (Ogden, UT), 19 March 1914, 1; cf. "Involves Lock of

Washington's Hair," *Chester Times* (Chester, PA), 1 November 1933, 4; and "Lock of Hair of Washington Found in Bank," *Wisconsin State Journal* (13 December 1939), 14, which notes the discovery of a lock of Washington's hair in a safe deposit box in Springfield, IL.

53. "Today," *Logansport Pharos-Tribune* (Logansport, IN), 21 November 1925, 1.

54. Russell B. Porter, "Orchid-Decked Venezuela Pavillion Takes Its Place among Fair Attractions," *New York Times,* 27 May 1939, 9; Meyer Berger, "At the Fair," *New York Times,* 9 May 1939, 19.

55. At mid-century, in 1953 a Pittsburgh newspaper ridiculed the idea of someone breaking into the "Historical Society's museum," stealing, then "fencing" a "lock of George Washington's hair." See "History Class for Crooks," *Pittsburgh Post-Gazette* (Pittsburgh, PA), 28 July 1953, 1. Beginning in the 1970s, there was recurrent reportage in American newspapers of Washington's hair being stolen in the United States and abroad. See "George Washington's Hair Falls to Thieves," *Corpus Christi Times* (Corpus, Christi, TX), 1 August 1972, 14A; "Washington's Hair Locked Up in Raid against Drug Dealers," *Chicago Tribune,* North Sports Final, C Edition, 29 January, 1991, 3, Proquest, *Chicago Tribune* (Pre-1997 fulltext); Alfonso A. Narvaez, "Washington and Hamilton Hair Stolen with Mourning Lockets: Items 'Priceless' Outside the Walls," *New York Times,* 12 January 1973, 40; Robert K. Whittman, *Priceless: How I Went Undercover to Rescue the World's Stolen Treasures* (New York: Broadway Paperbacks, 2010), 99–101; cf. *U.S. v. Medford,* 194 F.3d, 421 (3d Cir. 1999).

56. Head of state gift from Venezuela, presented to President Nixon during a White House visit on 2 June 1970, displayed in the Oval Office 22 February to 28 February 1971, artifact HS.1970.120, Richard Nixon Presidential Library and Museum (Yorba Linda, CA); Nixon quoted in Carl Bernstein and Bob Woodward, *All the President's Men* (1974; reprint, New York: Simon and Schuster, 2007), 340.

57. *USS GEORGE WASHINGTON (CVN 73) COMMAND HISTORY 1997,* 4, as enclosed in Commanding Officer, *USS George Washington* (CVN 73) to director of Naval History (NOgBH), Washington Navy Yard, 4 May 1998, https://web.archive.org/web/20130614182249/http://www.history.navy.mil/shiphist/g/cvn-73/1997.pdf; Facebook Messenger communications from U.S. Navy LCDR James Stockman, public relations officer for U.S.S. *George Washington,* to the author, 1 July 2013, and 7 August 2013.

58. Artifact EHA 239, National Park Service, Federal Hall. "Frame is elaborate gutta percha & gilded brass, c. 1850. Bottom left corner of frame

broken. On back of case is handwritten attestation that the hair was taken from George Washington's head at his inauguration"; artifact FEHA 1720, National Park Service, Federal Hall. "Strand of hair said to be from George Washington. Gray strand of hair is in an envelope." Both items are in the Messmore Kendall Collection of Washingtoniana, Federal Hall (New York), National Park Service.

59. Ruth Hargraves, Project Director, *Cataclysm and Challenge: Impact of September 11, 2001, on Our Nation's Cultural Heritage* (Washington, DC: Heritage Preservation, 2002), 15, http://www.heritagepreservation.org /pdfs/cataclysm.pdf, accessed 28 April 2013. Robert D. McFadden, "4 Killed, 44 Injured in Frauces Tavern Blast," *New York Times*, 25 January 1975, 57. Details inferred concerning the presence of the hair on both occasions were confirmed in a phone conversation between Jessica Baldwin Phillips, Museum Director, Fraunces Tavern Museum, and the author on 3 April 2013.

60. Erik Eckholm, "Using History to Mold Ideas on the Right," *New York Times*, 4 May 2011, http://www.nytimes.com/2011/05/05/us/politics/ 05barton.html, accessed on 28 April 2013; "The 25 Most Influential Evangelicals in America," *Time Magazine* (7 February 2005), http://content .time.com/time/specials/packages/completelist/0,29569,1993235,00 .html, accessed on 28 April 2013.

61. "Washington Had Rare B-Type Blood," *Portsmouth Times* (Portsmouth, OH), 4 July 1975, 13; "You Tried, George," *St. Petersburg Independent* (St. Petersburg, FL), 21 February 1977, 3A; "Washington's Hair Gets the Dry, Scientific Look," *Lawrence Daily Journal-World* (Lawrence, KS), 21 February 1977, 27; "Tests Seek George Washington's Hair," *The Vindicator* (Youngstown, OH), City Edition, 17 February 1994, A7; Sierra Bellows, "The Hair Detective," *University of Virginia Magazine* (Summer 2008), https://uvamagazine.org/articles/the_hair_detective, accessed 23 April 2013.

62. Federal Bureau of Investigation to Diane L. Dunkey[,] Museum Director and Chief Curator[,] DAR Museum, 31 May 1994, electronic facsimile conveyed by email by Jessica Baldwin Phillips, Museum Director, Fraunces Tavern Museum, to the author, 4 April 2013.

63. Micah Cohen, "Washington Shed Here: A Collectible," *New York Times*, 5 September 2007, http://www.nytimes.com/2007/09/05/us/05george .html, accessed 15 April 2013; Benjamin Rush to John Adams, 27 June 1812, excerpted in John A. Schutz and Douglas Adair, *The Spur of Fame: Dialogues of John Adams and Benjamin Rush* (Indianapolis: Liberty Fund,

2001), 247. E.g., there were eight listings of locks of Washington's putative hair for sale on eBay, http://www.ebay.com/sch/i.html?_odkw= washington+hair&_osacat=0&_from=R40&_trksid=p2045573.m570 .l1313.TR1.TRC0&_nkw=george+washington+hair&_sacat=0, accessed 23 April 2013; Eric Pfeiffer, "George Washington–Shaped Chicken McNugget Sells for $8,100 on eBay," *Yahoo! News*, 6 March 2012, http:// news.yahoo.com/blogs/sideshow/george-washington-shaped-chicken -mcnugget-sells-8-100-215736625.html, accessed 22 April 2013.

64. Micah Cohen, "Washington Shed Here: A Collectible," *New York Times*, 5 September 2007, http://www.nytimes.com/2007/09/05/us/05george .html, accessed 15 April 2013; *Sports Collectors Daily*, 27 May 2008, http://www.sportscollectorsdaily.com/baseball-cards-now-have-full -head-of-hair/, accessed 22 April 2013.

65. "Hair Force One," *Pawn Stars*, season 4, episode 132, 28 January 2013, as summarized in *TV Guide*, http://www.tvguide.com/tvshows/pawn -stars-2013/episode-132-season-4/hair-force-one/299236, accessed 15 April 2013; see also Chris Carlin, "Brag Photo: History Channel's 'Pawn Stars' Features Upper Deck George Washington Hair Cuts Autograph Card," *Upper Deck Blog*, 29 January 2013, http://upperdeckblog .com/2013/01/brag-photo-history-channels-pawn-stars-features -upper-deck-george-washington-hair-cuts-autograph-card/, accessed 15 April 2013.

66. See, e.g., "Finding a Lock of George Washington's Hair, and a Link to American History," *New York Times*, 18 February 2018, https:// www.nytimes.com/2018/02/18/nyregion/president-washington-hair -discovered.html.

67. "Union Demands Apology after Seeing Confederate Book Displayed in Congressman's Office," *CNN Politics*, 13 February 2019, https://www .cnn.com/2019/02/13/politics/confederate-book-us-government-union -members-congress-office/index.html.

68. "What Eight Presidents Who Weren't Elected Can Teach Us about Leadership," *Washington Post*, 17 April 2019, https://www.washingtonpost .com/business/2019/04/17/what-eight-presidents-who-werent-elected -can-teach-us-about-leadership/.

69. Cohen, "Washington Shed Here: A Collectible."

70. Susan M. Pearce, *Museums, Objects, and Collections: A Cultural Study* (Leicester, UK: Leicester University Press, 1992), 197, quoted in Nancy Martha West, *Kodak and the Lens of Nostalgia* (Charlottesville: University Press of Virginia, 2000), 141.

71. Penny Howell Jolly and Christina Christoforou, Opinion, "Op-Art[:] Heads of State," *New York Times*, 14 February 2010, http://www.nytimes .com/interactive/2010/02/15/opinion/20100215_OPART.html, accessed 15 April 2013.

72. Jackie Calmes, "When a Boy Found a Familiar Feel in a Pat of the Head of State," *New York Times*, 23 May 2013, http://www.nytimes.com/2012/05 /24/us/politics/indelible-image-of-a-boys-pat-on-obamas-head-hangs -in-white-house.html?smid=pl-share, accessed 15 April 2012; Lincoln, "Speech in United States House of Representatives: The War with Mexico."

INDEX

Page numbers in italics refer to illustrations.